WITHDRAWN
FROM STOCK

The Irish Administrative System

The Irish Administrative System

T. J. Barrington

Institute of Public Administration

© T. J. Barrington 1980
ISBN 0 902173 92 8

Published by
Institute of Public Administration
57–61 Lansdowne Road,
Dublin 4
Ireland

First Published 1980

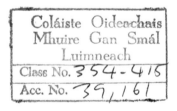
Set in 10/12 Plantin by Design and Art
Facilities and printed by Mount Salus Ltd.

Contents

Chapter 8 Review

Charts

For Patrick Lynch
whose concern for, and commitment to,
the development of Irish administration
has been an inspiration, challenge and
support to so many of us over the years.

. . . Flecte quod est rigidum,
fove quod est frigidum,
rege quod est devium . . .

Preface

This book has two main purposes, distinct but related. First, it attempts to look hard at the bewildering, many-faceted operations of an administrative system to reveal the essential unity of that system. This system is made up of a number of sub-systems and these of a great number of public bodies, all interacting. Through all these run discernible, but protean, elements appearing and re-appearing in a constant flow. But all this complexity has, I believe, a basic unity and simplicity that can be grasped without undue effort, and this book attempts to show what that unity is. From this high ground, as it were, we can get an overview of the principal features; but, as we move along, these features, and their relationships to one another, seem to change as they are seen from different standpoints, at different times, at different stages of the light. Nonetheless, if one can conceive of a single subject of public administration here is a sketch, in an Irish context, of what it seems to be like.

From this common base we can identify sets of problems and put them in some sort of perspective. Some of these sets relate to specific policy areas – agriculture, education, health – but others relate to the way the administrative system, and its parts go about their jobs, that is to say, the general *professional* problems of the administrative system. These latter are our concern here. Some of these sets, like administrative reform, are common to many administrations, others are more localised. The second purpose of this book, therefore, is to attempt to compose these sets of problems into an agenda for a programme of administrative development. This is, I believe, the special task of a profession that rests on the twin notions of public service and administrative science.

These are big loads to put on the study of public administration in one small country; but if one is concerned about how well the profession is discharging its overall duty of public service, and unhappy about the general state of administrative science, and one lacks the time, the learning and the insights to understand equally the problems of every administrative system, what can one do but stick modestly to what one knows and try to discern some universals in it? This book is, of course, primarily addressed to those concerned with Irish public administration, but I hope that enough of general interest emerges to encourage others to look likewise at their own administrative systems.

I have avoided attempting to test administrative theories for their relevance, or otherwise, to Irish conditions. This is partly because that is for another enterprise, partly because many of the theoretical insights seem to me not to be very helpful and partly because, given this theoretical poverty, more progress may be made by looking at the issues with a fresh eye, from working along the grain of the wood, from keeping one's feet firmly on the ground about one. (Choose your metaphor from the mix!)

The business of government is big business and it carries a heavy load of responsibility for national development. Much of this responsibility rests on the administrative system. What are the main issues internal to that system that impede it as a major means of national development? This book looks, therefore, not to the past but to the present and the future; it is concerned, not with achievements, but with problems and opportunities. The former would have been more emollient, but the latter is more bracing. What is attempted, therefore, is to present the subject for what it is in practice–lively, stimulating, intensely relevant to most of the major influences on our lives in the world of the present and the world of the future. To be concerned, therefore, with more sophisticated administration as a major dynamic of national development is to be concerned in an honourable task of some consequence to the general well-being.

Much of what is written here is the result of endless discussion and argument with many colleagues and friends at home and abroad, but especially in the Institute of Public Administration here. I am grateful to the Institute for the opportunity for putting these thoughts together; but needless to say, responsibility for them is my own. I thank particularly my friends Patrick Lynch and Basil Chubb for criticisms and suggestions. I am grateful to Gordon Hutton and Desmond Fennell who organised me to give a course of lectures at University College, Galway, from which this book grew; to my colleague Jim O'Donnell and his team for their skilful midwifery; and in a very special way to Colette Cullen for the calm and competent charm with which she coped with all my demands.

T.J.B.

November, 1979

Chapter 1: Consensus

1. What is Public Administration?

It will be recalled that Monsieur Jourdain, in *Le Bourgeois Gentilhomme*, discovered to his surprise that he had been speaking prose all his life. Practitioners of public administration are often equally surprised to learn that there is, likewise, a 'prose' of their activity. What is this?

Public administration must be one of the oldest professions. It has acted as the handmaid of government as long as government itself has existed, that is, for many thousands of years. Despite its age not a great deal is known about the subject. It has usually been taken for granted, much as usage in speech and writing was taken for granted up to the time of the grammarians in Imperial Rome. Secondly, the modern size and pervasiveness of public administration pose problems of scale and demand organisational skills that were not called for in simpler times. Thirdly, the realisation that public administration has a major developmental role to play in many modern states—and this is particularly true of Ireland—and the disappointments there have been in relation to ambitious plans for development, have made for pressure to get a clearer understanding of underlying rules that, being followed, may secure more successful development.

As government grows and grows we try to get, on the one hand, a bird's eye view of the whole situation, and, on the other, a greater understanding of the relationships between the very large number of public bodies involved and of their relationships with the citizen and with other bodies in the private sector. Hence, in recent decades there has been a rising interest in the subject of public administration.

I have been using the expression 'government' and 'public administration' without distinguishing between them. It is necessary to clarify the different, if overlapping, senses in which the two expressions are used.

But, first, let us distinguish the use of two similar expressions, 'the Government' and 'government'. By the first, we mean the fifteen ministers appointed under the Constitution who are charged with governing the

1

country. By 'government' we mean the processes by which 'the Government' discharges its duties and responsibilities. Over the years 'the Government' has accumulated a large number of such duties and responsibilities. The actual members of the Government will change over time, and so will the emphases that they place on some aspects of their duties rather than others. But, overall, the tasks to be performed by 'government' will carry on for long periods. It is these tasks and the activities of discharging them that we can class under the broad heading of 'government'. We can say that 'public administration' is the servant of 'the Government' but an intimate partner in the processes of 'government'.

The actual work of government is carried on by two classes of persons, the political leaders who tend to change every few years, and the permanent officials. In the United States the neat distinction is made between the elected and the appointed officials. The primary concern of the elected officials is politics, and the primary concern of the appointed officials is public administration. The common concern of both is government. We shall be considering later where politics ends and public administration begins, if such a distinction can be made; but for now let us think of public administration as that part of government that is carried on by permanent officials from day to day, from year to year, from decade to decade. This is, of course, done under the control—sometimes the very detailed control—of the members of the Government, or ministers.

A notable difference between the two constituents of government is that political issues and politicians in office change with considerable frequency, but their numbers overall remain about the same. On the other hand, public administrators have very considerable degrees of permanency but, certainly in recent decades, their numbers, and the range of their duties, have enormously increased. So, politics is highly mobile in content, but remarkably fixed in quantity, while public administration is remarkably permanent in content but subject to very considerable changes in quantity.

If we try to look at public administration more closely we can consider it under three headings. It can be considered as a *system*, of the interactions of the constituents of government, of the vast number of bodies that are comprised in public administration, and of the interactions of these with the private sector and the private citizen. Secondly, public administration can be considered as a *science*, that is as an object of careful study. Thirdly, public administration can be considered as an *art*, that is, in relation to the skills deployed by those engaged in day to day administration.

The principal institutions of the state have for long been divided into three kinds—the legislative institutions, the executive institutions, and the judicial institutions. When we talk about 'Government' we are concerned principally with the operations of the first two sets of these institutions, namely, the legislative and the executive. The political part of government is mainly concerned with legislation, that is, obtaining the powers, under certain limitations, to carry out what the Government believe the country requires them to do at any given time. The public administration part of government is mainly concerned with the execution, or carrying out, of that legislation. Let us leave aside, for the moment, where one of these ends and the other begins. This task of execution requires the setting up of various forms of public bodies to carry through the tasks decided by the legislature.

The place of government—and therefore of public administration—in modern society is very significant indeed. In a typical modern western society something like half or more of the gross national product of the society tends to be handled by government in all its shapes and forms. A notable feature of modern life is, therefore, the very great size and pervasiveness of modern government.

Perhaps more significant than the size of government is its inherent importance. Very many of the decisions that govern the way we live are taken by government and are carried into execution mainly by those engaged in public administration.

Thirdly, a great part of the most skilled human resources of a modern society are involved in government—that is, are employed by the public authority. Government is a great employer of educated, skilled and trained people—in Ireland, possibly the majority of such people are employed in government. Finally in modern democratic societies nearly one third of all *employed* people are employed by government in its various shapes and forms. That is a proportion that holds true also of this country.

So, whether we like it or not, government is very big and very important business. Modern government covers a wide range of activities, a great diversity of activity, occupies a large number of people, and is concerned with a great number of the most important decisions taken in the society.

At the risk of oversimplifying the issues, we have been thinking of government as consisting of two operations—'politics' which is concerned with the taking of decisions and 'public administration' which is concerned with carrying them into effect. As we shall see, this is a very substantial oversimplification of what goes on in practice. Nonetheless, it gives us one insight into the nature of public administration. It tells us that public administration is the system through which politics is transformed into governmental action. For example, if a party comes into power promising to abolish rates on domestic dwellings, the decision to do this is a political matter. It becomes the task of the system of public administration to prepare the necessary legislation in accordance with that decision, to work out the consequential financial arrangements, and to make whatever provisions may be necessary so that local authorities can carry on effectively under the new dispensation. So, this is the first proposition we can make in trying to understand what public administration is. It is the *system* through which political decision is transformed into governmental action.

As we shall see, it would be a mistake to deduce from the proposition that public administration is the system through which politics is transformed into governmental action, that the relation between politics and administration is not a very subtle one indeed. Of course, the administrative system is there to carry out the instructions of the politicians who constitute the government, but it is not only that. A number of complex interrelationships exist that are susceptible of cool analysis. Part of the science of public administration is to understand what, precisely, these relationships are and how they affect the behaviour of the various individuals and groups concerned.

The system of public administration itself is extremely complicated. In Ireland there are more than four hundred separate bodies within the system, and these themselves are grouped into various sub-systems, such as the civil service, local government, the state-sponsored bodies. The way these bodies and sub-systems operate, their strengths and weaknesses, their degrees of autonomy and the limitations of that autonomy, the extent of their contribution to the overall business of development, and a host of other questions, are also susceptible of analysis and of clarification.

There are many other issues that arise about the organisation of these bodies—about the people who staff them, about their management, about the systems for evolving policy—that call for study. Finally, a host of problems arise from the relationships of these bodies with the public in general, with the constitutional and legal systems, and with individual citizens.

The business of government is, therefore, a very complex matter and is carried out by a very large number of bodies whose relationships with one another and with the world at large are extremely diverse. Because of the importance of government and of the size of the resources, human and material, that it uses it is of great importance to have full understanding of these matters so that these great resources can be used to best effect. The study of public administration is, therefore, the attempt to get a scientific grasp of the complex interactions and interrelationships of these bodies.

So, a second proposition we can make about public administration is that it is a *science* concerned to study the behaviour of the public bodies in discharging the tasks of government. The realisation that there can be a science of public administration in this broad sense is a relatively new one. The science is, in consequence, still not well developed.

The practice of public administration is rather like the practice of medicine in that it is concerned with the skilled and detailed application of a variety of sciences. The sciences may be law, economics, sociology, mathematics, politics, engineering or a host of others applicable to the problems with which public bodies are concerned. This art, like any other, comes from flair, skill, understanding, training, experience, and sheer hard work.

So, the third proposition we can make about public administration is that it is an *art* concerned with the skilled application of knowledge to the business of government.

The art of public administration, like that of medicine, is learned basically by practitioners. This book is concerned with the first two of the propositions that we have uncovered – the nature of the *system* of public administration, and the approach to that system as a scientific field of study, or *science*.

The study of public administration is not at a very advanced intellectual level. Nonetheless, it concerns itself with matters of great importance to everyone in the community. It is the way of life of a large proportion of the people in our community. Above all, it poses a number of extremely interesting issues that are crucial to the life and to the development of our society as a whole.

One of the old chestnuts in the business has been: where does one draw the line between politics and administration? It is recognised that government consists of these two things: politics on the one hand, and administration on the other. What is the difference between them? Many answers have been given, but here we can concentrate on two opposing schools of thought. One school said there was a sharp cleavage between the two – that the politicians gave the orders and the officials carried them out according to their intrinsic logic (Wilson, 1887; Goodnow, 1900). Another school said there was virtually no difference, certainly so far as senior officials were concerned: they were manifestly in politics (e.g. Chapman, 1959). There is an element of truth in both views. On the one hand, a great part of the work of public administration is carried on according to rules that have been agreed, and politicians do not play any significant part in the applying of those rules in practice. The classic example here is the work of the Civil Service Commission. On the other hand, when a minister and his senior officials are engaged in a battle with entrenched interests to bring about a new scheme, to devise new legislation and new rules, they are all in the political arena together.

The conflict between these two views of the truth can be resolved if we look at government more closely as a system. One meaning of the word 'system', according to the Oxford English Dictionary, is: 'a set or assemblage of things connected, associated or interdependent, so as to form a complex unity.'

In the system of government are a number of sub-systems or lesser systems. Two major ones are *politics* and *administration*, each of them itself a system, but nonetheless composing between them the main part of the system of government. The work of government is assigned to one or other of these lesser systems, or to both together, according to the degree it meets the conditions of a third system, subtle, sensitive, elusive, the system of *consensus*. We shall later (in Chapter 8) be considering in some depth the system of consensus and its implications for the administrative profession, but for now, let us look briefly at how it moderates the relations between the two systems of politics and administration.

If we think of government as a process, we can see being fed into government at the political end a large mass of pressures, suggestions, conflicts as to what might best be done about the economy, social problems, taxing farmers, or whatever. The special task of the political system is somehow or other to work out ways and means that will reconcile the conflicts and will achieve some sort of general agreement on compromises for new schemes, and so on (Crick, 1964, Ch. 1; de Jouvenel, 1957, Ch. 1; Miller, 1962, Ch. 1). Very often—indeed usually in the continental tradition—this consensus is embodied in a legal instrument of some kind, and the terms of this law determine the conditions under which the administrators may act. Once that law has been settled, it becomes the task of the officials to administer the scheme and, as time goes by, to suggest various kinds of improvements in it. Sometimes, either because the circumstances have changed, or the scheme was not a very good one to begin with, or the officials were not very good at administering or adapting it, a fresh bout of conflict occurs and the situation is back again in the political arena. Eventually, some sort of consensus is achieved, and the scheme as amended is carried on by the officials once more. Sometimes this consensus will last for a generation or more, sometimes only for a few months.

We see in this the basic partnership between the official and the politician in government. The politician, supported by his officials when he is in office, achieves the consensus without which it is impossible to mount, much less administer, any scheme; the officials administer the scheme hopefully to the general satisfaction; but, if not, the scheme comes back into the political arena again and the politician has to do what he can to try to restore the consensus, on which the official can get to work once more; and so on, and on. Bertrand de Jouvenel has said that it is the task of politics not to solve problems but to settle them. One might add to this that it is the task of administration to solve them, and, so far as possible, to prevent them from becoming unnecessarily contentious. So, we see here a partnership between the politician and the administrator. Each has his job to do and, when each does it well, satisfactory government results.

The key factor here, so far as public administration is concerned, is this notion of consensus. On this consensus the whole business of public administration is erected. On this foundation of consensus are built the *institutions* and the various structures needed to implement the schemes that have been agreed upon. The rise, development, and fall of these institutions provide the material for some of the special studies that are contained within the general study of public administration.

The institutions once established have to be staffed and that staff has to be recruited, trained, deployed, remunerated and so on to give the best results. This gives a foundation for the various kinds of studies that relate to *personnel*, mainly psychological and behavioural studies.

The task of this staff, once assembled, is to devise *policies*, at the various levels of sophistication, to operate effectively those policies that are approved, and to adjust them to changing circumstances. These policies involve the application of economic, sociological, engineering, agricultural, and other knowledge and sciences to the needs of the tasks in hand.

These policies once devised and approved have to be implemented, and the effective *implementation* of these involves concern with management, and the various management sciences that help to improve performance.

Policies are not implemented in a vacuum. In the last analysis they affect people. Every administrative scheme relates to a *clientele* of one kind or another. If the clientele are not satisfied because some of the would-be beneficiaries of the policies do not get what they think they should have, the consensus may be destroyed and the issue will move into the political arena again. There are two main areas of clientele sensitivity. The first is the area of personal rights. People often feel themselves aggrieved because rights held out to them by the policies are denied to them in their actual operation. If there is no orderly method by which they can have these decisions reviewed and their own particular cases taken into account, these people will be forced into the political arena, with the effect, over time, of undermining the consensus. Hence, the whole area of administrative law and justice.

Again, political and administrative advance may be frustrated because the people do not understand the policies proposed, or distrust them. The second aspect of clientele sensitivity poses the problem of raising the level of public understanding and responsibility by information policies, 'open' government, and the various forms of public participation.

No policy ever turns out as planned; certain deviations occur willy-nilly and there has to be built in a means of *review* to ensure the necessary adjustments are made. If these are not made, objectives may not be achieved, clientele may grow increasingly dissatisfied, the consensus may be damaged or destroyed, emerging problems may not be recognised. In short, there will be professional failure.

The duty to supervise and maintain the administrative system as a smoothly going concern has profound implications for the *administrative profession* itself. These have not been fully identified, but they raise important issues about the dynamics of the administrative system as a whole which we shall be considering in Chapter 8.

At each of these stages we come back to the system of consensus and its requirements if it is to play its part as a sort of complex of air cushions around the system of administration, each with its fragile valve for pre-venting its contents – the result of the placatory work of the political system – from escaping back into the political system and the zone of conflict.

It will be apparent from what has been said that the basic premiss of the Irish administrative system, as in most genuine (if imperfect), democracies, is the full consent of the governed. It is possible to have a range of other administrative systems – indeed, these have been the norm in most countries – where the consent is coerced in varying significant degrees so that the consensus may not be able to assert itself except by violent fits and starts. By contrast, the democratic system normally permits the consensus to exercise its subtle, but decisive, discipline on a more or less continuous basis. It is this that gives administrative systems in healthy democracies their special character.

We have seen that the discussion of public administration as distinct, or as indistinguishable, from politics is misconceived. Something similar is true of another discussion, that public and business administration are really the same thing. It is true that both are concerned with the behaviour of organised bodies providing services of one kind or another to the public. Sometimes it is the same organisation, as when a business is nationalised and thus becomes part of the system of government. More frequently, we see people in the same occupational classification – busdrivers, typists, doctors, architects – engaging in precisely similar activities in both private and public sectors. In addition, many, at least, of the insights and tech-niques of management are common to the organisations in the two sectors. Where, then, is the difference between administration in the two sectors, if there is such a difference?

Administration is, basically, a *dependent* activity in both sectors, depen-dent on political consensus in the public sphere and on spontaneous enterprise in the private sphere. The condition for success in the public sphere is the maintenance of the consensus, and in the private sphere the (at least) avoidance of loss. The essential difference between the two is politics on the one hand and profit on the other. Of course, there is much overlapping between the two. Some public bodies are expected to be profitable. Some private business organisations, especially multinational ones, have to take account of political constraints. The general economic climate, insofar as it is affected by government action, provides opportun-ities and difficulties for both kinds of bodies. The business world is, in the short term at least, more uncertain than the world of public administration, and the penalties for failure are, usually, much more severe. The rewards for success are correspondingly good. But, through the hazards, the private body has one guiding light – to produce what is profitable, and normally not produce what is not profitable. The efficiency or otherwise of its activities is clearly quantified in the profit and loss account and the balance sheet at the end of each year. There may be ethical or political constraints on the *maximising* of profit; but the crucial guide in decision taking is the relative profitability or otherwise of any proposed project.

It is only occasionally that this kind of guidance is available in the public sector. One cannot decide the scale or pervasiveness of health services or income maintenance services or educational services by their expected profitability or otherwise! Moreover, the manner in which these services are provided may often be at least as important as the quality of the service; or, perhaps more correctly, the judgment on the manner may be a significant part of the judgment as to the quality. In the public sector it is essential, if one is not to fall foul of the law, to ensure complete regularity of procedure. Moreover, one must be scrupulous so as to be fair as between one client and another. There must be no discrimination. The public body is usually a monopoly supplier but cannot, or should not, take advantage of that situation. Wherever one turns, the opportunities for the exercise of discretion in the public sector are limited by different rules from those that operate in the private sector.[1] Of course, there are many management techniques that are equally applicable in both areas; but the task of running a public body, and consequently the skills and knowledge required for the successful performance of that task, are quite different from the task, skills and knowledge required in the private sector. This is not to say that there are not areas—for example, in the commercial state-sponsored bodies—where one shades into the other and both kinds of skills may be required.

Further problems arise within the public sector itself. Is public administration a term that can cover the whole of those employed in the public sector? Of the many thousands of people working in civil service departments, in regional and local authorities, in state sponsored bodies and so on, is it necessary to distinguish between those who are engaged in 'public administration' and those who are not? Or, are we to take it that every person employed in the executive side of government whose ultimate employer is the plain people of Ireland, is, by that fact, engaged in public administration? Quite clearly, there is a large body of activity concerned with the day-to-day operations of government—advising ministers, collecting taxes, designing roads, administering health services—that

---

[1] Professor Self, in evidence to the Fulton Committee, (Vol 5(2) p. 1121) highlights six differences. '(a) Government disposes of coercive powers which do not arise in the private sector. (b) Partly for this reason administrative decision-making is bound by rules of consultation, objection and appeal which have no parallel. (c) Management accounting cannot be be applied within government (unless in very modified form) to yield tests of efficiency. (d) Government undertakes or sponsors ventures in defence and technology which have no close equivalents. (e) While business management is strongly orientated towards market innovation, public administration can be said to be more concerned with 'market compression'—with the limitations of demands which cannot all be met. (f) Government co-ordination of economic action occurs at a much higher level, yet in more limited form, than is true of decisions made by even the largest firms.'

comes within the most narrow definition of public administration. Some would dispute that those in the army, the police, the teaching services and the public transport services should be included. Each of these has, of course, an expertise of its own – military administration, police administration, educational administration, transport administration. But if we think of the people in these organisations as part of a system by which the executive functions of government are carried on and if we think of the state, in the full sense of the public authority, as the employer of these people, then, insofar as they are assisting in the carrying out of actions of government they come, for that purpose, within the ambit of the term 'public administration'. This, indeed, helps to give us an insight into the nature of public administration – that is, that it is the process by which politics are translated into action. Those who are engaged in this process or activity are engaged in public administration.

Perhaps we might take a vivid example of this. The bus driver driving a publicly owned vehicle is in this sense engaged in public administration, while the bus driver driving a privately owned vehicle is not, although there may be no discernible difference between the work carried on by the two men. The difference is in the bodies that employ them and the conditions, as we have seen, under which these different kinds of bodies have to operate. In general, if we are thinking about government and public administration we are concerned with the *kind* of bodies they are. If we are thinking about transport, then they are both subsumed into that study. Here again it is not possible to have a precise cut-off point between the two kinds of study, and there is a good deal of overlapping and ambiguity between them.

Sometimes the boundaries of the subject are both hazy and ambiguous. Nowadays government participates with private bodies in a number of ventures – some of these are commercial, as Gaeltarra Éireann participates in private industries it helps to establish in the Gaeltacht; some are voluntary, as the health boards participate in relation to various voluntary social service bodies. In addition, the state funds, in one shape or another, a number of private bodies, sometimes providing nearly the whole of their income, as in the case of the Economic and Social Research Institute. The state provides a great part of the finances of the universities. Are they inside or outside the system of public administration? So, we have the difficulty not only of shifting boundaries, but also of hazy ones.

There is a second distinction that is often made within the system of public administration, that is between those who carry out reasonably routine duties, like driving a bus, and those who have to work out policy issues, for example, in relation to co-ordination of rail and road traffic. A fair bit of discussion of public administration is confined to the doings and preoccupations of the latter – that is those who are engaged actively in the policy making process. Here, clearly, the public administration issues arise in their most unambiguous forms. Nonetheless, the general proposition can stand that public administration comprises those who are engaged in government but who are not politicians, who carry out the work of government in bodies set up under statute for such a purpose.

2. The Study of Public Administration

Public administration is a subject of great diversity and complexity. How do we reduce that diversity to some sort of manageable groupings and terms? While public administration as an activity is extremely well developed and highly sophisticated, public administration as a study is in a very backward condition indeed.

Why should we study a subject of this kind? There are at least five reasons – the importance of government, its increasing role in society, the high proportion of trained people it employs, the importance of giving them useful and fulfilling jobs and the value of encouraging them to think more deeply about those jobs.

The first reason is, as we have seen, the inherent *importance* of government in modern societies both qualitatively and quantitatively. This is especially true of Ireland, where the responsibilities of government are very great because of the shortage of enterprise in the country and the lack of spontaneous economic development adequate to our needs and aspirations. It becomes the task of government here to try to bridge this gap between the aspirations of our people and their actual performance. On the whole, government has not been very successful in discharging this responsibility and is now faced with new challenges of great intensity such as that of providing for the employment of (relatively) great numbers of young people. These disappointments have not been for want of trying on the part of both politicians and administrators, but for lack of effective operation of the governmental machine as a whole. Hence, it is in the national interest to study how the machine may be made more effective.

Accordingly, there is the need for a continuing, lively scrutiny of old ideas and assumptions and their replacement where that is appropriate. Many failures of effective Irish government can be traced to two root causes, both on the conceptual level. These will be considered further later; but here let them be briefly put. The first has been the reluctance to grasp, at least until recent times, that the basic task of Irish government is development. The second has been the continuing failure to accept that government in action is a big and complex business calling for very special forms of management if it is to operate successfully. These failings, in their turn, come from the continuance of practices based on out-of-date ideas. The Department of Finance, for example, in its heyday as the (very effective) guardian of the public purse could find support for opposing developmental ideas that, inevitably, cost public money in the belief that public spending was necessarily less productive than private spending, and that public investment could occur only at the expense of private investment. That was once a largely unquestioned belief. It rested on the assumption that there was competition for resources between public and private enterprise when, in fact, there was a shortage of both kinds of enterprise, when, indeed, public enterprise was a condition for the development of private enterprise. It was thus quite inappropriate to the real needs of this country if development was to be stimulated and sustained.

Again, as we shall see in the next chapter, the basic system established to ensure the democratic accountability of government rested on the idea that the job of a minister in charge of a government department is very like that of a manager in charge of a small business—he should take all the decisions and have his finger in every pie. The framers of this legislation were themselves the products of shops and farms of which this was manifestly true. Government is not small business, but very big business indeed. Nonetheless, the system, based on such faulty analysis, continues.

Part of the case for the study of public administration is the need for an intellectual base on which a critique of such survivals can rest.

A second main reason for studying public administration is the steadily increasing role of government in all countries in relation to social problems, in the redistribution of increased resources within the society and the provision of great services such as education, health and, increasingly, transport. The orderly development of these services in line with the increased resources and needs on the economic front is essential to the orderly development of the society as a whole and to the maintenance of political stability. Success in this task makes heavy demands on the skill, intelligence and imagination of those concerned.

Thirdly, as we have seen, government is a great employer of educated, skilled and trained people. It is important for the overall progress of the society to ensure that these people give of the best of their abilities to the society, that the framework in which they operate should facilitate this, and that they themselves should have fulfilling jobs.

Fourthly, part of the fulfilment of any job is an understanding by the practitioner of the world he operates in. The less that world seems to be mysterious, unpredictable, irrational—the less it represents a Kafka novel—the more likely he is to feel at home in it and to make the best possible contribution to it.

Finally, one of the best features of human living is reflection, the ability, and the regular desire, to reflect constantly on what one is doing, to draw insights from it, to contribute in some way to the triumph of orderly thought over the random, the disorderly and the unpredictable, and so to increase the effectiveness of one's lifetime's activities.

Discussion in this country of these issues received a major boost from the publication of the report of the Public Services Organisation Review Group, 1966–69, (PSORG) usually called the Devlin report after the chairman of the Group, Dr Liam St J. Devlin.

Public administration in a recognisably modern sense existed, at least since the beginning of our era, in the Chinese and Roman Empires. However, it was not until the fall of feudalism and the rise of the modern nation states in the sixteenth and seventeenth centuries that modern European systems of public administration began to be established (Finer, 1961, p. 724 ff). Over the past four centuries we can see laid down the foundations of the subject—first, the concern for regularity, then for professional personnel, then for more efficient public bodies, then for more effective policy making, and, finally, for greater awareness of people as the clientele of public administration.

A major influence in continental Europe was the rediscovery of Roman law which led to the adoption of a unified, crystallised, codified set of legal principles, the logic of which decided the outcome of any particular case. This led to the first great insight into the study of public administration, namely, that of *regularity*. Acts of government must be authorised by law, the procedures followed must be within the law, actions must be carried on according to the spirit of the law, and—a gradual development—discretion exercised within the law must not be arbitrary or biased but must also conform to the general principles. With the rise of despotism in Europe, benevolent and otherwise, the lawyers elaborated various principles to justify the arbitrary actions of the 'prince'; but as democracy developed, the general principles of Roman law conformed to democratic requirements and these principles continue to dominate the systems of public administration in the continental European countries. Up to recently a great proportion of the higher civil servants in the continental European countries were students of law and very high prestige attaches still to those who are skilled administrative lawyers, for example, those who staff the Conseil d'État in France. This training gives a special flavour to the operations, nowadays, of the institutions of the European Community. British public administration, and consequently Irish public administration, did not receive this influence of Roman law as a firm moulder of the way public institutions carry out their business, and consequently have to adapt themselves in the European institutions to unfamiliar ways.

Nonetheless, whether the system of public administration has been directly influenced by Roman law as in the continental European countries, or by a mixture of common law and Roman law as in the United States, or by common law increasingly influenced by the practices of these other countries, as in Britain and Ireland, the first great principle of public administration is regularity.

The second great strand in the development of the subject has been concern with the *personnel* of the higher civil service, its methods of recruitment and its training, both before and after entry to the service (Finer, 1961, p. 729ff). Here the lead was given, most strikingly, by Prussia in the years after the Thirty Years' War which ended in 1648.

By the end of the century the holding of public office by hereditary right, and the holding of sinecures, had been substantially abolished. Gradually, from about 1700, appointees, first for the courts offices and then for the higher civil service generally, had to meet certain prescribed qualifications, have certain training, and pass written and oral examinations. For the higher civil service generally the King, Frederick William, was anxious to protect them from the training of lawyers and established three chairs of 'Cameralism' (that is, of general administration) in three Prussian universities for the purpose of training aspirants to the higher civil service. In the end, the lawyers won out to the extent that even still the typical German higher civil servant has been trained as a lawyer.

Orderly competitive systems of recruitment, and adequate preparation for public service, began to be adopted in the United Kingdom from the 1850s after the Northcote-Trevelyan report, and in the United States after the passing of the Civil Service Commission Act of 1883. In France the position was not fully regularised until after World War II, since when most aspirants for the higher civil service have been recruited through the École Nationale d'Administration in which they get a special preparation for their future duties for almost three years (ÉNA, 1975; B. Chapman, pp. 115–24). Conditions at the ÉNA often change.

The third great strand in the development of public administration has been the effort to make the various public bodies more *efficient*. Here again the Prussian civil service was a pioneer, but the modern approach to this question substantially derives from the rise of two movements in the United States towards the end of the last century. The first was the movement to reform public institutions that got its intellectual influences from university schools of politics (Wilson) and law (Goodnow). But the major impetus came from the rise, about the same time, of the scientific management movement, and a parallel rise, though a more limited one, in France in the early years of the present century. In the United States the management movement arose principally in the private sector and proved an inspiration for those concerned with the reform of various public bodies there. Enriched by the contributions of the sciences of psychology, sociology, and economics it made a dramatic impact on public service thinking in Europe after World War II.

The fourth main strand has been the rise in the interest in *policy making*. This got a great impetus from the economics of J. M. Keynes which showed that government could, by wise economic policies, help to accelerate economic growth and moderate the effects of economic slumps. As he wrote: 'The authoritarian state systems of today seem to solve the problem of unemployment at the expense of efficiency and of freedom. It is certain that the world will not much longer tolerate the unemployment which, apart from brief intervals of excitement, is associated – and, in my opinion, inevitably associated – with present day capitalistic individualism. But it may be possible by a right analysis of the problem to cure the disease whilst preserving efficiency and freedom' (Keynes, 1936, Ch. 24). For a generation after World War II it seemed that Keynes's ideas, coupled with sophisticated administration, would make for a speedy solution of most economic problems.

A further contribution came from the socialist ideas of economic planning, successfully operated in a democracy in France after World War II (Massé, 1962; Monnet, 1978, Ch. 10). This had a big impact on a number of other countries, including Ireland. Planning has since fanned out, in most countries, to cover not only economic, but social, infra-structural, cultural and other facets of public policy.

These two influences—Keynesian economics and planning—show that on the quality of governmental policy-making a great deal of the well-being of modern societies depends. It is perhaps typical of the human condition that the situation should now have turned full circle and that we are again faced with a western system plagued by unemployment.

The fifth strand derives from the increasing democratisation of society, the increasing acceptance of the well-being of *people* as the ultimate objective of government. So has arisen the modern interest in public administration as a social study, and as a means of synthesising the insights of the various social disciplines, including, by now, political science. The very growth in the size of government has, in a number of countries, raised critical problems of the relationship between the government and the citizens. These problems include the apparent alienation of large numbers of the citizens from the government elected to serve them, the intransigence of protest groups, the dangers of a break-down of law and order. Finally, there has been the growth of the idea that perhaps ad-ministrative efficiency consists less in technocracy and more in humaneness.

These issues have led a number of European countries to be concerned about the various structures and operations of government, in particular how to bring these operations closer to the people and how to get them to participate more effectively in them. This has led to renewed interest in the problem of remedying grievances, in systems of administrative law, in the Swedish institution of ombudsman, 'open government', and other similar ideas.

The history of the subject is one of increasing complexity. It is not enough that the public administration observes the rules of regularity; it must be staffed by people who are competent; it must be managed so as to give an efficient return for the resources employed in it; it must produce policies that are effective to solve the problems before it; and it must do all of these things in such a way as to preserve human rights and to win the acceptance and participation of the citizens.

What we see, therefore, is the growth over some four centuries of an increasing understanding of the nature of the tasks performed by government and the requirements for the effective performance of those tasks. In some respects, notably amongst the administrative lawyers in continental Europe, this has reached a very high level of sophistication indeed. In other respects, notably in the approach to administrative structures in the United Kingdom in recent years, it seems to have been little more than a running after the latest fashion.

So far as Ireland is concerned, where the need for effective systems of government is perhaps greater than with most other western European countries, the situation is, overall, very unsatisfactory. This has been, partly, because of the overwhelming influence of British ways of thinking about these problems, but mainly because of our refusal to realise that *what* it is possible to do about our problems depends greatly on *how* we tackle our tasks. A big intellectual task lies ahead of us if we are to improve our success rate.

There are a number of intellectual difficulties in approaching this study. The first is, as we have seen, the problem of description. What are the boundaries of the subject? This is made more difficult to answer because they tend to shift, as we have seen, both in relation to politics and to the business world and are in other respects, also, very hazy and ambiguous. So, it is very difficult to describe the boundaries of the subject with any degree of precision.

The second problem is that of categories. If one comes across a great jumble of what seems to be disorderly material, one's temptation is to sort like with like and put each category in a separate pile. In this way one gets some sort of conception of what is contained in the jumble. Public administration, from this point of view, is in a very jumbled condition indeed. The trouble is to decide, when one is trying to segregate one thing from another in one's mind, what intellectual pile each class of activity ought to be put into? One classification is into various kinds of things done; but this raises difficulties of its own. For example, a major activity of government is education. In Ireland, at the first level, primary education is substantially financed and almost entirely in practice provided by central government. At the second level, the older forms of secondary schools are financed only in part by central government, at least where fees are still being charged, so these secondary schools are still regarded as private bodies. The comprehensive schools are basically state-run schools, but the vocational schools are local authority schools. At the third level, the universities are established under statute or charter, are substantially financed by the State, yet are regarded in some way as private bodies. Similar problems arise in relation to health, to agriculture, and so on.

Another classification is the traditional one of central government, (or the civil service), local government, and the state-sponsored bodies. Here the categorisation is presumably intended to be substantially according to the analytical nature of the operation carried on, rather than the functional area in which it occurs. But in practice, this division is even more confusing than the other because no one seems to be able to define in any comprehensive way what services are basically central, local or functional. Any one of them could be anywhere and, as we have seen in the educational example, various types of schools–to take one of many examples–are distributed between central, local, private and functional bodies on no discernible principles.

These problems arise because of the higgledy piggledy growth of government. Institutions have been set up as ad hoc responses to needs, identified according to random pressures, and devised according to the fashionable form of public body at the moment. For example, in the early part of the nineteenth century it was fashionable to give a number of public services to government departments. Then, there was the tendency to give public services to local authorities. Later still boards–something like what we now call state-sponsored bodies–were all the fashion. At the beginning of this century the fashion changed back to government departments. For example, when the telephone service was nationalised, it was given to a government department. Nowadays, the fashion is for the state-sponsored body. In local government the accent in the last century was on small local authorities, in the earlier part of this century it was on larger ones such as counties, and now the fashion is for regional bodies grouping several counties together. Through all these ad hoc decisions can any sorts of patterns be discerned or any discriminating principles?

The answer one gives to that question depends on how one approaches it. The answer would be 'yes' if we tried to impose, for the purposes of description, some sort of order on the material before us. The answer would be 'no' if we accept that any such order is something purely subjective, in our own heads or textbooks, and unlikely to be seen in practice, unless, perhaps, over a very long period. Nonetheless, that is what science is about, attempting to understand the material and putting forward some sort of provisional answers that can be tested against the facts. It has been said that science has progressed not so much by providing the answers as by progressively clarifying the questions. We do this by arriving at an hypothesis that seems to explain the facts, testing this against the facts and then revising the hypothesis to take account of any deviations between the original hypothesis and the facts.

However, the notion of the detached observer is itself a myth. If there can be a Heisenberg principle in physics, how much more sensitive is this area! As we have seen, public institutions have been constituted according to prevailing fashions so that what goes on in our heads is likely, sooner or later, to affect some fashion and thus, to that extent, alter the data themselves. This may buoy up the conscientious reformer but it limits the pretensions of the scientist.

Nonetheless, we must do the best we can and, warily, adopt this sort of approach if we are to lay any foundations for an administrative science.

As we progressively begin to understand the problems and potentialities of the present state of intellectual and practical confusion, a more orderly system can be induced to emerge from it. Indeed this is essential if government is to keep on growing in size and importance in the way it has been growing over the past decades, and if those who make their lives within the governmental machine are to give of their best to increase the well-being, the mutual concern, and the intellectual and moral development of all the members of the community.

The first task is to try to get some perspective of the subject and of such unity as it possesses as the study of a very complex system. In a sense, this is to take a ridge walk in mountainy country with tortured geology, complex geography and beautiful scenery. One cannot, in such a walk, hope to understand fully the constituents of the shapes, the occupational patterns, the colours and the full causes of all this variety; but one can, nonetheless, get some overall conception of the whole, see it in a preliminary perspective, and relate what there is later to be learnt about detail to a single unifying concept of place. That is what this book attempts to do in relation to the complexities of the Irish administrative system.

3. The System of Government

The basic unit of study for public administration has been, within the broad range of government, the public body and its behaviour. Traditionally, a good part of this study has been about what goes on inside these institutions, in particular the relationships between each institution and those who staff it, and the policy-making process within the institution. However, as government grows more complex, increasing interest is being taken in the relationships of the various institutions with one another (O'Donnell, 1979). So we move from such long standing studies as 'The Civil Service', or 'Local Government' to what is known as 'The Machinery of Government' or, as I would now prefer to call it, 'The System of Public Administration'. Both these expressions, however, 'Machinery' and 'System' imply a rational ordering of the various institutions which to some extent begs the question of whether there is any such thing.

But first, some facts. Even in a small country like Ireland the number of institutions involved in public administration is very great. What one includes in any such count and what one leaves out are matters for some debate, but my count, as of January 1978, gives about 420 separate institutions. In central government there are just short of sixty of these bodies — eighteen government departments, and about forty commissions, offices, agencies. These latter range from very large bodies like the Revenue Commission to very small bodies indeed. There are about ninety state-sponsored bodies, again ranging in size from (by Irish standards) giants like Coras Iompair Éireann, the Electricity Supply Board and Aer Lingus, to minute bodies. In local government there are 115 directly elected bodies, 25 regional bodies, about 134 miscellaneous local bodies comprising vocational education committees, committees of agriculture, harbour authorities, fisheries boards, and game councils.

The constitutions, sizes, and duties of these bodies are extraordinarily diverse. For example, they range in size from the Department of Posts and Telegraphs, with a staff of over 25,000, down to very small organisations, such as the regional development organisations, with staffs of two or three. The total numbers employed at January 1978 amounted to about 274,000, made up of some 58,000 in the Civil Service, some 25,000 between the Army and the Gardai, some 60,000 in state-sponsored bodies, some 35,000 in local government, and some 53,000 in the health services, and about 42,000 employed in education (Administration Yearbook & Diary, 1979, p. 296). In all, about one-third of those employed (that is, other than those self-employed) in the State.

In all this diversity, what unifying factors can we identify? At least four:
(1) the Government;
(2) constitutional and legal constraints;
(3) the notion of 'the public service'; and
(4) common communication systems.

The first of these is the Government itself. The Constitution provides that there shall be not more than fifteen members of the Government, that is, full ministers, and that the business of government be distributed amongst them in accordance with law (Bunreacht, Art. 28). The division of functions has been done through a series of acts known as the Ministers and Secretaries Acts. Responsibility for the performance of those more than 400 public bodies and over 270,000 public servants is concentrated in the members of the government. Sometimes this responsibility consists in a duty of general overseeing, as is the normal practice in relation to state-sponsored bodies. Sometimes, however, the responsibility is for every detailed action taken by officers of the body—as is the general system in Ireland in relation to the civil service.

In general, ministers are accountable to the Dáil for the way they exercise these responsibilities. In relation to the civil service, this accountability tends to be very detailed. In relation to most state-sponsored bodies, at the other extreme, the accountability is largely in relation to overall performance. Ministers are held accountable by means of parliamentary questions, debates on the estimates for their departments, motions moved by members of the Dáil, and whenever they are proposing legislation to give additional powers or funds to any public body. The theory runs that by concentrating responsibility in the members of the Government, and their being readily held accountable by the public representatives in parliament, democratic control is maintained over the whole system.

However, many would argue that the methods used to effect parliamentary scrutiny are out of date and, in general, do not match in their effectiveness the very considerable powers that are vested in ministers. In practice, the great weapon of parliamentary control is publicity. In this way the media also participate in the democratic means of holding ministers accountable for the discharge of their functions (Chubb, 1974).

One can think of the system of government as something like a pie divided into segments. The diagram opposite illustrates one of these segments. At the apex of each segment is the minister. Immediately surrounding him are his principal advisers—those who, in Devlin terms, would constitute the 'aireacht'—and then at a further remove the rest of the staff of the department over which he presides. Further out in the same segment are the various non-civil-service bodies, the state-sponsored bodies, and local and regional bodies of various kinds that come within that particular minister's segment and that normally relate to him through his department.

So, the concentration of responsibility in members of the government and their accountability for the way they exercise these responsibilities to the Dáil—these constitute the first unifying factor in the whole system of public administration.

In effect this first unifying factor is the political process itself. The members of the government know that if they cannot hold the whole system together and drive it forward in the interest of overall development they individually, and their party collectively, will be held severely to account at the next general election.

The second unifying factor is the system of constitutional and legal constraints that governs the establishment of these bodies and their conduct once established. They must go about their business in accordance with the provisions of the Constitution and the general law of the land, as well as the particular laws that relate to them (Chubb, 1964). In addition, they must behave according to the general principles of these laws and in accordance with such rules as those of natural justice. These rules will, in effect, determine their manner of operation. Here, again, they can be held accountable—this time to the courts and, as the courts have been interpreting our present Constitution, they are steadily laying down ground rules that determine how these bodies may go about their jobs. Amongst other things, as is explained in Chapter 7, they have been whittling away at pretensions that ministers have inherited something of royal prerogative, and that raison d'état has a place under our Constitution.

The third unifying factor is the emerging concept of a single Irish public service. That is to say, there is increasing recognition of the fact that all of those who are employed in the business of government (or of public administration) ultimately are employed by, and serve, the same ultimate master, the plain people of Ireland. Of course, the jobs in an airline, say,

SEGMENT OF GOVERNMENTAL SYSTEM

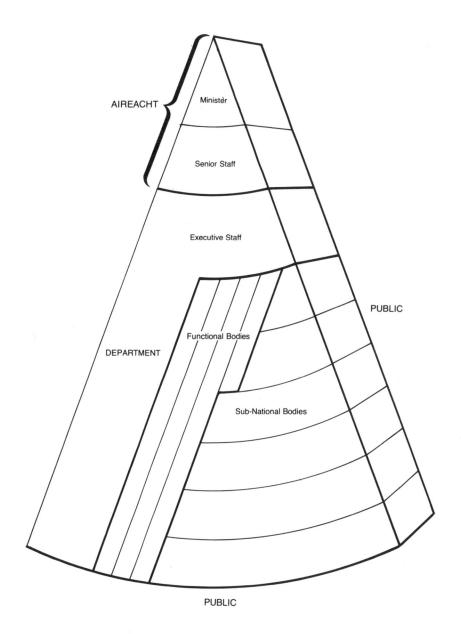

AIREACHT

Ministèr

Senior Staff

Executive Staff

PUBLIC

Functional Bodies

DEPARTMENT

Sub-National Bodies

PUBLIC

are not very like those in a health board or in a government department; but behind the diversity, there is the common task of providing a public service. To a greater or less degree of intensity the same political rules apply to all those employed by bodies in the public sector, and the same constitutional and legal ones. In the last analysis, the success or failure of any of these bodies will depend, to a quite remarkable extent, on the success or failure of the appropriate minister in handling its problems around the cabinet table, in securing resources for it, and, when legislation is necessary, in gaining the assent of parliament to what he proposes.

It was because of the increasing recognition of this basic public service unity that the Department of the Public Service was set up in 1973. Of course, one cannot speak of 'The Public Service' in the same sense as one can speak of 'The Civil Service' or 'The Local Government Service' because, so far at least, there are no common recruitment patterns, transferability, superannuation provisions and so on that are essential in order to constitute an operating 'service'. But many less tangible factors, such as professional commitment and ethics, are common to all branches of the public service.

Fourthly, there are common communication systems throughout all the various bodies. The Devlin Report (PSORG, paras. 12.4.1–12.7.7) identified four of these, activities that were common to all the bodies and therefore could, and do, act as channels of communication through them. These are finance, planning, personnel, and organisation.

The most prominent of these, is, of course, finance. One thing that is common to almost every one of these many bodies is that they spend significant sums of public money. Public money must be raised, it must be allocated according to some sort of common principles, it must be spent in accordance with common rules, and it must be accounted for to the ultimate fund-raising body, the Dáil. One has only to look at the book of annual estimates or the published appropriation accounts to see the extraordinary ramifications of finance and how it provides a common language for linking the most diverse of activities together.

Slowly, and with great difficulty, another communication system is being established, that of planning. The planners, and through them the Government, look out over the system of public administration and attempt to see it whole. Contradictions are identified and hitherto unsuspected linkages and conflicts are made manifest. Again, a common language is created for communicating throughout the diverse system.

The third of these communicating systems is that of personnel management which arises from the common factor of the public service, and the common manpower and personnel problems that it presents. Everybody has to be equipped with a method of enabling all these personnel problems to be dealt with in accordance with some common principles.

Finally, there is the as yet embryonic set of ideas of how to set about organising this whole complex of bodies into a freely functioning system where there will be a logical place for everything and everything will be in its place. This is what the Devlin Report identified as the organisation function.

At the centre of the administration there are, now, in addition to the general co-ordinating role of the Department of the Taoiseach, three specialised co-ordinating departments concerned with handling these communication channels. The present system of four co-ordinating departments and fourteen operating departments is set out in the chart on page 24.

The finance communication system feeds into the Department of Finance, the planning one into the Department of Economic Planning and Development, and the personnel and organisation ones into the Department of the Public Service. Part of the task of these three departments is to develop these channels so that communications run more freely and effectively through them. While the task of developing and improving the finance channel is considerable, the tasks facing the other two departments are, given the poor state of development of the planning, personnel and organisation functions, truly formidable.

The Department of the Taoiseach has become much more active in relation to the discharge of the overall business of government. There had always been provision for ensuring that the financial side of the business was co-ordinated by the Department of Finance; but there are many other aspects of government business that require co-ordination, the resolution of conflicts, and the development of agreed and coherent policies between different departments. This business has grown greatly in recent years, and is now a major preoccupation of what is still the very small, but increasingly important, Department of the Taoiseach. That department has also developed a significant rôle in relation to government information policy.

The main co-ordinating department has been the Department of Finance, concerned to advise the government about living within its means. This remains its function, a matter of crucial importance; but it has lost two other co-ordinating functions – concern for the public service, to the Department of that name, and planning to the new Department of Economic Planning and Development.

There are a number of ways of categorising government departments, but from the view point of government as a whole they can be seen to fall into two distinct categories – those departments (Taoiseach, Finance, Public Service, and Economic Planning and Development) whose main task is concerned with the co-ordination of government action, and the remaining departments, the operating ones, such as Agriculture, Health, Justice, and the rest. It is a matter for some thought whether *four* co-ordinating departments may not pose problems of co-ordination amongst

STRUCTURE OF GOVERNMENT
DEPARTMENTS, JUNE, 1979.

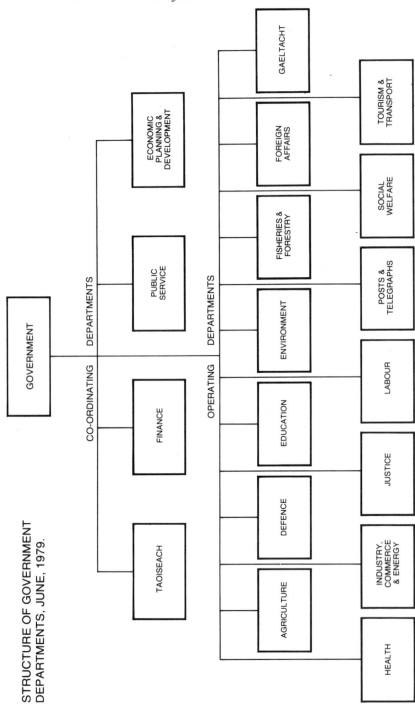

themselves (Clarke, 1971, p. 62). Quis custodiet . . . ?

Nonetheless, in all this it is possible to see common understanding and unification in the vast complexity of the system of public administration.

The expression 'machinery of government' has been used to describe the totality of the various public bodies we have been considering, and their complex interactions (Haldane, 1918; Barrington, 1975, Ch. 2). 'Machinery' implies a logic in the distribution of business as between these various bodies, and as to their relationships. It is almost impossible to discover any such logic. Nonetheless, discussion in this country and in others has brought the subject far enough to enable us to consider it in at least broad terms. So, let us try to stand back from the present confusion, itself the product of disorderly historical development.

The traditional division of the functions of government has been, so far as Ireland is concerned, into three – central government, functional government, and geographical government. In the continental European countries there is a fourth branch, which might be called appellate government, but, as we shall see later, this is virtually undeveloped in this country.

The chart on page 26 sets out, in perhaps more logical order than exists in practice, the executive system of Irish government. Within that system the first task of central government is to settle overall policy. The actual execution of the policies is done in the three traditional executive areas, each in terms of manpower, broadly equal in size. In the centre we have the executive services carried out by government departments and by the civil service agencies and offices. To the left we have the functional executive services carried out by the two kinds of state-sponsored body – the commercial state-sponsored bodies (such as Córas Iompair Éireann (CIE), Aer Lingus, Electricity Supply Board (ESB) and the non-commercial state-sponsored bodies (such as Bord Fáilte, Córas Tráchtála (CTT), Industrial Development Authority (IDA)). To the right we have the executive services carried out by the two kinds of geographical, or subnational, bodies – the regional bodies (such as the health boards), and the local government bodies proper (such as county councils).

It is very hard to get any coherent or logical system by which to describe the rôles of each of these kinds of bodies. They have grown up substantially by accident, and by reaction from the consequences of earlier fashionable thinking. For example, when the state was set up there was a clear determination to concentrate, so far as humanly possible, responsibility for the conduct of the system of government as a whole into the hands of ministers. This meant the wholesale abolition of various kinds of boards (or state-sponsored bodies as we might now call them) and of small local authorities, and the concentration, so far as local government was concerned, of all effective authority in the then Minister for Local Government and Public Health. However, this intense centralisation was no sooner achieved than

THE EXECUTIVE SYSTEM OF IRISH GOVERNMENT

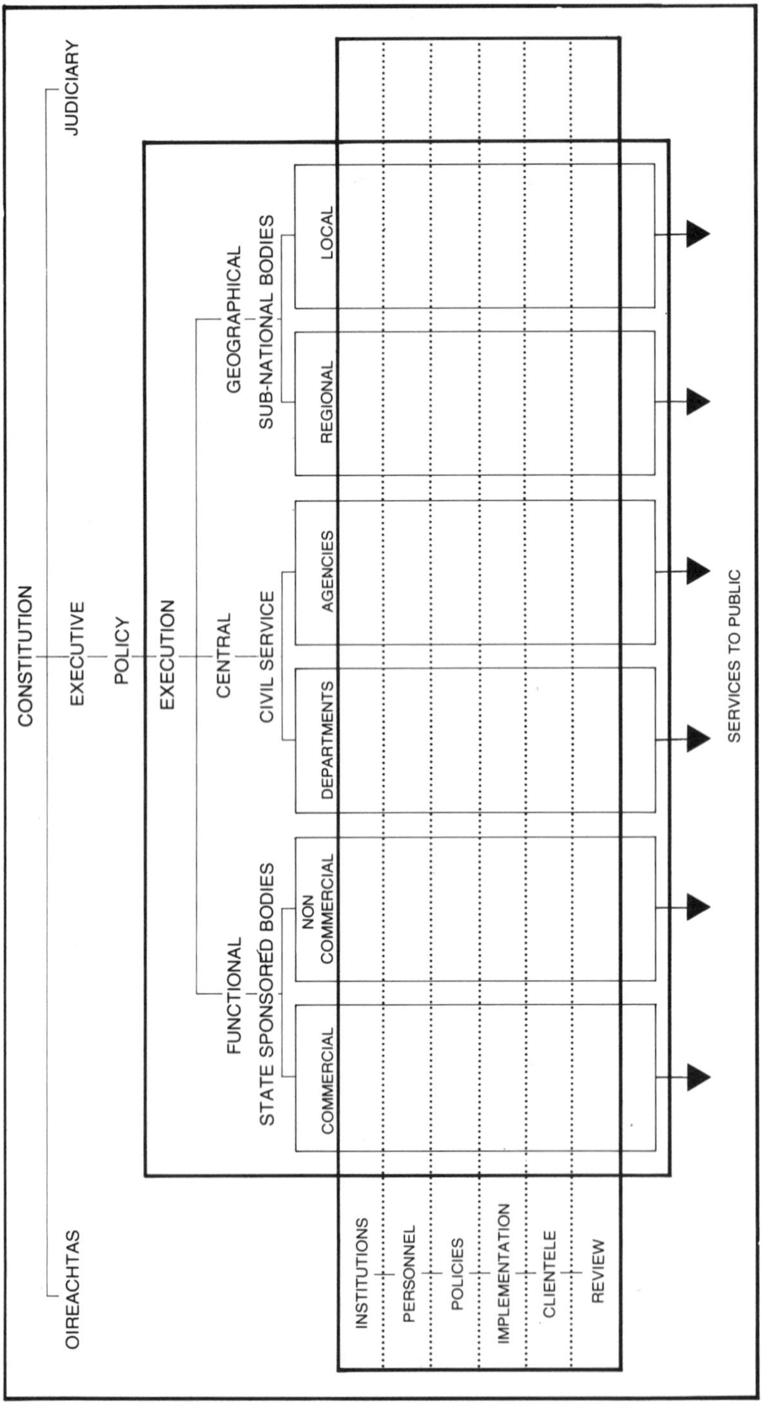

it began to break down and new state-sponsored bodies began to be established. As the years went by, these bodies became very numerous. No one really knew what was appropriate to a state-sponsored body and what was appropriate to a government department. In 1969 the Devlin Report tried to rationalise the functions of the two kinds of bodies (PSORG, Ch. 13).

Devlin's analysis of one of the major problems of Irish public administration was that the centralisation of detailed business in ministers was clogging up the centres of decision and interfering with the special task of the higher civil service, which was to advise ministers on the formulation of policy. They recommended that the administration of day-to-day work should be transferred to agencies rather like the non-commercial state-sponsored bodies. They did not, apart from my Addendum (reprinted in Barrington, 1975, Ch. 3), tackle the question of the rôle of local government.

This was the beginning of an attempt to get a logical differentiation between the rôles of the various types of bodies. The task of central government would be to deal with overall questions, to improve the formulation of policy and to raise the level of co-ordination of government activities by means of improved financial procedures, by means of planning, by means of overall policies for the effective use of the personnel of the public service, and by means of rationalising the structures of government.

The task of the functional branches of government would be to carry out various commercial activities, to deal with specific promotional and developmental functions, and to deal with such overseas functions as were not directly related to foreign policy (PSORG, Ch. 13, Part II passim). No line was laid down for the functions of local government, but it has certain distinctive characteristics. It is operated under the general control of local representatives directly or indirectly elected. It tends (in other countries to a greater extent than in Ireland) to provide particularly those services that impinge directly on people. It may also, in consequence of this, have some relevance to those governmental services that are 'thick on the ground', as it were.

There has been a slowly awakening interest in these problems of how to distribute the business of government to the most appropriate agencies. This arises partly from the growth, the size, and the pervasiveness of government. It arises because the people now have more leisure and are better educated and are, therefore, more concerned to play some active part in public affairs. Finally, it arises because of the increasing anxieties about the effectiveness of this very large body of governmental activity.

We have a certain amount of discussion nowadays about centralisation and decentralisation of government work and agencies and, in relation to the latter, of the concepts of deconcentration, devolution, and dispersal.

Following the Devlin lines there is a very strong case for the centralisation of policy making and overall governmental management in the interest of making that management more effective. But what about decentralisation?

First, it is important to know what we mean by each of the terms we have used. The decision to move the Department of Lands to Castlebar (and the actual implementation of that decision by moving a fragment of the Department there) was a decision for the *dispersal* of a government department.

This was also true of the decision about the Department of Education moving to Athlone. Dispersal is often confused with decentralisation, but it is not *decentralisation* because the department, or its appropriate part, remains just as centralised as before. Dispersal may have its own advantages, but it does not come under the heading of decentralisation.

Decentralisation can be either deconcentration or devolution. If the decision has been, say, to reorganise the Department of Education on a regional and/or county basis and to give real authority and discretion within the department to a regional or county director, that would be *deconcentration*. In this way decision-making is decentralised throughout the country.

The further step of transferring these departmental, regional or county functions to a regional or county authority—as is the practice in many countries—would be devolution. In this, decision-making would be devolved from ministers and their direct representatives, to other bodies such as regional or county authorities (Barrington, 1975, Ch. 3).

It is clear that certain functions of government could not be decentralised. Overall economic and financial policy, foreign policy, defence, final responsibility for the well-being of the society in its broadest sense—these must remain with central government.

Certain other technological functions, where economies of scale are of great importance—such as the generation of electricity—are best, also, dealt with on a nationwide basis, by a functional body such as a state-sponsored body. Other commercial and specialised promotional functions—especially those relating to activities outside the country—are also clearly appropriate to centralised state-sponsored bodies.

However, the vast mass of detailed government business falls outside these classes and the question remains: what sort of body is best fitted to discharge them?

We will discuss these issues later. For the moment it is perhaps only necessary to point out that great perplexities exist in all of these questions and that it is the task of those who study public administration to try to produce some sort of principles by which these problems could be tackled so that what we might call 'institutional development' can be got going. We have had too much hunting after fashion in fits and starts, and too little thought about how best to produce a gradually developing model of a system of government coherently organised to meet the political, infrastructural, economic, social, and cultural needs of the people if the consensus, on which the whole enterprise depends, is to be maintained and enhanced.

Chapter 2: Institutions

1. Central Government: The Civil Service

Central government is that branch of public administration carried on by the civil service under the direct or general supervision of ministers. Strictly, there are two civil services – the civil service of the government and the civil service of the state, that is of the other branches of the state administration, specifically, of the Oireachtas, of the Attorney General and, I would hazard, though the issue does not seem to have been decided, of the Courts (*McLoughlin* v. *Minister for Social Welfare*, 1959; Staff of the Houses of the Oireachtas Act, 1959). However, the civil service of the state need not detain us. It is very small in relation to the civil service of the government and raises very few issues of its own.

In total the civil service is very large. In 1978 it comprised about 58,000 people (Administration Yearbook and Diary, 1979, p. 25). Even when one excludes what are called 'industrial civil servants' (e.g. forestry workers, Board of Works labourers etc), it numbers close to 50,000, half of whom are in the Department of Posts & Telegraphs running the postal and telecommunications services.

When we talk about the civil service we usually have in mind a fairly restricted number of people. We think particularly of those who are grouped in the administrative class, whose special task is advising ministers and dealing with the higher work of government departments. These number about 1,100 people. They are flanked by two other important groups: a group of generalists in the executive class, numbering just 2,800, and a group of specialists, including professional officers, numbering just 4,000. These three groups of rather less than 8,000 people attract most of the attention. But their work rests on a base supplied by over 40,000 persons employed in other groups. These are the 'outdoor' staffs–inspectors, technicians, postmen; the great body of 'clerks'–the clerical and typing staffs and their supervisors; and the messengers, etc. When we talk of 'policy' it is the 8,000 with which we are mainly concerned; but when we concern ourselves with questions of institutions and personnel in central government then the whole body of civil servants is included

(Dooney, 1976).

The temper of our civil service is substantially governed by two things. The first is the tradition of the British civil service which was inherited when we achieved independence in 1922. At that time some 21,000 civil servants were transferred to the service of the new state and these transferred officers occupied the greater part of the significant posts in the civil service for many years after that (Fanning, 1978, Ch. 12). Given the very considerable traditions of the British civil service, and the quality of professionalism it displayed, this was a formidable asset for the state. Above all, the civil service has proved itself to be loyal, diligent, intelligent, austere and honest.

Certain weaknesses were also inherited, particularly the lack of overall concern for the performance of the system as a whole, as distinct from the day-to-day operation. One of the maxims of the British civil service was 'clear sight over short distances'. This became very much the mark of the Irish civil service. Coupled with this was the tradition, reinforced by the bent of the Irish temperament, of being suspicious of any thinking that claimed to be systematic and concerned with the long-term. These still remain, overall, significant criticisms that can be made of our civil service.

The second main influence was that embodied in the Ministers and Secretaries Act, 1924. This act provided that the business of government would be divided over eleven departments. In the years before the war two extra departments were created under acts amending the Ministers and Secretaries Acts – Lands and Supplies. Both of these departments have now disappeared. One department – Fisheries – lost its separate existence. Since the war eight additional departments have been created, the most recent (in 1977) being the Department of Economic Planning and Development. There are now eighteen departments. In addition there have been a number of changes of name and of transfer of duties from one department to another (Administration Yearbook and Diary, 1979, p. 25). The departments and principal offices are listed and categorised on p. 153 below.

The most significant feature of the Ministers and Secretaries Act of 1924, which has not been altered in all the subsequent amending acts, has been the creation of the minister as the 'corporation sole' of the department (Section 2(1); PSORG, 4.1.1-11). That is to say, the legal personality is the minister and the department is no more than an extension of that personality. Legal powers, with very few exceptions, are given to the minister and, to be validly exercised, must be performed by him or under his explicit direction. In this way the attempt was made to ensure that ministers would be fully in control of the business of government and thus fully answerable to the Dáil for their performances. It may have been feasible in the early days of the state for the minister to decide everything of significance in the department, but, as the business of government grew, this became increasingly impracticable. Nonetheless, this remains the legal foundation of the intense centralisation of Irish government.

If the minister personally could not decide everything then he could informally, if strictly illegally, delegate his powers to a small number of the most senior officials in the department. These officials would readily know the minister's mind on broad classes of questions and decide accordingly. If there were any later question about these decisions, he would have ready access to whoever took the decision. The consequence of all this was that an immense quantity of detailed business came to be discharged at the very tops of the departments. The senior officials, instead of being preoccupied with broad questions of policy, became more and more burdened with matters of detail (Whitaker, 1961).

Thus the legal and constitutional position reinforced the natural traditions of the service and the temperament of the Irish people. But the special steps taken to ensure that the minister would be in control of the whole operation proved selfdefeating. He could be in control, with his most senior advisers, of a great mass of detail; but who would be in control of the whole drift of policy in his sphere of operation? Exceptional ministers and exceptional civil servants broke out of this constricting situation; but, overall, the majority have been unable to transcend it.

Balancing this concentration of authority and responsibility in ministers was a widespread acceptance of the need to depoliticise much of public business, to have it carried on 'in a businesslike way'. Notwithstanding the still surviving popular belief that public administration is steeped in 'politics', they have to a considerable extent been kept apart. Politicians, even in the ministries, have struggled to keep politics out of the day-to-day conduct of public affairs, and officials have stayed out of politics. The extent to which public administration has been depoliticised in this country is, on the whole, unusual. The clearest manifestation of this striving towards depoliticisation was in the attempts to make local government – heavily politicised on independence – more 'businesslike'. But the most striking example, adopted almost in an absent-minded way, as a solution to the problems raised by concentrating so much responsibility in ministers, was 'hiving-off' from government departments by committing new services to state-sponsored bodies and, from time to time, breaking off services discharged by departments to specialised, newly established state-sponsored bodies. Again, 'business' seemed to provide a suitable model for depoliticisation. This hiving-off enabled particular activities to get specialised care without overburdening ministers and senior officials; but it raised all sorts of difficulties of its own. There was confusion about the rôles of such bodies, and how they could be fitted into an overall administrative system. The members of the Dáil were unhappy at the transition from the system under which ministers answered details about actions by their departments and, indeed, by local authorities, to the situation where ministers would not answer in relation to the detailed activities of state-sponsored bodies.

Eventually, the Devlin Report of 1969, grasping that out of these confused, and confusing, but long-sustained attempts to centralise responsibility yet depoliticise public business, a genuinely Irish set of institutions was struggling to emerge, recommended (Ch. 13) that a clear-cut division be made between policy duties, which were matters for ministers and their immediate advisers, and executive duties which should be handled by state-sponsored bodies or other executive agencies outside the day-to-day control of the minister. However, to ensure that these bodies in their operations had clear lines of overall policy to which they would be expected to adhere, and to provide means by which they would have an input into such policy making, Devlin recommended that the policy formulation side of the government department should be strengthened by the addition of four staff units concerned with finance, planning, personnel and organisation, and that these units should be duplicated, where the size of the state-sponsored body warranted it, by corresponding units within its organisation. These units would have to be staffed by qualified people (PSORG, 12.4.1-12.10.4). In this way ministers would be in charge of the really important policy-making and deciding function, they could co-ordinate and maintain overall control of the business in hand, but they and their immediate advisers would be protected from the mass of executive detail. At the same time the state-sponsored bodies and the agencies would be given broad guidance as to the policies to be followed and then would be permitted to get ahead with tackling their various jobs.

Ministers have recognised the relevance of this analysis, and efforts—most of them agonisingly slow—have been made to bring it about in practice. So far, the only department that has taken significant steps towards adopting the new system has been the Department of Health (Health, 1973). Its main executive functions are, of course, carried out by the regional health boards. It is flanked by a very large number of state-sponsored bodies, some of them very small, and it has set up three special executive agencies from its own staff. Nonetheless, the remainder of the department—or aireacht as Devlin called it—still remains many times the size of the typical Swedish ministry which, in conception, resembles the Devlin aireacht, and old habits of control and expectations of ministerial intervention in executive problems die hard. Some progress has also been made with the department of Transport and Power (now Tourism and Transport) (Transport, 1974). The job of equipping the remaining departments with the necessary skills to provide the four staff units—planning, finance, organisation and personnel—has made even less satisfactory progress. So, we have the increasing realisation that the special rôle of government departments is policy formulation, but the two steps needed to realise this in practice—the hiving-off of executive detail and the equipping of the departments with the necessary skills for new policy formulation – make very poor headway indeed.

Another feature of the 'corporation sole' concept derived from an older tradition of government still. If the King through his officers caused me a grievance, I would approach him directly or indirectly, and seek his clemency in having the grievance removed. It was within the royal prerogative to do this. Some vestige of this was carried over into the new Irish state and even seemed to survive the republican Constitution of 1937 (see Chapter 7). If the situation was that the minister had refused me some benefit that I felt I had a claim to, then, perhaps, if I got the ear of the minister he might, as far as his discretion extended, remedy my grievance. Sometimes, this was formalised as when a statutory right of appeal was given to an aggrieved person to the minister who, in law, had actually caused the grievance! With a few exceptions (for example, the Land Commission, the Appeals Office of the Department of Social Welfare, etc.) the appeals tended to be handled by exactly the same people as those who had in effect taken the decision in the first place. Where no statutory right of appeal existed approach to ministers was made either personally or, more usually, by approaching local representatives whose task was to 'service' constituents by passing on the problem to the appropriate minister. Thus has been developed the very remarkable Irish political institution of 'brokerage' by which public representatives establish their value to their constituents by making representations on their behalf to public bodies. This exists, to some extent, in most countries but the degree to which it exists in this country is quite exceptional; its implications do not seem to be fully grasped (see further Chapter 7).

An exception to this leaning on ministers to alter decisions taken, or to influence them before these decisions are taken, has been in relation to the institution, within the civil service, of commissions, such as the Revenue Commissioners, the Civil Service Commission, the Land Commission. Here it is well recognised that the commissioners are expected to take their decisions on the basis of the law and the facts, and they are not expected to – and indeed do not – bend to representations from public representatives, including ministers.

Here, again, Devlin tried to limit the role of government departments by moving in some way towards the practice in other countries where formal systems of appeal exist for the remedying of grievances separate from the ministries themselves. The Devlin proposal was for the appointment of a commissioner for administrative justice whose task it would be to get appropriate appellate systems established throughout the public service. This proposal has not really got off the ground (PSORG, 15.5.1-3, Appendix I). This question of appellate organisation and procedures is dealt with in some detail in Chapter 7.

If, to follow Devlin, policy formulation is the basic task of the civil service, what is the overall purpose of policy-making? In effect, what are the overall tasks of government? Empirically, they are as set out in the tasks of the eighteen government departments. All the other public bodies relate, in some way, to the responsibilities of those departments. So when we list those departments we get, in a broad way, a list of the responsibilities of modern Irish government. The range of these duties spans the whole life of the community. Similarly, to anticipate the argument of Chapter 6, the effectiveness of government can be measured by how developmental it is. If we have to put all of this in a nutshell, we can say that the overall task of government is that of national development.

A good part of the policy-formulating side of civil service work is concerned with the identification and analysis of problems, and the sorting out of possible ways of tackling them. Usually, special interest groups make it their business to bring problems, or their perceptions of problems, to the notice of government departments and they usually have their solutions to those problems as perceived. The task of the civil service is, however, to try to survey the whole field to make sure that significant aspects of the problem are not being overlooked and that solutions that look well in the short term will be likely to stand up, also, in the longer term, or at least be readily adjustable to changing conditions.

There is, of course, the more general political dimension to the policy-formulating process. Clearly, if the party in power has a clear-cut policy or ideology on the matter at stake then the process of policy formulation at the administrative level is, basically, to explore the feasibility of the detailed application of that policy. But, if the broad outlines of the issue have not been settled in this way, if the party is itself divided, or if the issues are so new that no lines of battle have been drawn up or, conversely, if there is fierce public controversy on the issue, then the task of devising an acceptable and workable policy becomes pretty formidable.

Once a decision has been taken on the broad outlines of the policy—here the minister or, in major matters, the Government will take the final decision—it becomes the task of the administrator to consult the various interests—particularly other government departments—with a view to a generally acceptable working out of details, if that is possible. Here, very considerable skills of persuasion and negotiation may be necessary. This side of administrative activity is, of course, now greatly increased because of the large number of negotiations that must take place in Brussels at meetings of officials of the European Community. If negotiation fails at the official level, either in Brussels or in Dublin, the issues have to be put up for decision at a higher level—in Brussels to the Council of Ministers, in Dublin to the Government. At home a major issue will usually result in proposals for legislation and this involves extended work with the parliamentary draftsman, other departments, and eventually assisting the minister as the legislation goes its way—sometimes a very protracted way – through the two houses of the Oireachtas.

When the legislation has been passed it is usually necessary to draft various statutory regulations and administrative rules to give effect to the intentions of the act. Usually, again, it is necessary to get money from the Department of Finance, accommodation from the Office of Public Works, office equipment from the Stationery Office, and staff from the Department of the Public Service and the Civil Service Commission to implement legislation. It may also be necessary to have detailed negotiations with the various interest groups concerned. Sometimes these may be very difficult, and the price they may demand for their co-operation, in terms of money or otherwise, may be too high, so another round of often protracted negotiations must begin. In the end when the scheme is got off the ground it is necessary to keep it under control to ensure that its objectives are achieved, that money and other resources are not wasted, that there is enough staff to ensure that good service is given, and that even-handed justice is at all times maintained.

A cycle of this kind, from the first beginnings of a new policy through legislation to the implementation stage can often last a number of years so that there may, during that period, be a considerable turnover of civil servants dealing with it.

We have been dealing with the operation as it is to be seen at the administrative levels. This is, of course, under-pinned by the work of many junior officials. Members of the executive grade will have had to prepare endless notes and memoranda, keep minutes of meetings, and generally look after a great volume of paper work and correspondence. They will be, of course, assisted by clerical and typing staff. Where the scheme relates to some area of professional expertise – for example, the attempt to eradicate brucellosis in cattle – there will be an input from the appropriate professional and technical staffs. All of this must be co-ordinated and managed in a careful, consistent and orderly way so that the reasons for the various decisions are well rehearsed, and are recorded for the future, or for the defence of actions that lead to public criticism.

The civil service has long been regarded in many countries as a profession, in the sense that it demands special qualities and qualifications at recruitment, it requires for its successful operation a high level of personal dedication, it has a strict code of ethics, and it operates according to some very special constraints.

Like members of all large organisations – except those at the very top – the civil servant works, nearly always, under a cloak of anonymity. At the senior levels he is the shadowy adviser of the minister who gets nearly all the praise, and suffers nearly all the blame, for the success or failure of the operations concerned; either way, the official maintains discreet silence.

Although civil servants, especially at the highest levels, are involved in the political process, they give their loyalty in equal measure to whatever

minister, of whatever party, is in power. This means that they are required
to refrain from involvement in politics in the normal sense of the word.
There is some debate as to how far down in the hierarchy this prohibition
should extend. The tendency has been to relax it for the lower reaches of
the service, but to insist on it for the higher reaches. In this, Irish (and
British) practice varies from that of a number of other European countries.
For example, in France, the Federal Republic of Germany, and Sweden,
senior civil servants have often clear-cut political loyalties and withdraw,
from time to time, to become, for example, members of parliament. Civil
servants must not only be loyal, they must also be – and be seen to be –
scrupulously fair and honest. They must not, of course, use the information that comes to them by way of their jobs for their personal gain.

One of the arguments for the secrecy with which the civil service, to the
public eye, goes about its business is that it enables officials to be perfectly
honest in the advice they give to ministers. Ministers are, of course,
perfectly free to reject advice; civil servants are not free to give only that
advice that they think will be acceptable. The secrecy that surrounds the
advice given to ministers makes it difficult for civil servants to practise
what is known as 'open government'. Many people think that this is now
one of the requirements for running a modern democracy. In Ireland
however, the task of providing information to the public is, to a very great
extent, left to ministers. There are big issues here, discussed in Chapter 7.

A good part of the Devlin Report was devoted to the question of how to
improve the systems for formulating and co-ordinating policy in government departments. The system proposed resembled the Swedish system,
but also, it should be added, the practice of certain large business firms.
The proposal was that the special rôle of the civil service should be the
preparation of material for policy decisions. This need not preclude, of
course, civil servants inviting specially qualified outsiders to participate in
working parties and committees so as to assist in this task. In other
countries there is doubt whether civil servants, working by themselves,
have sufficient political commitment to help ministers to think through
both the political, and the administrative, sides of the policy formulation
problems.

In a number of continental European countries there is a further problem
of the co-ordination of the work of the department itself. In these countries
the British (and Irish) system of a single permanent head as the co-ordina-
tor of the department's work and as the chief adviser of the minister does
not exist. In France, for example, policy formulation at the top, and
expecially co-ordination, is substantially the work of the minister's
'cabinet'. This may include civil servants from the department itself and
others from other departments, as well as a small number of outsiders.
This system has influenced, to some extent, the 'cabinet' system of the
European Commission where each commissioner has his own co-ordinating

and advisory group to help him not only with his own departmental responsibilities but also in playing a full part in the collegiate work of the commissioners as a whole. Various forms of the 'cabinet' idea are used in other countries, such as Belgium, where its use has led to serious criticism.[1]

A good deal of thought has been given to the question of policy formulation in Britain. There the suggestion of the Devlin group here, that executive work should be 'hived off' to something like our state-sponsored bodies does not seem to be acceptable to British public opinion, and it was not recommended by the 1968 Fulton Committee. Their recommendation was that flanking the permanent head of the department there should also be a senior policy adviser to the minister, who would also be head of the planning unit (Vol. I, pp. 58–62). The units have been installed, but the proposal of a senior policy adviser does not seem to have been implemented. However, a number of the Labour ministers in Britain have, in recent years, brought into their departments politically committed persons who would act as their personal advisers. A minister might have one or two of these advisers. Something similar was adopted in Ireland by members of the last coalition government, principally the Labour members.

Both in this country and in Britain there seems to be some confusion between three distinct, but related, problems. The first is the need to assist the minister to play an informed part, as a member of the government generally, in relation to the overall tasks of the Government. As things stand in this country he has no special assistance for that responsibility. The second is the task of co-ordinating the work of the minister's department. This, in our system, is the work of the permanent head of the department: but in France, where there is no such head, it is a function of the 'cabinet'. The third is, as Devlin insists, that the overall task of the senior civil service is to raise the quality of the departmental advice given to ministers. Devlin proposes to do this by having *systems* for the preparation of well-thought through and adequately concerned policies (PSORG 12.2.1–12.7.7). Fulton proposes the special policy adviser leading a planning unit.

Generally, the civil service—especially the extreme ministerial form that has been adopted in this country—is faced with an acute role problem. On the one hand it has a unique and irreplaceable role to advise ministers and to formulate policy. On the other hand, it is also to *implement* policy. What is the place of the geographical and functional forms of government—the local authorities and state-sponsored bodies—which are basically implementing bodies? They conflict with the logic of the daily business of government centralised in ministers, but there is fairly general acceptance

[1]Notably in the Belgian periodical *Res Publica* by Baron Snoy and Leo Moulin. The latter contributes a pungent chapter on this topic in Dogan, (1975), pp. 163–84. More discreetly, Molitor (1974), pp. 251–7, shows the abuse of the system and the constant breaching of the rules to control such abuses. In 1973 the number employed in Belgian 'cabinets' was 1,887, of whom 330 were senior officials. Dogan's book has an interesting chapter on French 'cabinets'.

of the criticism that this daily business, by its constant pressures, prevents the longer term thinking needed for policy formulation. Something must give; but what? The civil service seems quite unable to make up its mind on this issue.

2. Geographical Government: (1) Local Government

The geographical systems of government are, primarily, the local government bodies—the county and district directly-elected bodies as well as the statutory committees of these—committees of agriculture and vocational education committees; the regional bodies, which are indirectly elected for the most part; more miscellaneous local bodies such as fishery boards and game councils; and a group of community and residents' associations that have not, with rare exceptions, been absorbed into the governmental system. These do not cover all the operations of governmental bodies in a particular area. There are, of course, the field-services of the various government departments, many of which are based on provincial, regional, county or sub-county areas. In addition, there are the field-services of some of the larger state-sponsored bodies, notably the Electricity Supply Board (ESB) and Córas Iompair Éireann (CIE). The question of the relationships of these field-services to the more generally recognised geographical bodies will be discussed in the next section.

First, let us take local government proper.

One can see operating in our society two very different conceptions of democratic government. The first is the one that is predominant in this country, that of centralised democracy. The belief is that the country is best run by committing not only final responsibility for the conduct of business, but, day-to-day responsibility, to ministers in Dublin who can be elected and dismissed by the people at regular intervals, depending on their promises and performance.

There is very little room in this conception for the other conception of democracy, which operates at its most developed in Switzerland, but is well accepted in most European countries. That is that there are horses for courses. Under this other conception there is, certainly, a task to be performed by central government, but this need not conflict—and should not conflict—with the tasks to be performed by the smaller units of government; they have their rights too. In this conception, which is very well developed in the Federal Republic of Germany, for example, a positive benefit is seen in local freedom, local diversity, and, if you like, local pig-headedness. This is the acceptance in practice of the notion of the 'principle of subsidiarity' which could, but does not, have great significance for the organisation of our governmental system.

Local diversity is something that in our cultural life we prize, but are suspicious of in our political life, and have little time for in our administrative life. How, then, do we fit our inheritance of the local government system–one of the contributions of Anglo-Norman and English influence to Ireland–with our overall conception of democracy? The answer is, basically, that we do not try. Local government is, like any other historical ruin, something that we are perhaps reluctant to see removed wholly, but which we are prepared to see moulder away.

Nonetheless, local government in its various forms continues to be a significant part of Irish government. It is also a significant part of Irish democracy. The directly-elected members of the Dáil and Seanad amount to some 200 people. This can be contrasted with the some 1,700 people directly elected to local government bodies. So, if popular representation is a feature of democracy–and most people would claim that it is–then local government has at least a quantitative claim on our attention.

It is not, I am afraid, too cynical to say that our national politicians, when they are out of power, display some interest in the development of local government. But when they return to power, this interest rapidly evaporates. Why should this be? There are, I think, both political and administrative reasons.

Politically there is the fact–which is basic to a healthy democracy–that competition for public office is extraordinarily intense, and, when one is in office, one is conscious all the time of being surrounded by other people who would happily take one's place. So ministers, whatever they may say in public, feel themselves threatened by locally elected public representatives, members of the Dáil may feel that their tenure of their seats could be undermined, members of county councils are overtly or covertly jealous of local community groups, and so on.

Apart from all this, there is the cut and thrust of party politics. No party in government is happy when the opposition party has a dominant role in the affairs of some other significant public body. There are significant–if not very long-sighted–arguments, therefore, on the political side, for not unduly exerting oneself to ensure that the local government system keeps abreast of the times.

There are also administrative reasons. Centralised government in a small state is very widely believed to be more efficient than decentralised government. Administrators claim to have tidy minds, and like to think–even against the evidence–that centralised administration of services will provide common standards throughout the country as a whole. Many of them are obsessed by the engineering analogy that bigness makes for efficiency and smallness for inefficiency. Officials also distrust the willingness, or ability, of directly-elected local representatives to take responsible views about the spending of money, the making of appointments, and the rest. Finally, if one's parish is the country as a whole, one has often reason to be shocked by the views of those who concentrate on the local parish pump. Not all of these political and administrative arguments stand up to close examination, but together they make a pretty formidable case to answer.

On the other side, there are also political and administrative arguments. The political ones rest, for the most part, on the longer view. For example, there *is* a considerable sense of historical continuity in our society that has helped us through hard times in the past. This is an asset not to be thrown away.

Secondly, a healthy democracy depends on the development of greater self and community realisation. Initiative and creativity of this kind tend to be frustrated unless opportunities for exercising responsibility are made available. If one wants to preserve some reasonable balance between the various parts of this country, one has to provide throughout the country – and not only in Dublin – opportunities for the exercise of creativity and leadership by the most gifted people; otherwise they will continue to be sucked into Dublin. On the existence, and on the moral nourishment, of such people a great part of the future of local and regional development, in all its shapes, depends. If man is naturally a political animal, and if politics is one of the highest forms of human endeavour, and the disposition to public service a foundation of democracy, then all reasonable steps should be taken to develop the whole man, and his commitment to the community, both as a whole and locally, wherever he may be. Moreover, to widen the opportunities to exercise responsibility, including the need, from time to time, to take very tough decisions, raises the level of responsibility in the community as a whole. Similarly, the experience of the need to bargain and to compromise enhances the spirit of realism within the society. Indeed, the 1971 White Paper on the reorganisation of local government (Ch. 2) could speak of local government as a 'school of citizenship', as in this connection fulfilling 'a higher purpose' than merely the supply of public services – fine sentiments, of course, unsupported by action.

Finally, a crucial feature of democracy is the representative system. In this country we have relatively few opportunities for electing to public office those whose disposition or commitments prevent them from aspiring to national office. One consequence of this has been a certain 'holier than thou' attitude – most unhealthy in a democracy – by non-elected people to elected ones.

The administrative arguments revolve around the question of efficiency. What is efficiency when it comes to dealing with people and communities, often bewildered and distracted? Do centralised services, *in fact*, provide a common standard of service throughout the country? If, in fact, they have an advantage here, does the fact that, in practice, they operate in watertight compartments independently of one another more than outweigh this advantage, such as it is? Given that services tend to cluster around certain individuals in the society, certain families, and certain communities, is there not a formidable advantage in having these services operating flexibly with one another, co-operating instead of operating in isolation? In this connection are not local knowledge, local discretion, and the toleration of local diversity likely to relate the diverse remedies more closely to the facts of differing local situations? The argument is basically that local knowledge, local discretion, and local linkages may, over a wide range of the personal services, be more efficient and more humane than the operation of standardised, remote and very distinct services operated a long way from the point of the service.

A second argument relates to the pervasiveness of services. If there are local organisations, covering every part of the country, that administer individual services, changes and improvements in those services can be brought into effect throughout the country very rapidly indeed. With centralised services this is, in practice, much more difficult. A large number of relatively small authorities doing a large number of things may provide a speedier and more effective set of services than a relatively small number of authorities each doing its own thing.

This is not, of course, an either/or situation. There are certain functions that are best done centrally – above all overall policy. But when it comes to execution, a two-way linkage can be highly efficient – that is, a linkage between central policy and local execution, and a linkage, at the local level, between the various executive activities.

Finally, an essential constituent of efficiency is communication, and knowledge of what actually needs to be done and of what actually is happening. Given the existence of certain standards defined by the overall policy makers, this local knowledge can lead to effective review of the success or otherwise of the operations and, if there is reasonable local discretion, the taking of whatever remedial action is required. This is what subsidiarity is about. It is not just a high moral principle: it is a principle for the efficient management of diverse human services that have to be delivered to a wide diversity of people, families and communities through-out the country as a whole (Barrington, 1975, Ch. 8; NESC 41, Ch. 4).

Local government in Ireland has a number of diverse origins, some of them going back to Anglo-Norman times. The latter part of the nineteenth century saw the widespread creation and democratisation of local bodies, culminating in the Local Government Act, 1898, which set up democrat-ically-elected county councils on a broad popular franchise. It was the schooling in democratic institutions provided by such bodies that gave much of the training in the public management of affairs for the revolution-ary Dáil immediately prior to independence.

One of the first actions of the newly independent Irish government was to consolidate the various types of local authorities into, substantially, a single system and to bring this under the very tight control of the appropriate government minister. The first step was to base the system on the county and its legal counterpart in the four cities of Dublin, Cork,

Limerick and Waterford, the county borough. To this end all the small rural authorities were wiped out. The smaller urban authorities close to the county boroughs were also absorbed in them. The urban authorities within the counties were maintained, but, to an increasing extent, their functions were gradually taken over by the county councils. The result is that local government in the Republic of Ireland, now consists of twenty-seven county councils (two of them in Tipperary) and four county boroughs, thirty-one in all. There are eighty-four other directly elected urban authorities, only four of them of any significant size—Dun Laoghaire, Galway, Dundalk and Drogheda. Even these are, for management purposes, the overall responsibility of the relevant manager for the county council. By the standards of other small democracies, we have very few directly elected authorities, and if we accept that, in practice, we have only thirty-one with a significant range of functions, extremely few by the standards of any other country.

We have also some indirectly elected authorities of some marginal significance—the committees of agriculture, now being absorbed into a state-sponsored body, and the vocational education committees in all the counties and in some of the larger urban areas. In relation, however, to the total public activities for agriculture and education, these committees are very peripheral bodies indeed.

The second step was to ensure that these local authorities were adequately staffed. Accordingly, in 1926, the Local Appointments Commission, a counterpart for the local government service of the Civil Service Commission—which is responsible for recruitment to nearly all posts in the civil service—was appointed to look after recruitment to the most important posts in the local government service. This remedied a substantial abuse in relation to the local government system, and in a relatively short time provided the local government service with a· highly professional corps of officers.

The third step, given the fact that the local authorities were now relatively large and relatively well staffed, was to ensure that they were also well managed. Experience in central government, and in the business world, has shown that day-to-day management needs to be divorced from overall direction. Accordingly, at first gradually, from 1929, in the four county boroughs, and then from 1940 in the counties, a system of a full professional manager in charge of the day-to-day activities of the local authorities was established.

These three changes—the drastic reduction in the number of local authorities, the establishment of the Local Appointments Commission, and the introduction of city and county management—were all highly distinctive features of the Irish local government system in the first twenty years of independence. They all arose from the assumption by central government of responsibility for raising the level of efficiency of local government according to the conceptions of efficiency in the 1920s and 1930s (Collins, 1963, pp. 28–35).

The other side of this coin was the subjection of a great part of the day-to-day operations of local authorities to the most intense subordination and control. This, also, was highly exceptional (Barrington, 1975, p. 201). Since 1942 the impetus towards further local government reform and development has almost entirely disappeared, but the subordination and control have been continued.

If there ever was a belief in the value of a local government system under a native government it has ceased to be practised for the past generation, notwithstanding many official protestations (e.g. Local Government Re-organisation, 1971 and 1973). In consequence, the system has been losing its market share, as it were. Either it has lost some of its existing functions, or it has failed to acquire new ones as the system of government became more and more extensive.

Exceptions to this were the establishment of the County Development Teams in the underdeveloped counties in the early 1960s. These were an attempt to link the local government system with the processes of overall development. However, this innovation, while it still survives, has been largely superseded by other developments in state-sponsored bodies. About the same time, also, under the Local Government (Planning and Development) Act 1963 local authorities were given extensive powers not only to control the development of building activities, but also to play a positive part in overall development and so become 'development corporations' (Third Programme, p. 163). Some progress was made here, but, again, the real action was to lie elsewhere.

The most striking failure during this time was the neglect of the problem of local finance. In the past a number of local authorities, including quite small ones, were able to raise their capital needs in the open market; but this gradually became more and more difficult and the capital needs of local authorities are now almost entirely met by the state, by making loans through the Local Loans Fund.

So far as current expenditure is concerned a number of ad hoc measures were taken to assist local authorities to provide specific services by means of percentage grants, and also to mitigate, by a general grant, the heavy effect of rates on farmers, especially the smaller ones. Usually financial support on capital and current account for specific purposes was given at the price of a very high degree of interference in the discretion of local authorities. Up to, and including, 1976, about 40 per cent of their current expenditure was supplied by the state. With the decision that the state should, in effect, pay the rates on private dwellings and some other buildings, this proportion is now just over 60 per cent (Dáil Debates, 307.5, 854).

There is an old saying that men pay their taxes in sorrow but their rates in anger. This anger was, to some extent, intensified by the failure of the central government to reform the local taxation system. Rates are assessed on dwellings and land according to their nominal letting value, but these values are related back to values current when the great valuation of Irish land and property was made in the years 1852 to 1865. The result has been that very great anomalies have been tolerated, and the actual levels of nominal annual letting value have been left far behind by the decline in the value of money (McElligott, 1955). In consequence, the rates, which are struck on the basis of so much in the £ of this net annual letting value, appear exceptionally high, and provoke a good deal of resentment. In addition, no real attempt to tackle the problem of equalising the burden as between the different local authorities was made. The very poor counties along the western seaboard had to strike very high rates and yet were not able to provide as good services as the richer counties on the eastern side of the country (IPA, 1977; de Buitleir, 1974, Ch. 10; Walker, 1963, p. 12; Hughes, 1961).

The failure, over a very long period, to tackle these two questions of the archaic tax base and the problem of equalisation has led to the inevitable result. Administrative failure almost always ends in political irresponsibility.

Local government without its main taxing power is almost a contradiction in terms. Nonetheless, other local government systems (e.g. Denmark and Holland) draw the bulk of their finances from the state and are still vigorous.

Apart from this, the local authorities lost their health functions, which represented about half their total expenditure. This happened under the Health Act, 1970. These functions were transferred to special health authorities on which the county councils and county borough councils were entitled to nominate a bare majority of the representatives; but, in practice, the control of the health services has slipped from their hands.

For Programming, Planning and Budgeting (PPBS) purposes, local functions have been grouped into eight 'programmes', namely, (1) Housing and Building; (2) Road Transportation and Safety; (3) Water Supply and Sewerage; (4) Development Incentives and Controls; (5) Environmental Protection; (6) Recreation and Amenity; (7) Agriculture, Education, Health and Welfare; and (8) Miscellaneous. The big spending occurs on the first three. The second three are small operations, and the last two are vestigial ones.

It is hard to say just what functions ought to be carried out by local authorities and what functions should not be carried out by them. But if we compare the functions performed by Irish local authorities with the functions that are performed by local authorities in other countries, we see a substantial shortfall in this country.

Let us look at one of the oldest functions associated with local government in this country, and indeed many others, the preservation of law and order. In Ireland, what do we find? Irish local authorities, unlike so many others in other countries, have no policing functions, no functions in relation to the lower courts, no functions in relation to prisons. They have, it is true, the duty of maintaining court-houses!

In another long-standing area, the cultural, local authorities provide libraries, and to some extent museums, and have some vestigial interest in national monuments; but in relation to the development of the artistic, linguistic, and heritage responsibilities of government, nearly all the action in this country—little as it is!—lies elsewhere. So far as our European partners are concerned, we are, in the cultural area, both nationally and locally, totally outclassed. It is normal in other European countries for education, below the university level, to be a local government function. Here the involvement of local government is marginal in the extreme.

In the last century Irish local government got its great shot in the arm by being given responsibility for tackling poverty in all its forms. Now, the last vestige of social welfare has been removed from it. The same is true of the health services, though here some institutional links remain. In other countries it is commonplace for health and welfare services to be managed by local government.

In the infrastructural area our local government system is at its strongest and it is concerned with roads, houses, water and sanitation. This is commonplace for local government elsewhere; but, in other countries, transport is also, where it is local, a function of local government.

In the newest area, that of economic development, most of the action lies, of course, with other bodies. As we have seen, in the 1960s a brave attempt was made, through the county development teams, to link in some counties a number of local services with the process of economic development; but county development itself has never developed, except to spread in its restricted form to other counties. Through the Local Government (Planning and Development) Act, 1963 local authorities were given a number of functions to provide infrastructural services to facilitate industrial activities. This is perhaps one area where local government has been permitted a real developmental rôle.

Again, one crucial attribute of governmental systems in the full sense is to be able to tax. We are now, in this context, living with the consequences of the total failure to update the basis of local taxation, legally untouched for a century and a quarter.

We have been considering *functions* of government, but there are other aspects, too. The second of these is the existence within the institutional structure of the power to exercise *discretion* and to take *initiatives*.

In the developmental process initiative, discretion, individual judgment are held to be crucial and essential. So we have set up state-sponsored bodies explicitly to exercise these qualities. But our local government system remains shackled with archaic legal and administrative impediments to the displaying of such qualities. Unless the central authority sanctions, supports and legislates for a new initiative little or nothing can be done. With one or two exceptions, there has been no disposition by any government to give local authorities anything approaching the freedom to engage in developmental activities that is possessed, as a matter of course, by the promotional state-sponsored bodies. Ours remains one of the most centrally controlled of local government systems.

Thirdly, if we think of local *government* in the wide sense as being concerned with what is carried on by all the institutions of government in one place, we would expect to find, as we find in other countries, some system by which local government can be institutionally linked with the other bodies operating in its area so that concerted activities can be engaged in. But we have no such formal, comprehensive system. Such informal systems as we have vary greatly from place to place and from service to service. 'Government' has no single or formal presence in any area smaller than that of the state itself. We have no local functionary comparable to the prefect or the provincial governor of other European countries. In the smaller areas we see only fragmentary—often conflicting—manifestations of individual national services.

In the Mid-West region a most valuable initiative was taken, arising out of the requirements of physical planning, to establish a region-wide focus where, in the interests of concerted development, as many as possible of the representatives—elected and appointed—of these official bodies could be gathered together around a single table. The logic of this, and its effectiveness, were so compelling, that central government reeled back a little and decided that similar bodies should be called into being in the other regions. But the new bodies were allowed neither the powers, the resources, the skills nor the mandates that would enable them to realise their potential.

This is not to say that all the functions, discretions and responsibilities, listed are everywhere local functions; but it is clear that the possible range of local government functions, discretions and responsibilities, if the experience of other countries is to be a guide, is, in general, much more extensive than it is in this country.

What, then, are the problems of local government in Ireland today? The first is the very inadequate acceptance of the democratic value of the directly elected local representative, and of the significance for a developing democracy of increased local discretion. As our society is changing, and as people throughout the country are becoming more conscious of community and of the need for local decisions, for the relating together of various services, and for development, there is increasing conflict with a local representative system that is limited in size and is concerned with a relatively declining number of ageing functions.

Secondly, there is the problem of administrative efficiency. The extraordinarily wide range of governmental functions, looked at from the periphery, grows increasingly complicated and bewildering. If one thinks of the services as radiating from the centre like the spokes of a wheel, one can see, at the periphery, that there is no rim on the wheel to link various spokes together at the point where they meet reality, where they touch the ground.

Thirdly there is the problem of areas. For some functions the counties and the county boroughs are too small; for others they are too big. For administrative reasons the country is covered with a network of very small, or relatively small, areas in respect of which officials of central government, and of local government, have responsibility but virtually no inter-relationships. Moreover, these areas tend to be different for every service. But this network of administrative areas is most inadequately matched in the representative system. We see the rise of local community groups both in the rural areas and in the cities struggling in a rigid, and often, but not universally, hostile, environment to acquire some recognised rôle. We see, at the sub-county level, a network of administrative areas concerned substantially with personal services that are, for the most part, not only outside the representative system but largely unresponsive to local views and special local problems. We see in the larger developing cities — especially in Dublin — on the one hand, the remoteness of the local government system from the ordinary people and, on the other, its inability to cope with the dynamic problems of growth typical of a modern conurbation. There is a clear need to look again at local government at the sub-county level and its relationships there to the extensive administrative network. There is the need to look, also, in this context, at the survival in local government of the medieval walled town defending itself in a hostile environment. Now that the county town is the centre of a substantial community, urban and rural, there is a case for ensuring that the form of the smaller local authorities takes this into account. At the highest level, there is the chaos that exists in relation to the areas and functions of regional bodies. But this is a matter we shall consider further in the next section.

Lastly, there is the problem of how the local government system, if it is to survive, can be got to adjust itself to the changing circumstances. Our system, as it has evolved, prevents, or neutralises, any local initiatives. Under the local government system, as we have seen, a local authority cannot in practice assume new functions, unless it can persuade the Minister for the Environment to promote the necessary legislation. This almost completely wipes out the opportunities for local initiative, so far as the formal local government system is concerned (IPA, 1971, Ch. 5).

A corollary to this tight central control is firm central leadership to enable the system to move with the times. But, as we have seen, there has been no such leadership for over a generation. What will happen, what will give? The most likely outcome is the increasing obsolescence of the local government system. The modernising, innovating spirit moves to where flexibility can be found. That, in the administrative sense, is in relation to the state-sponsored bodies. So we are left with an increasingly irrelevant local representative system, and, to repeat, more and more spokes unrelated together by means of a wheel rim at the point where the wheel meets the human problems of people, families, and communities.

3. Geographical Government: (2) Regional Government
The word 'region' is highly imprecise. It has been defined as that area either bigger or smaller than that one which was last talked about. South America is described as a region. For the purposes of the European Regional Fund the whole of the Republic of Ireland is a region. But in administrative practice in this country, a region is, typically, a grouping of three to five counties. Sometimes it can contain as many as seven, in one instance, or as few as one. Overall, the number of regions in the country varies according to their purposes, but typically, there are seven to nine of them.

Some regions have both a representative and an administrative function – these are, notably, the Health Board regions. Included in this category are also the Regional Tourism Organisations and the Regional Development Organisations.

One regional organisation has a devolved function – the Shannon Free Airport Development Company (SFADCo), which has been, apart from its specific functions in relation to Shannon, the agent of the Industrial Development Authority for the Mid-West region. Perhaps one might also include under this heading Gaeltarra Éireann, which carries out developmental and cultural activities in the Irish-speaking fragments of several counties.

Other regions have purely administrative and managerial significance, notably the five regions or 'areas' of Córas Iompair Éireann (CIE), and the twelve 'districts' of the Electricity Supply Board (ESB). These represent the deconcentration of significant powers to the appropriate managers. One might also include here, though they are outside the system of public administration, the eight regions of the Circuit Court – the first attempt to establish regions, dating from 1924. Other bodies, such as AnCO (The Industrial Training Authority), the Industrial Development Authority and the National Manpower Service also practise some degree of deconcentration to their regional officers (Roche, 1973, p. 27; NESC, 22).

One may also see some vestiges of regional organisation, but here almost entirely for the purposes of internal supervisory and organisational purposes, in the major government departments and services, notably the Department of Agriculture, the Land Commission, the Office of Public

Works, the Garda Síochána, etc. (IPA, 1971, App. 4).

Broadly, however, one can think of regional structures as being of two classes, namely, those which have both a representative and an administrative structure, and those that exist simply for administrative purposes, with such bodies as SFADCo and Gaeltarra Éireann falling somewhere between the two.

One striking feature of the Irish geographical system of government is the absence from it of responsibility for education, except for the very limited part played by vocational education committees. It is normal in other countries for first and second level education to be the concern of geographical government – in our terms, at the county and regional levels. Suggestions to remedy this lack have been made, but without success.

In 1967 the Steering Committee on Technical Education (p. 30) proposed to the Department of Education that 'consideration be given to the establishment of Regional Education Councils having accountability in as much as possible for all education in each of the regions'. Nine regional technical colleges were established in the following years, but were not put under regional authorities. In 1973 the Department of Education put forward outline proposals for a system of regional education bodies; but nothing developed. In 1973, also another committee, this time the Murphy Committee on Adult Education, put forward (Ch. 4) at regional and county levels a two-tier system, with the county body as the basic education authority, and responsibility for all non-university third-level and for some specialist education services at regional level. Nothing has come of this proposal.

One can date the beginning of regional bodies proper from the decision of Bord Fáilte in 1964 to move for the disbanding of the largely ineffective Irish Tourist Association, a national body, and its replacement by eight regional bodies, representative of the various tourist interests in each region. The functions of these bodies are somewhat limited, but they represented a substantial move towards the involvement of tourism interests throughout the country in the work of tourist development.

However, the major step towards regional bodies in this country was taken in 1970, and represented a move in the opposite direction. This was the setting up of the Regional Health Boards and the assignment to them of the health functions that had, with a few exceptions, been up to that date discharged by the county authorities, the major local government bodies.

The third type of representative regional authority, the Regional Development Organisations (RDOs) – but this time with very little administrative underpinning – began in the Mid-West region (that is Clare, Limerick City, Limerick County and Tipperary North Riding) in 1968. This was, unlike almost anything else in recent Irish administrative history, a local, non-statutory initiative to pull together as many as possible of the official bodies operating within that region and to get public representatives and officials working together on problems that were common to the region as a whole. This idea was taken up in 1969 by the then Department of Local Government, and spread to the eight other planning regions, that is areas delimited in that year for the purposes of the Local Government (Planning and Development) Act, 1963.

These three kinds of regional bodies can, therefore, be seen to have had three diverse origins. The first was an attempt to replace a national body by eight more locally based ones, the second was to replace a large number of health bodies by eight regional ones, and the third was designed, not to supersede either national or local bodies, but to address itself to problems that are common to both.

The present day move towards regional groupings of counties has resulted in great confusion about the regional boundaries – there has been a tendency for each service to make its own groupings of counties. Fortunately, most of them at least stick to the county boundaries, but a number of so-called regions cut across even these, notably the catchment areas for the Regional Technical Colleges (More Local Government, App. 4 and maps; Roche, 1973). This confusion about areas is not only untidy in itself, but it effectively frustrates the assembly of common data for all administrative purposes within the regional areas, and the clear-cut pinning of responsibility for concerted action by the various bodies within a single common region.

Part of the impetus towards regional thinking has come from the increasing interest in regional development in various countries. Regional development as a problem comes from two aspects of development – relative overdevelopment in metropolitan regions, coupled with gross decay at the heart of the region, and relative underdevelopment in mainly rural areas.

By overdevelopment is usually meant the excessive size and the excessive role of a large city with the conurbation that tends to grow up about it. Great problems of transport, traffic, water and sewerage services, pollution, law and order, etc., pose themselves in these areas. The sheer size of these conurbations permits a number of services to be supported – notably cultural ones – that smaller areas lack the resources for. Against this, other aspects of the 'quality of life' take a heavy beating in such conditions. Too much of the wealth, talent and resources of the country get sucked into these large areas. Part of regional policy in most countries is to try to devise systems that will enable the advantages of large areas to be maintained while reducing the disadvantages. For example, the French government have a very rigid policy attempting to prevent the further growth of Paris, and attempting, also, to divert activity from Paris to other regions of France. The problems of the Dublin area are small in relation to those of the great conurbations, but they are growing (Walsh, 1978) and they do pose, acutely, the need for some form of authority that can look at the general problems of the area as a whole and can get them tackled.

At the same time, there is, at the heart of all these big conurbations, a sort of spreading decay, as traditional forms of economic activity become superseded by new ones, as people who were content in the past to live in crowded urban conditions move out to suburban and ex-urban areas, leaving behind pockets of poverty and deprivation and decay that exact their own price in human misery and delinquency. The classic example here is, of course, New York; but even in a small way Dublin is displaying some of these symptoms. So one has the paradox of too much development on the one hand, and spreading decay at the heart of this development on the other.

In many countries these issues are tackled by a 'greater authority' (for example like the Greater London Council) which is supposed to concern itself with the overall problems. We lack any such authority in the Dublin area. In place of this we have had individual policies—such as the decentralisation of factory work, centralisation of office work, or indiscriminate house building—which are either short-sighted, or absent-minded, or which compound the difficulties. Some method by which the diverse systems of government that operate in the Dublin area can be knitted together in such a way that the problems of this area, which comprises about one-third of the population of the state, can be considered in relation to one another and as a whole is essential. The Regional Development Organisation has some remit in this connection, but it spectacularly exhibits the weaknesses of the rest of these organisations throughout the country, which are discussed later.

The other big problem, and the one that looms largest in the public mind, is the relative underdevelopment of the other regions of the country. Much of the discussion about regional development is about how to hasten the process of economic and social development in those regions so as to reduce the disparity in economic and social wellbeing between, say, the Eastern (or Dublin) region on the one hand and the North Western and Donegal regions on the other (NESC, 4). Very considerable disparities are to be found under a number of headings such as demography, income, productivity, the supply of social goods (educational, medical and other provisions), as well of course as in the opportunities for employment. For example, in 1973 average income per head in the Eastern region was something like 50 per cent higher than that in the North Western and Donegal regions (NESC, 30, p. 21). These disparities arise because of the 'backwardness' in economic terms of the state of economic organisation in those regions. This sort of problem exists in every country but, so far as the European community is concerned, our Western regions are amongst the poorest of all. A major aim of regional policy is to reduce these disparities and eliminate them if possible.

A second aim of regional policy is to release, as it were, the capacity for growth in the less favoured regions and, by these means, to increase the overall level of growth.

The special case for a regional organisation to deal with these problems of regional growth is to achieve a 'synergy' by which the various forms of growth that are stimulated in a particular area will interact on one another so as to produce a 'virtuous cycle' that will enable the growth process to take off. One of the major constituents of any such operation is the providing of opportunities for the best educated and the best talented people to remain within the region – instead of being sucked off to Dublin – so that they, in themselves, reacting on one another, will stimulate various kinds of managerial initiatives. In fact, the contrary has occurred – 59 per cent of all Irish office jobs are in the Dublin region, and an overwhelming proportion of the most senior jobs (NESC 28, pp. 83–5).

Finally, a number of these regions may be deprived economically and socially, but they are well endowed with those mysterious constituents of what is called the 'quality of life'. The stimulation of greater activity, and the growth of greater resources, in the regions enables the development of cultural activities – in the broad sense – that tend to make a significant contribution to this quality, so helping to maintain within the area various kinds of leader groups who otherwise might be tempted to migrate elsewhere. These, in turn, help to raise the possibilities of managerial spin-off and so contribute to the overall synergistic potentialities.

Our membership of the European Community has, of course, made everyone in the country familiar with the notion of regional development. One unfortunate effect of the decision by the European Commission to regard the whole of the Republic of Ireland as a single region is that it has reinforced the belief that the regional problems of the country can be tackled almost exclusively by the central government in Dublin and that no other organisational arrangements are really needed for that purpose. That is to say, as between Ireland and the other members of the community, we are regionalists. So far as Ireland itself is concerned, we are centralists.

This needs to be qualified in two respects. First, energetic and successful efforts have been made to distribute factory jobs throughout the country. (Indeed, this may have gone too far, in the sense that the massive redundancy problems arising from obsolescent industrial activities of the past in the Eastern region have, only very recently, entered into the consciousness of public policy).

The second qualification is the decision to establish regional development organisations in each of the regions.

The purpose of the RDOs was to encourage the discussion of regional problems – that is, those problems that were greater than the responsibility of any single agency operating within the region – with the hope of achieving a consensus on how they should be tackled. This was the first attempt to establish an exchange, as it were, into which all the problems and the administrative activities carried on within the region could be plugged.

It was also important in providing a table around which all those concerned with public activities in the region could be seated, whether they be public representatives or officials. So the RDOs represent the various public bodies operating in the region, local and regional, as well as the field services of central departments and agencies and of state-sponsored bodies operating within the region. From these two mixtures, of central and local agencies, and of representatives and officials, it was hoped that the development process in the region would get a substantial reinforcement. On the whole, this formula worked well in the Mid-West region.

Discussion on strengthening the regional development organisations has tended to concentrate on giving them statutory functions. Much less attention has been given to providing them with adequate administrative underpinning. If there is to be a regional input into the overall process of economic and social planning and if there is to be effective implementation within the regions of whatever may appear in the plans, a significant regional administrative apparatus is required. It is required to collect the data, demographic and other, relevant to the preparation of regional plans. It is required to analyse that data and to determine regional priorities. It is required to achieve some degree of concertation of the programmes of the various implementing bodies within the region, and to achieve agreements and enforceable commitments to that end (NESC 22, p. 9). The diagram in NESC 22, although not comprehensive and slightly out-of-date, illustrates some of the complexity of the situation. Finally, an administrative apparatus is needed to review the effectiveness or otherwise of the programmes and the plans. The RDOs are aiming to tackle that kind of job, but have not got much further than the identification and analysis of common problems, and the achievement of some degree of consensus about how they should be tackled. One has only to compare them with the strength of a number of the functional agencies with some regional activity, notably SFADCo and Gaeltarra Éireann. These possess much more in the way of managerial and analytical resources than has been dreamed of for the RDOs.

There are, as has been indicated in relation to our dilemma so far as the European Regional Fund is concerned, two approaches to the idea of a regional development. The first is that the whole of Ireland is an underdeveloped region and that the best results are likely to be got from concentrating on the overall problems. One argument is that to impose 'extra tiers of government' into the system of a small country is to make it too complicated to work. Another argument, but an unstated if fundamental one, is the fear of those who possess power that the division of power will reduce their own effectiveness.

The other line of argument is that if one can mobilise the resources of initiative, inventiveness and intelligence of people throughout the country, and can get agencies to work closely and co-operatively together, one can enhance the whole process of development. Those who hold this viewpoint are not unduly impressed by the 'extra tiers of government' argument, because, they point out, these tiers already exist in an organisational sense, they are not well developed, they exist in isolation within each agency, and they have little or no input from public representatives, so that overall, they are largely sterile. We already have the extra tiers, but they are bureaucratic tiers, and lack democratic input and responsibility except to ministers of central government. An inquiry has been underway into these 'sub-national systems', but as it is being conducted by the representatives of the very agencies that operate our highly centralised system one may doubt the chances of a creative solution to these problems.

The problem of tiers is well illustrated in relation to the Health Boards. The strong argument for having larger areas of operation than the existing counties which led to the establishment of the regional health boards rested, basically, on the technological problems of general hospitals. Medical science is such that it has become highly diverse and a good hospital needs a number of highly qualified and specialised staff and a lot of extremely expensive equipment. This requires it to have a substantial catchment area, and regions were settled on for this purpose. Indeed, in many respects, the regions themselves may be too small for some of the most advanced specialisms. At the time the change was made nearly two-thirds of all health expenditure went on hospitals. The proportion tends to remain at about this level, rather higher than the OECD average (OECD, 1977). But of this expenditure two-thirds—that is, about half the total expenditure on health services—goes on the acute hospitals which demand large catchment areas. Acute beds, however, numbered some 14,000 of the country's hospital beds (FitzGerald, 1969, p. 51), that is, about a quarter of the total of some 60,000 hospital beds in the country. The other beds were in special hospitals—mental hospitals, geriatric hospitals, homes for the mentally handicapped and so on. For the vast bulk of these people large hospitals, and, consequently large catchment areas, are not technically necessary. It is now believed that both economy and efficiency are to be obtained by keeping these units as small and as well-distributed—that is as close to the local community—as possible. The size—and the cost—of the acute bed problem seems to have obscured the very different problems of the great majority of hospital patients.

The third broad element in health activities is what has come to be known as 'community care'. The argument is that if the costs of the health services are to be kept within any reasonable bounds, people and communities must be encouraged to take their own health care problems in hand before they develop into the great premature killers of modern society, i.e. heart disease, strokes, avoidable forms of cancer, and accidents. So we find the community care organisation moving down once more from the region to something like the county and below that to sub-county areas.

This illustration gives some idea of the remarkable complexity of trying to arrive at an appropriate area for particular services. One argument pulls one way, another argument pulls another. At one time one argument is dominant, subsequently the other. To enable the appropriate adjustments to be readily made we need both a more clear-cut and a more flexible system. A means of achieving this is to have clearly defined, uniform levels—whether region, county, or district—for all purposes, and to provide for the movement of services up and down this scale as changing conditions require. The analogy might be with a large building where there are clearly defined and unalterable floors, but a system of lifts that move freely from one floor to another as circumstances require. One illustration of this is how the Danes handle education: pre-school and primary at the level of small authorities (15,000 average population), secondary at the level of relatively large authorities, and university at the national level.

In brief, the picture about regionalism in Ireland is extraordinarily confused and, in consequence, inefficient. Through all the confusion, however, one can see two significant forces operating. One is the almost instinctive, and often inarticulate, one which tries to relate levels of government to sub-national areas of varying size that seem to many people to be both more manageable and more appropriate as well as being, on occasion, more susceptible to direct democratic control. It is this instinctive urge for some form of sub-national systems that has led to the proliferation of tiers of authority, both in the administrative and the democratic sense. On the other hand, there is the tenet on which the state was substantially founded, that a democratic government established in Dublin must be in unfettered control of the country as a whole if it is to be held democratically accountable for its successes and its failings to the people of Ireland as a whole.

The issue between these opposing viewpoints has not been resolved, and it is difficult to see any sign that it will be resolved in a measurable period. Until it is, the whole issue of regionalism will remain confused and, largely, ineffective. If we add to this the steady decay of local government, it is clear that a geographical system of government in Ireland will have to struggle very hard if it is to make its potential contribution to the better government of the state.

Chapter 3: Institutions Continued

4. Functional Government: State-Sponsored Bodies

The expression 'state-sponsored bodies' covers some ninety bodies established since the foundation of the state to deal with specific functions of government. They have been defined by Garret FitzGerald (1963, p. 5) as:

autonomous public bodies other than universities and university colleges, which are neither temporary in character nor purely advisory in their functions, most of whose staff are not civil servants, and to whose board or council the government or ministers in the government appoint directors, council members, etc.

These bodies are often called 'semi-state bodies', but there is nothing 'semi' about the state's involvement in the overwhelming mass of them. Occasionally the state and private enterprise enter into partnership, either a direct relationship, as when the Minister for Industry and Commerce took shares in Bula Mines Ltd, or indirectly where the Industrial Development Authority or Gaeltarra Éireann take shares in some enterprise that they sponsor, or, occasionally, where there is some private participation in what is basically a public operation, such as the Irish Life Assurance Co. Ltd or the Agricultural Credit Corporation Ltd. But these are exceptional. The overwhelming mass of the state-sponsored bodies are totally owned by the state. Hence, 'semi-state bodies' is a quite inaccurate term.

Another term often used is 'public enterprise'. This clearly covers some of the commercial state-sponsored bodies, such as the Electricity Supply Board (ESB), Córas Iompair Éireann (CIE), Bord na Móna, Irish Shipping, Aer Lingus. Such bodies as these comprise most of the employment, and most of the capital investment, of the state-sponsored bodies as a whole; but 'public enterprise' does not cover more than a fraction, by number, of the state-sponsored bodies. It is one category, if an extremely important one, of the whole (Coyle, 1973).

State-sponsored bodies are to be distinguished from government departments in two respects. The first is that they are primarily executive bodies, established for the purpose of implementing certain overall policies. The second is that they are, basically, single-purpose, or functional, bodies, unlike government departments which tend to range over a wide variety of purposes. They are similar to local authorities in that they are primarily executive bodies, but dissimilar in that local authorities usually have a number of functions.

State-sponsored bodies represent the attempt to bring a business pattern of organisation to the discharge of public affairs. In this they are quite distinct from both government departments and local authorities. Overall responsibility, that is the 'direction' of the body, is committed to a board of about seven or eight members, appointed by the shareholder(s), usually a minister. The members of the boards are very often businessmen, who serve part-time. They may have, on appointment, little or no knowledge of the business conducted by the appropriate body. Sometimes they are supporters of the party in government at the time of the appointment. A number of members of boards are civil servants drawn from the relevant 'parent' departments; this is held to facilitate communication between the two types of bodies. Occasionally, the board members represent specific interests with which the body is concerned – this was a notable feature of Bord Báinne when it was a state-sponsored body and before it became a co-operative enterprise: there the various agricultural interests elected members of the board. Recently, under the Worker Participation (State Enterprises) Act, 1977, provision is made for worker representation on the boards of seven of the state-sponsored bodies – Aer Lingus, Bord na Móna, B & I, Comhlucht Siúcre Éireann Teoranta, CIE, ESB and Nitrigin Éireann Teoranta.

Normally the chairman of the board is, like the other members, part-time, the management of the organisation being in the hands of a chief executive. However, occasionally the chairman is also the chief executive – this used to be the situation in CIE and the ESB. At present, there are, for all practical purposes, fulltime chairmen of these two bodies, in addition to separate chief executives.

The rôle of the board of a state-sponsored body has been summarised in the Devlin Report (PSORG 5.2.21) as follows: it is to

1. implement government policy,
2. appoint top management,
3. exercise financial control,
4. stimulate development,
5. maintain liaison with the minister,
6. supervise personnel policy,
7. measure management performance.

However, this austere statement of functions may obscure the crucial rôle of the board as the meetingplace of two major influences. The first is, of course, the overall policy of the minister, where he has articulated this. Policy, however, seldom springs, like Pallas Athene, full-panoplied from the head of its progenitor. Instead, it becomes progressively defined by the interaction of overall ministerial objectives with the second major stream – the flow of proposals from the management to the board. These proposals aim to reconcile objectives to feasibilities. They pose new developments both of board and ministerial policy in the light of operation and experience and of the new insights to which these give rise. Finally, these matters are discussed and weighed by board members of broad general experience from many walks of life. The development of policy, therefore, is a broadly participative affair in which the board plays a central rôle.

The ink was barely dry on the Ministers and Secretaries Act of 1924 – which set out to abolish independent boards and concentrate the business of central government in ministers – when other bodies, outside the day-to-day control of ministers, began to be set up. The first four were the Agricultural Credit Corporation, the Dairy Disposal Company, the Electricity Supply Board, and the Medical Registration Board. The legislation under which all of these were established was passed in 1927. These illustrate the diverse origins of the state-sponsored bodies. The Agricultural Credit Corporation was intended to fill a gap arising from the shortage of credit to farmers at that time. The Dairy Disposal Company was established to take over agricultural processing industries that were collapsing. The Electricity Supply Board was established to provide for a major piece of infrastructure for the society. The Medical Registration Board was established, like the Dental Board in 1928, basically to control the profession by means of registration. All these bodies were intended to be, and were, self-financing, at least so far as current expenditure was concerned, so the business form of organisation seemed specially appropriate for them. Later this form of organisation was used for promotional bodies which drew all their current expenditure from the state, such as Bord Fáilte, Córas Trachtála, the Industrial Development Authority. It was also used for research and cultural bodies, such as the Medical Research Council, the Medico-Social Research Board, an Foras Forbartha, the Arts Council, the Abbey Theatre, etc.

There is no common constitution for these bodies. Some have been set up directly by statute, such as the ESB, CIE, Bord na Móna, so they are called statutory corporations. Some have been set up under, but not by, statute, such as the Agricultural Credit Act 1927 under which was established the Agricultural Credit Corporation – this is called a 'statutory company'. Other bodies have been established under the Companies Acts, but without any specific authority from an act of the Oireachtas, for example Irish Steel Holdings Ltd, Irish Shipping Ltd, The Agency for Personal Service Overseas. Others, such as the Hospitals Joint Services Board, have been set up under a general enabling act, The Health (Corporate Bodies) Act, 1961. The striking feature of the state-sponsored bodies, therefore, is the diversity of their origins. They were established to meet specific problems as they arose, and operate under no general rules or statutes.

In the aggregate they employ about one-quarter of the public service, and consume about half of the state's annual investment programme.

According to the Devlin Report (PSORG 5.2.1-33; 13.5.1-11) the state-sponsored bodies can be broadly divided between the commercial bodies, representing about a quarter by number of the whole, and the non-commercial bodies. These non-commercial bodies can be broken down into (1) marketing bodies, (2) promotion bodies, (3) research, advisory and training bodies, (4) bodies for registration and regulation of professions, and (5) miscellaneous bodies providing services, mainly in the health field. But there are many other possible ways of categorising them.

The significant distinction is, however, between the so-called 'commercial' and the 'non-commercial' bodies. In general, the 'commercial' state-sponsored bodies, because they have to operate in a business environment, fit naturally into the general constraints and freedom of the business world. To survive in that environment, they need a high level of autonomy and discretion. On the other hand, because they draw so much of their capital from the state; because some of their activities are classed as 'social' —maintaining uneconomic railway lines, extending electricity services to uneconomic areas, etc.—they receive direct subsidies; because they are such big employers their salary and wage policies have a profound effect on the economy as a whole, and the public service in particular; because their activities may have significant political repercussions, such as those of Radio Telefís Éireann,—for all these reasons total commercial freedoms are not feasible in relation to them. The question is, where should the line be drawn between autonomy and control.

A similar problem arises in relation to the other state-sponsored bodies. The main reasons for establishing them outside the civil service proper—that is, outside the day-to-day control of ministers, the various constraints that apply to the civil service, the direct accountability to the Dáil—could not rest on 'commercial' considerations because they are not trading bodies: they engage in promotional, regulatory, research, etc., activities, financed by direct subsidies. Why, then, 'commercial' freedoms? Why, therefore, should there be a distinction between, as they have been described, 'the bond and the free'? (Collins, 1953, p. 31). The reason is that there are certain practical advantages in this type of body that are not possessed by the traditional civil service or local government bodies. The unplanned, ad hoc, spontaneous, and increasing recourse to the 'non-commercial' state-sponsored body seemed to suggest that there was a tacit acceptance of the need for a special kind of body to implement policy. And, by implication, for another kind of body, the government department, to formulate, co-ordinate and review policy. Once this logic was grasped, as Devlin grasped it (PSORG 13.2.1), then there was the argument for an organisational dichotomy between policy work and the implementing of the policy. Accordingly, it was logical to hive off all the executive work from the government department proper. If this were done, there would be a great increase in the number of 'non-commercial' state-sponsored bodies or their equivalents.

The other argument for this change was that executive work is more effectively performed if the body concerned with it has a clear mission and, as far as possible, a 'single' function. Even allowing for the necessary constraints on a public service body, there is room for a substantial increase in the autonomy of bodies required to show performance. Moreover, performance itself can be reasonably well measured against the task to be performed. A clear mission, concentration of responsibility, and clear-cut accountability are the most effective ways of ensuring that an executive organisation does a good job. On the whole, this is what has happened with the experience in this country of state-sponsored bodies. They do offer a means for the effective implementation of policy (Lemass, 1958; Colley, 1973; Ryan, 1973).

This is not to say that there have not been problems. The ad hoc way by which the state-sponsored bodies have been set up, the tendency inherent in them towards the fragmentation of public work, the confusion about their roles vis-à-vis the parent departments, the consequent tensions that arise, the confusion as to who is responsible for the articulation of policy, the occasionally erratic application of controls and interference from ministers and departments, the lack of clarity in the methods of financing – all these are substantial difficulties; but were not seen by Devlin as being irremediable or, necessarily, inherent in the system. The task was, in effect, to create a *system* where the roles of the various types of bodies would be fairly defined, and fitted into an appropriate network. The three ingredients of success were seen as policy planning, task definition, and reasonable autonomy (PSORG 13.2.1-3; 13.3.11; 13.6.5).

The more the business of government increases in scale and quantity the more important it is to ensure that what is done in government is mutually consistent and operates on the most appropriate levels for achieving the ends of government. Present-day thinking is more and more persuaded that for this to happen there must be some system of planning running throughout the whole operation of government. It is of the nature of planning that, so far as is possible, the various operations by the various bodies be concerted – that they serve common overall objectives, that they adhere to the priorities that have been marked out, and that their results are subjected to cool analysis. This, as we have seen, is primarily the task of the civil service; but it would be a mistake to think that it is for the civil service to prepare the plans and for the various executive instruments – geographical or functional – to carry them out.

If plans are to be realistic they must take diverse rôles fully into account and they must be based on the practical experience, knowledge and insights of those who are engaged in the day-to-day operations. It is essential, therefore, that the executive instruments have their own plans in relation to their own activities, and that these plans, in so far as they affect other agencies, be fed into some overall planning agency. If we wish to have an overall transport policy, for example, the knowledge and the expertise of the various transport agencies—in our case almost exclusively state-sponsored bodies—must be fed in some orderly way to the department concerned with transport. That department's own planning, then, must try to establish priorities for the transport area as a whole, ensure that investment in that area gives the best return, and that the activities of the various agencies assist, and do not impede, one another. When all this has been worked out—and some hard bargaining is inherent in this process, both in relation to the state-sponsored bodies on the one hand and the Department of Finance and the Department of Economic Planning and Development on the other—an overall transport policy gets worked out and the state-sponsored bodies concerned proceed to operate it. From the experience of operating it they see new potentialities, or snags, within it, and feed this information, with their proposals, to the department concerned with overall policy. This is the sort of vision that the Devlin group had of the role in planned policy formulation of the state-sponsored bodies, not only in the transport area (PSORG 12.5.1-10).

But even if one has a relatively clear-cut system for the formulation of policy and its implementation by the state-sponsored bodies, a number of problems remain. The first problem is how to balance the autonomy that is inherent in the state-sponsored body system with the need for some sort of overall control. One control is, of course, an overall planning system and the observation of whether the state-sponsored body is in fact making its input into overall planning and is implementing the agreed policies to the desired level of satisfaction. To ensure that this was being done with a reasonable level of efficiency and economy, Devlin proposed that there should be periodic administrative and efficiency audits for executive bodies, though not, normally, for commercial state-sponsored bodies (PSORG 14.6.6-7). However, this proposal has not been adopted, so far at least. But then neither has the proposal about integrated planning.

In recent years there has been an increasing degree of unionisation of the staffs of public bodies, so that a staff concession—particularly in relation to pay—granted by one of them tends to find its way through the others very rapidly. Sometimes, the pay given to the most senior officers of state-sponsored bodies tends to provoke envy and emulation in the more tightly-controlled organisations, such as the civil service. In consequence of all this the Department of the Public Service has now, substantially, concentrated into itself control over the pay of all levels of employees of the state-sponsored bodies. Standard salaries, gradings, pension rights, etc. tend to be established throughout the whole public service. This, of course, tends to cut across the possibilities of fully responsible direction by the boards of the state-sponsored bodies.[1]

This might be tolerable if there were a real attempt to create a single public service, providing the conditions for mobility in relation to recruitment and pension rights, etc. so that there be an open market for talent in the whole area of the public service; but this has not been, and is not being, achieved; though there have been a few small steps in that direction. Indeed, the very unionisation of the state-sponsored bodies has tended to make for the filling of the higher jobs within them by internal promotion. There is, increasingly, being brought about the sort of situation that operates in the civil service, where uniformity in staff matters is pursued to the detriment of innovation, motivation and creativity, while the opportunities for free movement become even fewer.

The formal system of control over the state-sponsored bodies is, primarily, that exercised by the minister by appointing his nominees to the chairmanship of the board and membership of the board. In this way, by keeping a channel of communication open between the minister personally and the chairman of the board in particular, a balance can be struck between the overall policy requirements of the minister, and the necessary degree of operational autonomy and discretion that makes for responsible management within the body.

A further system of communication which is used in relation to some bodies is to have a civil servant from the parent department a member of the board. There are two views about this. One is that it puts a civil servant in a very difficult position when, as inevitably occurs, there is a difference of view between the board and the department. The other view is that most differences of this kind come from failures in communication and the existence of the civil servant tends to reduce the number of these failures. Here it is important to distinguish between two levels of communication. Where the problem is not day-to-day relationships at the official level between the department and the state-sponsored body but a question of ministerial, or major board, policy then, of course, the correct channel of communication is directly between the minister and the chairman of the board.

Sometimes ministers and departments may wish to influence board policy in a direction which, in the opinion of the board, may not be in the best interests of the body. Usually, these matters are ironed out in negotiation. There is a special statutory provision in relation to Radio Telefís Éireann which gives the minister power to issue a formal direction requir-

[1] In May 1978, the Minister for the Public Service required the board of the Agricultural Credit Corporation to cut the salary of their chief executive to the approved level, i.e. by 25 per cent. This they did.

ing the board to do, or to refrain from doing, certain things in relation to public security (Broadcasting Authority (Amendment) Act, 1976, s. 16). A general power of ministerial direction is envisaged in the United Kingdom (*Nationalised Industries*, p. 11).

The main administrative control over the state-sponsored bodies is, of course, financial control. The non-commercial ones are almost wholly financed from central funds, by means of money voted each year. Some of the commercial state-sponsored bodies receive an annual subsidy, for example CIE. Others receive a subsidy for a specific social purpose – for example the ESB in relation to rural electrification. But apart from current expenditure, almost all of them are dependent on capital that comes either directly as advances from the state, or indirectly under guarantees given by the state. Moreover, their borrowing limits tend to be governed by statute. The extent to which money is provided, either directly or indirectly, by the exchequer has, of course, a profound influence on the operations of the body. Up to the end of 1976, total state investment (apart from subsidies and grants) in these bodies was some £340m, about one-third share capital, the rest loans. Overall return is about 2 per cent annually. In addition, there is a big contingent liability under the guarantees given for loans raised from other sources.

The parliamentary control on the state-sponsored bodies is substantially related to this financial control, either in relation to the annual voting of subsidies, or in relation to legislation that authorises borrowing. On the whole, however, the Oireachtas does not have much control over the state-sponsored bodies – parliamentary questions and motions about them are unusual. In late 1976 a committee of both Houses of the Oireachtas was established to consider the reports and accounts of a number of commercial state-sponsored bodies. This met twice before the dissolution of the twentieth Dáil. It was reconstituted in 1978; but it is not yet clear what its effect will be.

So far as the commercial state-sponsored bodies are concerned, there has been a good deal of discussion about their economics, the return for the capital invested in them, and their pricing policies. Where a commercial state-sponsored body can operate on a wholly commercial basis there is no great problem; but where the capital investment does not yield a market rate, or where the commercial activities get mixed up with a social service of one kind or another, then considerable complications occur.

On the whole, for example, the Electricity Supply Board is able to secure enough revenue to enable it to finance its current and capital expenditure. But it is required, as we have seen, to provide a service in rural areas that is uneconomic. It was required, while the price of oil was very low, to pay a relatively high price for using peat as a fuel. In so far as this raised costs, it also raised the price to be charged for electricity, itself an essential ingredient in a great part of economic activity.

Acute problems arise in relation to Córas Iompair Éireann (CIE). On accounting principles, the railways are almost wholly uneconomic,[1] but CIE is required to maintain them as a public service. Given the cost of fuel and wages, and the traffic congestion in such places as Dublin, the cost of providing a public transport system tends to be more than the public are prepared to pay. In the thinly-populated and remoter rural areas it is quite uneconomic to provide a public transport service at all. What should be done? Should public transport be regarded as 'a public service' like the health services or the education services, supplied according to need and basically financed from taxation? Once one begins to raise questions like this about the operations of even the so-called 'commercial' state-sponsored bodies one realises that the distinction between commercial and non-commercial is not so great. They are, basically, instruments of government.

A number of the state-sponsored bodies are now engaged in activities outside Ireland, mainly in the Third World. Sometimes this is direct trading with an opposite number in developing countries, as when Aer Lingus—which has extensive operations of this kind—or the ESB carry out tasks for their opposite numbers in those countries. Sometimes it is diversification, as when Aer Lingus engages in hotel activities in Britain and the United States. Sometimes it is work done for an international agency, as when the Shannon Free Airport Development Company (SFADCo) carries out a Third World contract for UNCTAD.

More than thirty bodies have come together in an organisation called DEVCO in order to develop the potentialities of Irish state-sponsored bodies for exporting their skills and expertise to the Third World. There is also a state-sponsored body, the Agency for Personal Service Overseas, operating under the aegis of, and financed by, the Department of Foreign Affairs for encouraging Irish people to provide a personal service to developing countries.

Apart from this, some state-sponsored bodies maintain offices and missions in the developed world. These include Aer Lingus, Bord Fáilte Éireann, Córas Tráchtála and the Industrial Development Authority concerned, respectively, to attract tourists, to sell goods and to obtain industrial investment.

All of these overseas activities have some impact on official Irish operations abroad.

The Irish state-sponsored body is very much a native growth though its counterparts exist in a number of other countries, especially developing ones. Overall, it has shown itself to be a very considerable instrument for development. It has played a big part in raising the level of management in this country. In an unstructured, unplanned sort of way, the state-spon-

---

[1] The CIE loss for 1978 was estimated by the National Prices Commission (Report no 71, March 1978, p. 35) at £35m, of which just £31m was attributable to railway services.

sored bodies have contributed very effectively to the development of the country, and represent a most interesting adaptation of a form of organisation from the private business world to the needs of public administration. This has not been without its problems, and there are other problems still to be faced; but, overall, one cannot but be impressed by the record. This record, if accepted, poses major challenges, and opportunities, for the future of Irish public administration.

5. International Institutions

It is no longer possible, if it ever was, to consider a national system of public administration in isolation. The growth in the size and scale of modern business, and in the number of multinational companies, together with the speed and ease of modern communication and transport systems, have meant that even a small off-shore island like Ireland cannot remain immune to what is going on in the rest of the world. For example, the 1973 war between Israel and Egypt, and its consequences on the reactions of Arab oil producing states, have had the most profound effects on the economy of this country, as on others.

But less dramatically, we are part of a world that is becoming, to an ever-increasing extent, inter-dependent. It is no longer possible to carry on our system of public administration without constant reference to what is going on in other countries. No matter what sector of our system of public administration we take, we can find its counterpart, not only in other countries, but in international bodies that have a significant effect on the way bodies in this country go about their business. By such means skills, experience and insights get exchanged and general rules get drawn up, not only for activities performed on an international scale, but also for activities at home. Information is exchanged, collated and compared. The results often have significant inputs into the formulation of domestic policies.

This increasing involvement with international bodies has led to the development of a new kind of official. In former times, foreign relations were a matter for a specialised group of officers concerned with foreign affairs; but, increasingly, the role of the political generalist is being supplemented, if not to some extent supplanted, by experts talking and negotiating about common problems across national boundaries. As we have seen, some official bodies have extensive dealings abroad, and some of them maintain missions of their own.[1]

In addition to formal international organisations and conferences, where governments as governments are represented, there is also an increasing number of less formal bodies where governments, officials, and academics

---

[1] Dr P. J. Hillery, when Minister for Foreign Affairs, is quoted (Keatinge, 1978, p. 1) as saying that 'Ireland's foreign relations in the true sense are broader than anything done by my Department'.

mix freely for the purpose of arriving at better understanding of common problems. Not only are there formal negotiations as between countries, but there are also less formal exchanges of views and experience.

This notion of international exchange of views and of negotiation about detailed matters of administration, both internationally and nationally, arose towards the end of the last century. It is claimed that the first of the international vocational bodies was, not surprisingly, the Universal Postal Union. With this body and others in the communications field, our Department of Posts and Telegraphs keeps a close liaison. At a very early stage of our independence we eagerly joined the League of Nations and played an active part in it and in its fellow organisation, the International Labour Organisation (ILO), in the years before World War II. The ILO now belongs to the United Nations family of organisations, and our Department of Labour is actively concerned with it. A number of its international conventions have been incorporated into our national law. Similarly, the Department of Health and the Department of Agriculture relate to two other members of the UN family, the World Health Organisation and the Food and Agricultural Organisation respectively. The Department of Education relates to another member of the family, UNESCO in Paris. And so it goes on. There is constant coming and going between these bodies and the relevant departments – international officials coming to Dublin and Irish officials attending meetings and conferences at the headquarters of these organisations. In addition, Irish officials have served on projects sponsored by these bodies in Third World countries.

After World War II the government of the United States launched a major aid programme to put the shattered economy of Europe back on its feet. To concert the actions of the recipients and to set priorities amongst them, there was established in Paris the Organisation for European Economic Cooperation (OEEC). This represented eighteen European countries. When the economy of Europe had been substantially restored, and other forms of European economic co-operation established, as we shall see, this organisation gave way in 1961 to the Organisation for Economic Co-operation and Development (OECD). There are twenty-four members, nineteen European countries and five countries outside Europe, namely Australia, Canada, Japan, New Zealand and the United States. In addition, Yugoslavia participates in certain activities of the organisation. OECD's aims are to promote economic and social development by assisting its member governments in the formulation of policies designed to this end and by helping to co-ordinate those policies; it also strives to stimulate and harmonise its members' aid efforts in favour of developing countries.

The various studies and conferences sponsored by this body have had a profound effect on economic policy and management in Ireland, firstly by making clear that Irish economic development in the 1950s was lagging behind that of other countries, and secondly in suggesting solutions to major problems of policy that occurred as a result of the efforts to accelerate growth. Unfortunately, Ireland's very poor official efforts in relation to overseas aid (Sutton, 1977), has meant that we have been able to play little or no part in the second side of the OECD's operations. Departments particularly concerned with the OECD are the Department of Finance and the Department of Industry, Commerce and Energy, as well as the Department of Foreign Affairs and, now, the Department of Economic Planning and Development.

Three other major bodies in the economic field are the World Bank, the International Monetary Fund, and GATT, the General Agreement on Tariffs and Trade. These bodies are concerned to stimulate trade throughout the world and, to maintain, so far as possible, a monetary balance in relation to it. The Department of Finance is concerned, primarily, with the first two of these, and that Department and the Department of Industry, Commerce and Energy with the third.

On the broad political front Ireland was substantially isolated for a number of years after World War II. When the North Atlantic Treaty Organisation was established in 1949, Ireland, pursuing its policy of neutrality, rejected an invitation to join the other twelve countries which became members at that time. We have remained aloof from that alliance since.

When the United Nations Organisation was established after World War II, Ireland's membership, with that of certain other countries, was vetoed by the Soviet Union as a bargaining counter to exert pressure to have withdrawn the veto on some countries that were friendly to them. However, a deal was struck in 1955 as a result of which Ireland became a member of the United Nations Organisation. From the beginning we played a very active part in the councils of the United Nations, and contributed troops and other personnel to a number of peace-keeping operations. The most notable of these was in the Congo (now Zaïre), where the military Commander in Chief of the UN forces was an Irish soldier, General Seán MacEoin. Irish troops have also served on peace-keeping missions in the Middle East and in Cyprus. It was in large measure due to the tireless diplomacy of the Irish Foreign Minister, Frank Aiken, that the nuclear non-proliferation treaty was agreed upon. In more recent times Irish concern with activities in the United Nations – although we continue to participate in peace-keeping forces – has been over-shadowed by the moves towards European integration. Freedom of manoeuvre and scope for independent action have, from time to time, been limited by the need to concert some actions with our European partners.

The first significant step towards European integration was taken with the foundation of the Council of Europe, with its headquarters at Strasbourg, in 1949. At present the members number nineteen West

European States. Membership is limited to parliamentary democracies. The Council operates a very wide-ranging programme of co-operation between governments on, chiefly, public health, legal, human rights, scientific, educational, social and environmental matters. Over eighty international conventions on these subjects have so far been concluded.

The organisation consists of an executive committee of ministers (the foreign ministers of member states) and a parliamentary assembly of 154 members appointed by the national parliaments. The assembly makes proposals for action by the council and constitutes a broad parliamentary forum for the free expression of public opinion on major issues.

The council is active in the following policy fields: public health standards, social policy, foreign workers, women workers, population questions, the environment, local authorities and regional planning, international, civil, and administrative law, criminology, science and technology, freedom of the press and development aid.

Perhaps the most notable achievement of the council has been the European convention on Human Rights. This convention is policed by means of the European Commission of Human Rights and the European Court of Human Rights. Each of the member states has a member on each of these bodies. Ireland has had some prominence in this connection. The first case to be taken by an individual against his national government before the Commission of Human Rights was taken by an Irishman, G. Ó Laighleis, who was interned during the period of IRA activity between 1956 and 1961. He petitioned the Commission that the Irish Government was denying him his rights under the Convention. The Irish Government successfully defended itself against this charge.

But the most notable case so far taken under the Convention has been the complaint by the Irish Government that the British Government by its agents in the North of Ireland had engaged in systems of interrogation that breached the Convention. The charge was made on a number of counts, but the Commission found for the Irish Government only on the major one, that the practices complained of were 'torture' under the Convention. The role of the Commission is substantially to act as a conciliation body as between the parties. However, the Irish Government pressed the case to the Court, which agreed with the Commission on all accounts, except that it reduced the finding in relation to the practices complained of from 'torture' to 'degrading and inhuman treatment'.

The net effect of all of this is that the interrogation practices complained of have now been found contrary to the law of the democratic countries of Western Europe. Thus, there is the beginning of a system of jurisprudence in relation to human rights, and the limits of action by a member state in applying pressure to its citizens. There is a long way yet to go before citizens and suspects can be protected from the brutality of governments; but at least a beginning has been made.

The realising of a number of the aspirations towards European union came as a result of the skilful political pressure and leadership of a remarkable Frenchman, Jean Monnet (Monnet, 1977, Chs. 12-14) supported by three notable political leaders, namely Konrad Adenauer in Germany, Alcide de Gasperi in Italy and Robert Schuman in France, and later, the Belgian, Paul-Henri Spaak. The political conditions for this were eased by the spin-offs from the joint activities engaged in both in the Council of Europe at Strasbourg and at the OEEC in Paris. As a result, the 1950s saw the founding of a number of bodies designed to achieve forms of union in western Europe. The first of these was the European Coal and Steel Community, founded in 1951 (discussed later). Another was the Western European Union, founded in 1955 on British initiative, after the collapse of the negotiations for a European defence community. Its primary purpose related to defence, but it had social and political objectives as well. Its seven members were the United Kingdom, France, the Federal Republic of Germany, Italy, Belgium, Netherlands and Luxembourg. It has not played a very active part since its foundation, and has been largely superseded by events. The European Free Trade Association (EFTA), with its headquarters in Geneva, was established by the Stockholm Convention of 1959, and consisted of those members of the OEEC who wished to have closer integration in relation to industrial products (but not agricultural products) and who were particularly concerned to avoid political integration. Ireland did not join. The member countries were Austria, Denmark, Norway, Portugal, Sweden, Switzerland, and the United Kingdom. Iceland and Finland joined later. However, Denmark and the United Kingdom withdrew from EFTA at the end of 1972 to accede to the European Community on 1 January 1973. The remaining countries have made trading arrangements with the European Community.

The root cause for the desire for union in Europe was to prevent a recurrence of the Second World War, particularly the further struggles between France and Germany. On 9 May 1950, at the prompting of Monnet, Robert Schuman, the French Foreign Minister, declared that a united Europe was essential for world peace and as a first practical step towards this end he proposed 'to place the whole Franco-German Coal and Steel production under one joint High Authority in an organisation open to the participation of the other countries of Europe.' Germany, the Netherlands, Belgium, Luxembourg and Italy agreed to enter into negotiations and these six countries accepted the proposed principles. Britain expressed sympathy for the Schuman plan, but failed to agree to the necessary commitment. In consequence these six countries established, under the Treaty of Paris in 1951, the European Coal and Steel Community.

Following the failure to establish a European Defence Community and the European Political Community over the next two years, the negotiations began in 1955 which led to the signing of the Rome Treaties in 1957 under which the European Economic Community and Euratom were established. The two Treaties came into operation on 1 January 1958.

Each of the three European Treaties provided for similar institutions: a Council of Ministers, a Commission (or in the case of the Coal and Steel Community, a High Authority), a Court of Justice, and an Assembly. However, by 1967 the institutional structure had been simplified, so that now for all the three Communities there is a single Council of Ministers, a single Commission, a single Court and a single Assembly. The Council consists of the foreign ministers of the member states, but when specialised issues such as agriculture or finance are being dealt with, the appropriate national ministers attend. The national governments appoint the members of the Commission, the Court and formerly the Assembly. The Assembly was directly elected by the people of the Community in elections held in June 1979.

In 1961 Britain decided to negotiate for membership of the Community, and Ireland, Denmark and, slightly later, Norway—all of them with strong links with the British market—decided to do likewise. The British negotiations broke down in 1963 and the other applications were not pursued at that time. Eventually, Britain, Denmark and Ireland joined from 1 January 1973; the people of Norway rejected membership in a referendum.

There were two main motivations for Ireland in joining the Community —the first was to break out into a larger grouping that operated as a *community* and to dilute the ancient confrontation with, and dependence on, Britain. The second was to diversify our trading pattern as much as possible—the Community was the fastest growing economy in the world.

This need was particularly felt in relation to agricultural exports, on which both the balance of payments of the country as a whole, and a great number amongst the poorest people in the country, were dependent. Because Britain had pursued traditionally a cheap food policy it maintained an open market for agricultural products. This meant that Irish farmers received very low prices for their products, and had little incentive to increase production. The Common Agricultural Policy of the Community, on the other hand, was based on the principle that efficient farmers should be as well-off as efficient producers in any other sector of the economy. This meant high prices, stable prices, and, so far as we were concerned, a market for our traditional agricultural produce.

This policy has had a dramatic effect on the whole social situation in Ireland. The best farmers have done well, and the poorest farmers have had much of the worst of their poverty alleviated. A great part of Irish political and administrative activity in relation to the Community has been concerned with the Common Agricultural Policy—its maintenance, improvement, and, so far as we are concerned, its extension to such areas as sheep meat and to disadvantaged areas where it had not originally operated. The struggles that go on in Brussels in relation to sea fisheries – covering the two broad areas of conservation and the development of the very under-developed Irish sea fishing industry – vividly illustrate the Community system at work. They are, however, but a pale shadow of the struggles that achieving the Common Agricultural Policy involved.

Another major interest of Irish policy has been in relation to regional development. Originally it was thought that the Regional Policy would be taken seriously by all the members of the Community, and this would involve substantial transfer of resources from the richer countries to the poorer ones, notably Italy, because of its very poor southern half, and Ireland. This has not occurred because the redistributive effects of regional policy have not been taken seriously enough, possibly because – as we can see in this country – those who stand to gain from it do not themselves take it very seriously.

There is a substantial body of opinion that sees the achievement of economic and monetary union (EMU) as the next crucial step forward for the Community. This is almost certainly so. During 1978 EMU proposals received powerful reinforcement. If EMU is achieved, or if the significant step towards it of the European Monetary System succeeds, it is difficult to see that the 'peripheral regions' (which include Ireland) will not be greatly imperilled as a consequence, unless there is a really massive and effective development of regional policy. These are very serious problems for the future of this country.

As things are, another effort at equalisation is made by the Community's Social Fund which underpins a number of good works in this country, notably several programmes of An Comhairle Oiliúna (AnCO), the industrial training body. But the dramatically effective social and regional instrument affecting this country has been, of course, the Common Agricultural Policy which has transformed Irish rural life.

But these are some of the big issues. There is also a great mass of day-to-day pieces of administration that involve Irish civil servants and other Irish representatives, parliamentary, vocational and the like. One gets some idea of the range of these from the staffing of the office of our permanent representative to the Community. Apart from officers of the Department of Foreign Affairs, there are representatives of the Departments of Finance; Agriculture; Fisheries and Forestry; Industry, Commerce and Energy; Tourism and Transport; the Environment; Social Welfare; and Labour. That is, half the departments are directly represented. In addition, the evening plane to Brussels is usually half-full of civil servants – a substantial number of them from the Department of Agriculture – travelling on business connected with the Community. Travelling also one may find representatives of various interest groups, such as industry, trade unions, agriculture, the universities, etc. Most of the work that they are engaged in gets settled through a vast committee structure that operates both in relation to the Commission and the Council of Ministers.

However, from time to time it is impossible to settle these issues at the official level and ministers, at the various meetings of the Council of Ministers, engage in these long drawn-out, well-publicised bargaining sessions by which the toughest decisions relating to the Community finally get taken. Large decisions that transcend these specific policy issues tend to be taken by the European Council, that is, the meeting of Heads of State and of Government held three times a year.

The experience of working in the Community and in its multifarious agencies has posed probably the greatest challenge to the Irish public service – especially the civil service – since World War II. There is general agreement that Irish public servants have taken to this very different milieu with some degree of success. There are still problems, amongst a number of them, principally, of insufficient general exposure to the European background as a whole, and in particular, the limitations in relation to the languages of the Community. This tends to restrict, to some extent, free and easy personal relations – which are so valuable in the negotiation process – to English-speaking groups. Given the difficulties that the British are experiencing in adjusting themselves to the ways of the Community this can be a drawback for a small country like Ireland. Certain public servants, who have to operate both at home and at Brussels, have to carry very heavy loads of work. On the other hand, a relatively small bureaucracy has certain advantages. Its members have easy access to ministers. They can negotiate over a broader range than representatives of bigger countries who, while they are more specialised in their knowledge – and therefore likely to be better informed in a narrow area – have, for that very reason, less freedom of manoeuvre at the negotiating table.

Whatever the present strengths and weaknesses, in the long run there may be a more serious drawback still. Granted that survival in the Community is a matter of constant and hard bargaining, it would be unfortunate if this country saw its role in the Community as being one of being constantly 'on the make', as it were. The Community grew out of one of the greatest creative ideas in history. It demands from its members not only hard heads but also some corresponding degree of creativity. That is a major challenge to all of us in this country, whether we be politicians, public servants, farmers, fishermen or whatever.

A major problem is the virtual absence of means of studying international relations in this country, so that the level of knowledge of politicians, officials and academics of emerging trends in other countries of Europe, and of the Third World in particular, is disconcertingly low and quite inadequate to our new responsibilities and opportunities.

Whether at home or abroad the modern public servant – whether he be a civil servant, a local government officer, in the service of a state-sponsored body, or an international civil servant – is operating amongst a great mass of institutions set up for all sorts of reasons in all sorts of different ways. Through all this diversity, however, there is one single thread. The individual public servant works with his colleagues in his own institution, under the appropriate political masters, to achieve some overall improvement in his region, in his country, in the international community. This is the reality behind the vast mass of detailed and confusing day-to-day business that flows through this great complex of institutions. It is likely that this growth of direct contacts with officials abroad will bring about big changes in the role of professional diplomats (as the recent British 'think-tank' report has urged CPRS, 1977), and for other officials cross-fertilisation of ideas, policies and practices (Chapman, 1959; Fougère, 1967; Johnson, 1973; Molitor, 1974; Plantey, 1971; Oliver, 1978; Vinde, 1968).

As one looks to the future one sees the emerging development of One World, as it has been called. What occurs in some (to us) remote place can have direct effects on our daily lives. The problems of other countries become our problems too. As we emerge from our long period of eclipse by our powerful neighbour we find ourselves faced with increasing problems of foreign relations, of foreign trade, and of international finance. Our own undertakings – public and private – become involved in international activities and the advantages and the complications that these inevitably bring for government. On the other hand, great problems arise over the impact on our country of the multi-national firms. World preoccupations with such problems as energy vitally effect us all – the householder, the big business, the small farm.

Just as within the nation there are great structural imbalances as between the more and less advantaged, so, to a vastly greater extent, there are structural imbalances between the less advantaged countries – containing the vast majority of mankind – and the more advantaged. Just as happens within the national community, at least in the short term, the very process of economic development tends to make these imbalances greater still, unless corrective action is taken. As members of the European Community we are committed at the supra-national level to attempt to reduce these imbalances by enabling developing countries to trade freely with us, by helping to guarantee some stability in the volatile prices of primary products on which so many of them depend, and by the transfer to them of skills and technology. What has been done so far goes nowhere near what needs to be done if there is to be some balance in world development. For that reason there have been the attempts to achieve at the *international* level various initiatives summed up by the expression the 'New International Economic and Social Order' to prevent the present gaps between rich and poor nations from growing wider and to help the poorer nations to achieve rates of development in some way commensurate with their needs. One way of doing this is to help them to industrialise themselves more rapidly and to produce goods that will compete with established industries in (e.g.) Ireland. If this is to be done without too much hardship at home some sophisticated *national* adaptation policies will be required.

Overall, if Ireland is, on the one hand, to play a part in an increasingly international world, and on the other is to serve its own best, longterm interests, it will have to equip itself with institutions for much more information, study and research into foreign affairs and to develop degrees of knowledge, exchange of personnel, and of sophisticated action much beyond anything that has so far been conceived of, much less achieved.

6. Problems of Institutional Development

There are a number of levels at which one can consider the problems of Institutional Development as far as public institutions are concerned. The more one examines these the more important it becomes to try and see them in their full context. This context is concerned with three levels: that of *individual* organisations, that of *structures* of organisations, and of a *system* constituted of these structures.

To illustrate this complexity let us look, if only in a very simplified way, at how far social organisation is supplemented by elaborate governmental organisation, concerned to underpin, for example, the movement of people. So we find the need for elaborate systems of transport. We find that government is responsible for providing air transport through one company (Aer Lingus) and sea transport through two of them – B & I and Irish Shipping. (The British government is responsible for others.) To provide places of arrival for these craft it is necessary to have ever larger harbours and airports. To move the people it is essential to have a significant public system for internal transport and, for this and for those who provide their own transport, an adequate system of roads. To accommodate the tourists and other travellers there must be an adequate system of hotels and other amenities. In all of these things modern government is concerned – in Ireland directly to a very great extent, but also indirectly.

As the population rises there are problems about providing sufficient jobs for young people. So, the government is concerned with the promotion of economic activity in agriculture and industry. It is concerned with assisting the selling of the products, with creating the conditions by means of economic management and taxation policies that will stimulate enterprise, and with creating the economic and political ties that will provide expanding markets for the goods produced.

Economic development of this kind has to be supported by a substantial social programme that, for example, provides houses for the workers who can get employment, and that provides health and welfare services for their dependants and for themselves in old age and retirement.

As economic activities become more sophisticated higher levels of education and skills must be provided for the population and these in turn lead to the demand for the development of various cultural activities.

There are two points to be noted here. The first is that none of these activities can be considered in isolation – they are all related to one another in some way. The second is that all of them are underpinned by public institutions. In very many cases these services are provided directly by public institutions, and in others the institutions provide them indirectly as, for example, the Arts Council provides support for writers and artists, or Bord Fáilte grants for improved hotel accommodation. What has been set out above is a very simplified version of the activities for which government has found itself, willy-nilly, responsible. But the outline is sufficient to give some idea of the extraordinary complexity of all the activities of government taken as a whole.

We can look at these activities in several ways. One way is to look at them in relation to their closeness or distance from the direct supplying of a service, such as, in the examples given above, the operation of a ship, an aircraft, or an hotel. At a second level one can think of the problems of infrastructural development – the provision and development of harbours, airports, internal transport systems, roads, amenities. At a third level one can think of the systems for the promotion of economic activity – organisations for promoting the sale of exports, or the attraction of tourists, or foreign enterprises. At a fourth level one can think of the tasks of developing the educational, technical and cultural skills of the people who will be working in the factories, operating the hotels, or whatever. At a fifth level one can think of the problems of overall economic management – attempting to maintain stability, stimulate enterprise, to guide the flow of investment. At a sixth level one can think about the problems of the equitable distribution of the results of economic development, so that there is some concept within the society of caring for the needy and of 'fair shares'. At a seventh level one can think about the problems of the effective operation of the institutions that are to look after all of these services. Finally, at the eighth level one can think of the problems of the overall political management, so far as it is feasible, of the community as a whole.

It is not necessary, of course, to stress that these layers of government are not watertight – nothing in all of this business is clear-cut or precise. Nonetheless, these different sorts of levels are to be discerned in the operation of government in practice.

Because of the sheer size of these operations, their comprehensiveness and their different levels of sophistication, considerable institutional problems arise. They arise especially when we are concerned to improve the overall performance of these institutions and to reduce waste and conflict. These institutional bodies are susceptible to some form of rational analysis and prescription. This is not to deny that they are not, like anything in the human condition, subject to unpredictable forces that beat on them from outside, and, indeed, to almost as unpredictable forces that, unless there is very careful management, will convulse them from inside.

Nonetheless, it is important to hold on to one point. That is: each institution has reasonably defined objectives and reasonably substantial resources. Its task is to achieve its objectives by the rational use of these resources. This applies both in the public and in the private sectors. Many thousands of managers, public and private, in this and in other countries, are preoccupied with the tasks of removing the internal impediments to the more effective use of resources and with the speedier attainment of the objectives that have been identified.

For a single organisation, the removal of the impediments and the necessary degrees of internal reorganisation are, relatively speaking, easy so far as that single organisation is concerned. But these organisations do not work in isolation. Many of their activities are with and through other bodies. It is when one comes to the problems of the linkages as between a number of organisations engaged in achieving a common objective that the difficulties become very much greater. These linkages may be *horizontal* or *vertical*.

The horizontal linkages may be primary, secondary or more sophisticated still. Let us, first, look at examples of primary and secondary horizontal linkages.

An objective of government policy is to develop deep-sea fishing off the west coast of Ireland. For that there are required ships of substantial size, which themselves call for very heavy investment of capital, for a high level of training for the skippers and crews, and for adequate deep-sea harbours. One decision to this end was to develop a deep-sea harbour at Rossaveal on the Connemara coast. This involved specifications from the Department of Fisheries and Bord Iascaigh Mhara, Gaeltarra Éireann (because it is a Gaeltacht area) providing additional resources, the Office of Public Works acquiring the necessary land and designing and constructing the harbour works, the Galway County Council in putting in roads and water supplies, the Department of Posts and Telegraphs in putting in telephone equipment, the ESB in providing power, CIE in providing transport facilities, and somebody or other being induced to establish processing facilities in the harbour.

This whole operation began in 1968 and ten years later had not been completed. It is, in consequence of such delay, likely to have been very wasteful. We lack any means for ensuring that the activities of all these public bodies are dovetailed in such a way that the overall time for providing the whole is the minimum that is technically feasible.

One can see the same need for binding together diverse policies and diverse organisations if one looks at a secondary level, the problem of industrial development. There is a shortage of private industrial enterprise in this country and a major part of government activity is to try to reduce and, if possible, remove that shortage. The Industrial Development Authority and, in their special areas, the Shannon Free Airport Development Company (SFADCo) and Gaeltarra Éireann exist to deal with this problem. So they attempt to encourage native industrial enterprise and woo foreign enterprise to establish factories in this country. They give substantial grants of money, and give access to other concessions in the taxation field. They establish industrial estates, and put on them advance factories and arrange with local authorities and other public bodies to provide the necessary infrastructural services. So far as the work-force is concerned arrangements are made to develop industrial skills in technologists, technicians, and workers generally. Arrangements exist through, for example, An Comhairle Oiliúna (AnCO) for training and retraining of workers. The National Manpower Service exists to provide guidance to both employers and workers as to availabilities, and to encourage mobility, both geographical and vocational. Local authorities and the National Building Agency are engaged in providing housing for these workers. Other infrastructural services such as transport facilities, roads, communications, etc. must be provided to facilitate enterprise and to cope with the products that emerge as a result.

There are here some very difficult questions of phasing all these operations, and the activities of a large number of public bodies, in such a way that there is produced, overall, a smoothly operating system for the encouragement and development of industrial enterprise. These are two examples of the system of government operating on the horizontal, as it were. In the Rossaveal case there is a reasonably specific objective and, hopefully, a limited time-scale. In the instance of industrial development the objective is much more general, and the time-scale necessarily much less specific.

But one can look at all of this in a vertical context also. The various horizontal linkages are themselves bound together by vertical linkages. These come from certain overall policies of government that run through the activities of the individual agencies—or ought to run through them. Planning systems, if they were effectively installed and well operated, could make a big contribution here. But there is needed, at a more abstract level, clear-cut overall policies. For example, in both of the examples given the overall objective is the development and encouragement of enterprise and, in consequence, employment. For encouragement to occur in the area of enterprise, or in any other areas, a set of coherent, consistent and complete policies must exist to achieve an effective attack on the problem of overall employment. Obstacles within the control of government must be removed, and incentives must be mutually reinforcing, neither too little nor too costly, to achieve the required objective. Policies to stimulate private enterprise, whether home-grown or imported, if they do not seem to be sufficiently effective, may need to be supplemented by other policies, for example, as was done in the thirties, by means of public enterprise. Similarly, if industrial enterprise cannot meet the overall needs of employment policy, may not comparable degrees of energy and creativity be needed to develop service employment? What is required here is, overall, the high-class management of the various operations to tackle this problem. The same issues arise in other areas of overall policy (Barrington, 1976).

At a higher level of sophistication there is need for other, more general, qualities of government. One expects here good order, stable, predictable and *comprehensive* policies, the development of a more equitable society and, in consequence, higher levels of harmonious development.

In the last analysis government is, to use the hackneyed phrase, about the quality of life in the society and the great variety of government interventions must result in some transformation from quantity to quality.

In general, the work of government has to be underpinned by public institutions. As we have seen there is the problem of combining a number of institutions into various horizontal systems so that they will work effectively together to achieve certain common specific objectives. There is the problem of achieving vertical structures so that there will be coherence and consistency within and as between all of these systems. If we are to have anything approaching efficiency in government as a whole, common objectives, both specific and general, must be defined, clear-cut roles and programmes must be allocated, unnecessary frictions and uncertainties removed, and various forms of lubrication applied to ensure smooth communications and harmonious working.

The need for clarity of approach has been thrown up by the difficulties there have been in this country in trying to achieve an adequate planning system. In many ways a plan for economic and social development should be something like a blueprint for a machine. It is when one begins to try to put all the pieces in some sort of order and to remove the avoidable frictions that one discovers the extraordinary difficulty of, even conceptually, considering the whole question in mechanical terms.

However, there are certain broad guidelines that are available. We have seen in Chapter 2 the crucial importance of distinguishing between the formulation of policy and its implementation. We have seen also in Chapter 2 and in this Chapter the sorts of problems that are appropriate, both in number and in kind, for being dealt with at the centre, and the sorts of problems that are capable of being dealt with at the periphery of the system. We have just now been looking at analytical categories of problems, horizontal and vertical.

One can also look at all of this from the functional viewpoint, of the division of responsibility as between ministers into what have been called

'portfolio areas' (Whelan, 1975); as well as the consistency of responsibilities and operations as between the portfolio areas. If one thinks of the
business of government as being divided rather like a pie, one expects,
so far as possible, the pieces to be functionally distinct as between one
piece of pie and the other, and coherent as within each slice. So there is
the need to divide out the business of government in a consistent and
coherent way so that like functions are grouped together as far as possible,
as Devlin tried to do (PSORG, Chs. 18–38).

There is the need, within each of these functional areas, of ensuring
common objectives and consistent operations. And there is the need to
ensure that, as between the various groups of functions, there is overall
consistency and coherence, as well as co-operation, in the full sense of the
word, in practice.

In a political sense there are means by which all of this can be achieved,
certainly in the short run. The coherence of the party system, the constant
meeting of members of the government around the cabinet table, the
pressure of the opposition, the ruthlessness of the electors at election
time – these are strong forces making for political coherence and consistency. In theory, this is transmitted from the political system through
ministers to the administrative system and, again, in the short run this is
reasonably effective.

But, overall, as the experience of nearly every country can show in
recent decades, there is need for something else, something that will
clarify, simplify and make more effective and humane the whole complex
of administrative bodies and get them, in the best sense of the word,
under control.

7. Institutional Reform

In September 1976 I attended a meeting, organised by the European Group
of Public Administration, in Tampere in Finland. It dealt with 'Administrative Reform' (RFAP 5, 1978). Countries from both Eastern and
Western Europe were represented there. In every one of these countries
action in relation to 'Administrative Reform' was going on. In most of
them the results so far were disappointing. In the same year was published
case studies of reform efforts in four 'developing' and four 'developed'
countries with two major analytical studies by the editor. The same general
impression emerges (Leemans, 1976). Earlier, there appeared a thoroughly
depressing analytical study (Caiden, 1969).

Why should so many countries be concerned about the state of their
administrative apparatus? There seemed to be a number of reasons. But
first let us look at three concepts that are often used in this connection.
They are the concepts of change, of reform, and of development.

Continuous and rapid change is a commonplace of our world. Public
institutions are no exceptions to this requirement of constant change.

Indeed, it may be more necessary in relation to them for a number of reasons. First of all, they are themselves a part of the world in which change is a regular feature, so they themselves are subject to the normal processes of change. Secondly, they are a significant part of any given society and thus specially subject to the changes induced in that society. Thirdly, most of them exist precisely to promote change. This involves them in constantly adjusting their methods to deal with the consequences of their own activities.

The second concept is that of reform. Where change is resisted – we have for a long time seen this in relation to the problem of local government finance – or where the changes accepted are inadequate to the needs of the situation, the processes of external change will, sooner or later, refuse to be held up indefinitely. These processes will then take their own paths, sometimes highly irrational or violent ones. In such circumstances the institution becomes an obstacle to this movement, or else it becomes irrelevant to the situation as a whole. It has lost its foundation, in whole or in part, the consensus that gives it its raison d'être. Eventually, something *must* give, and this breaks out in a demand – and eventually action – for a once-for-all reform of the institution. It is a matter for observation that the momentum of this kind of reform often suffices for some twenty or thirty years. Then the whole process begins again, a kind of extended stop-go operation.

The third concept is that of development. Even where a public institution is, in Churchill's expression, 'in continuous and harmonious relationship with the progress of events' that is, responsive and adaptive to externally induced change, this may not be sufficient to prevent it from falling back into the need for reform. This is because the role of most public bodies nowadays is not simply to react to events, it is to shape them in some way. Nearly every public body has a promotional role and shares in the responsibility of any governmental institution to lead and influence that part of the society to which it relates. This calls for a positive approach to change, for using it as a dynamic for achieving a better society. This is what we mean by development. Institutional development is necessary within the individual institutions (Lawrence and Lorsch, 1969); but it is also necessary as between institutions and within and as between the structures and systems formed from these institutions.

But to return to the concern of so many countries with the state of their administrative apparatus. There are at least six reasons for this concern – the growth of '*bureaucracy*', the results of *incrementalism*, anxiety about public service *efficiency*, the demands of *planning*, the problem of popular *alienation* and preoccupation with *devolution*.

The first reason for this concern is the size of modern government, and the corresponding growth of administrative institutions, of 'bureaucracy' and in the number of bureaucrats (Albrow, 1970). This poses problems of political control of the powerful institutions that have grown up in every country and the fear that those who man these great institutions do not adequately reflect the opinions and the values of the people of the country. Where there was a very pronounced class structure, as in Britain, the higher civil service in particular seemed to be the preserve of one class, a class, moreover, unable in the opinion of its critics to tackle the needs of a modern, egalitarian society (Expenditure Committee, 1977, lxxviii–lxxxiii).

The second main reason arises from the phenomenon of incrementalism, that is from the ad hoc way that the public institutions have been established and have grown and proliferated. If one can imagine this incrementalism as a steady drip into a bucket, sooner or later the bucket overflows and some action has to be taken about it. In Marxian terms a 'transformation' has occurred and the whole situation has been forced onto another plane.

A third reason is the problem of efficiency, especially if we consider efficiency in engineering terms. If one recalls that an electric fire returns energy in the form of heat rather less than one-fifth of the energy required to produce that heat, one has some sort of a picture of the anxieties of many people in modern societies as to the efficiency, in this sense, of the public institutions. They absorb large quantities of highly-qualified people and consume great resources. Is the output commensurate with these inputs? Or is there good reason to draw the analogy of the electric fire? No one really knows, but there is mounting disquiet on this head (Cogan, 1978; NESC 43).

A fourth reason is the need to clarify and rationalise the various forms of state intervention by means of planning systems, and to ensure that the objectives laid down in the plans are in fact, so far as humanly possible, achieved. Such achievement is not a common experience and there is mounting anxiety as to why plans are not better devised and as to why there is not better implementation of what is contained in the plans.

A fifth reason arises from the increasing articulateness of the governed. In a number of places there is evidence of the alienation of the people from the system of government, leading to active hostility to various government measures. The reaction in some countries is to increase the opportunities for the exercise of real responsibility by as many people as possible, and to involve them in the processes of government, where this is feasible, and by these means to increase the level of knowledge and understanding amongst the people of the steps that have to be taken to increase overall welfare. This involves some drastic changes in government institutions and their method of operation.[1]

[1]The most drastic, so far, has been the large-scale decentralisation of powers to local authorities in Denmark, caused, at least partly, by concern on this issue. See also the 'Proposition 13' revolt in June 1978, of taxpayers in California. A similar revolt was narrowly averted in Switzerland. Note that these are all very rich places. What seems to be happening is the alienation of the well-heeled.

Sixthly, and related to the fifth point, is the rise of regionalism in all its forms and the consequent movement in a number of countries for devolution from central government to subordinate bodies, notably in Italy, but also in Spain, Belgium and, possibly, Britain.

Reasons such as these have impelled most modern governments to be concerned about the overall health of the institutions they rely on to provide the quality of government that in all its complexity they, and their peoples, require. What is striking is the variety of the methods used to this end. But, overall, efforts have been largely concentrated on two broad areas—on the one hand the civil services of the various countries, and on the other, the geographical systems of administration, namely, the regional and local government systems.

One can see a great variety of efforts made to improve all the aspects of administrative activity—proposals to improve structures, to stimulate personnel, to improve policy making, to raise levels of management, and to bridge the gaps between government and people. The need for change, where it is accepted, varies from country to country, and within countries, in relation to each of these aspects. Nonetheless, taking the picture as a whole a large panoply of instruments can be discerned.

One of the most common changes has been to re-allocate functions as between ministers. For example, in this country the number of government departments has risen, in just over thirty years, from eleven to eighteen. There has been an attempt to clarify and to concentrate functions under individual ministers. This has been done in a rather unplanned way, and the Devlin proposals (PSORG, Chs. 18–38) for rationalising the distribution of functions as between ministers have been largely ignored.

In Britain there has been a great deal of chopping and changing of ministries—a recent writer has pointed out that over the past decade what used to be the Board of Trade has gone through a number of major transformations (Henderson, 1977). But the main thrust of altering ministries in Britain has been to attempt to tackle the problems of co-ordination by concentrating large numbers of cognate functions under nine or ten super ministries—for example, Foreign and Commonwealth, Health and Social Security, Industry, Environment, Defence, Education and Science. In this way the business of government would be parcelled out into large blocks, each under the supervision of a super minister, supported by a number of assistant ministers. There are mixed views as to how successful this has been. A persuasive case for the giant department—and its implications for the system of co-ordinating government business as a whole—is made by a former permanent secretary of a 'giant' (Clarke, 1971). A less agreeable picture emerges from an outside analysis (R. A. Chapman, 1977). Moves along the same lines have been made in France. It will be recalled that one of President Nixon's projects was to reduce the Federal Government to seven departments.

A second structural change has been to establish a special agency concerned with institutional reform. In France and in Britain this office comes directly under the Prime Minister. These two offices are concerned with the civil services of these two countries. The French one operates primarily through the other ministries, so it is not easy to gauge its effects. The English one, on the contrary, has substantial powers of its own. It was set up following the Fulton Report in 1968, and began its operation with great vigour and dash. But it seems to have fallen on evil days. The recent eleventh report of a sub-committee of the Expenditure Committee of the English House of Commons has recommended that, for all practical purposes, it should be wound up (paras 85–90). There is a Ministry of Administrative Reform in Italy, which has been concerned substantially with the major changes in establishing regional governments in Italy; but otherwise its performance has been disappointing. Our own Department of the Public Service which has the remit of the whole public service, its overhaul and development, has been able to achieve disappointingly little (Ó Nualláin, 1978). In the Federal Republic of Germany an administrative reform committee operated under the Chancellor for some seven years, producing some specific recommendations that have had some success with the Federal ministries and some valuable general reports which have been substantially ignored. In consequence, the committee has been wound up. Overall, the idea of a special agency for administrative adaptation and development has proved to be a very weak engine indeed.

The third main class of structural change has related to the geographical forms of government – local government and regional government.

So far as local government is concerned, there has been a move in nearly every country to enlarge the unit of local government from the very small and very local to a larger size. This has meant in most countries the drastic reduction in the number of local government units. However, it must be borne in mind that after these changes have been made, for example in Sweden, Denmark and Holland, there still remain many more local authorities in those countries than we have in this country. Here in the 1920s we carried the slaughter of local authorities to remarkable lengths. In Britain there has also been a reduction in the number of local authorities and substantial reform of the system, now giving rise to a good deal of disquiet. The most bizarre change has been that in Scotland where a single local authority – Strathclyde – covers just half the population!

The second major local government change has been towards decentralisation of central government activities and their devolution to the new local authorities. This has been most strikingly carried out in Denmark. It is likely that in both Holland and Sweden steps will be taken in the same direction.

On a much larger scale is the issue of devolution to large sub-national bodies. This has happened, most strikingly, in Italy where the great part of what was formerly central government activity has been devolved to specially established regional governments. Something similar appears to be occurring in Spain and, in a curious way, in Belgium. We can see the travails being endured in Britain about the proposed devolution to Scotland and to Wales. In France, at one time, it looked as if there would be established significant regional authorities. It was the rejection of his ideas in this connection that was the occasion for General de Gaulle to leave office. It looks now as though such regional bodies as exist in France will have their functions confined to administrative, and not political, roles.

The most striking example of a system of government relying on geographic units to carry out the main duties of government is, of course, the Federal Republic of Germany. The Federal ministries are, for all practical purposes, planning, policy formulating, and controlling bodies. The day-to-day administration of Germany is substantially carried out by the governments of the Länder. There is also a very strong and complex local government system.

A fourth structural change has been 'hiving-off'. The most radical suggestions in this regard have been those of the Devlin group which recommended the hiving-off of executive functions to functional groups rather like our existing state-sponsored bodies. Very little has come of this so far. In Britain, following the recommendation of the Fulton committee for the establishment of centres for 'accountable management', a few such bodies have been established, mainly to supply goods and services to government agencies. There has also been set up an airports authority. The most striking example of the system of a governmental system relying on a small ministry surrounded by functional agencies is, of course, Sweden. In Finland, a somewhat similar system operates.

A further form of 'hiving-off' is in the wider use of private sector and non-governmental bodies to carry out by contract certain functions for government. The practice is well established in certain areas—e.g. research, house-building—but it is, of course, open to much wider use. Its protagonists argue that it makes for greater efficiency and lower costs; but they have to overcome formidable centripetal forces.

A good part of the problems of reform have related to the personnel of the public service, especially of the civil service. The Fulton Report is substantially concerned with this problem—with simplifying the grading structure in the civil service, with ensuring that there is adequate training for civil servants (both formal training and in relation to work experience) and so on. We will be dealing with this in more detail later. The Devlin Report, on the other hand, took the view that if the structures of the public bodies were correct, they would, of themselves, ensure that these personnel questions were adequately tackled. Subsequent experience suggests that this was a serious misconception.

Perhaps the most original, and far reaching, idea in this area was the

Devlin notion of a single public service incorporating the civil service, the local government service, and the services of the state-sponsored bodies and, by implication, the post-Devlin health service. But, although a Department of the *Public* Service has been set up, virtually nothing has been done to give reality to this idea, except in one particular. That has been in relation to pay. The heavy inflation of recent years has posed very significant problems in relation to pay in the various kinds of public institutions and the number and importance of the people involved has meant that public pay policies could have repercussions throughout the economy as a whole. Hence here and in Britain there has been a good deal of activity in trying to control the pay of public servants.

Strangely enough, there has been much less concentration on the problems of policy formulation. Most countries have been struggling with the problems of planning as a discipline for policy formulation. In this context, perhaps the French and Dutch have made the most progress. In such countries as Sweden and the Federal Republic of Germany the central ministries are almost wholly concerned with planned policy formulation. In Britain planning units have been established in the departments but, following the resounding failure of the National Plan of 1965, have not been worked into a *system* of planning. In this country we now have our new department of Economic Planning and Development and, at last, some progress in installing the long promised planning units in the other departments.

As we shall see in subsequent chapters there has also been much discussion and some experimentation, and action, in the areas of public finance, management services, and clientele.

There has been no shortage of discussion, and proposals, for making systems of government in most countries more efficient and more adaptable, and for developing the institutions of government along reasonably clear-cut lines. Here and there some progress has been made; but, overall, the results have been profoundly disappointing. The problem is to discover what dynamics can be harnessed to bring about the necessary changes.

So far, the most substantial changes have arisen from exogenous factors. The big changes in Denmark, for example, were brought about to a great extent by the *political* need to close the gap between government and people. So far, the only significant Devlin success has been in relation to the implementation of the Aireacht in the Department of Health: that department found the Aireacht essential – so it informed the Public Service Advisory Council (Third Report, 1976, 2.1.2) – in the task of making a success of the big changes being brought about in the health services. That is to say, the dynamic here was an *administrative* need. Substantial changes have occurred in relation to public finance in Britain, caused by an *economic* need, exacerbated by the great inflation of prices.

Are we to conclude, therefore, that significant administrative reform will be brought about only where it can be harnessed to a critical political, administrative, or economic reason, calling for significant change? Must we rely on advance by sporadic crises? Or can we identify some continuing exogenous pressures that will ensure continuous and orderly institutional development? It is often said that we can only expect to look for these in the political system itself, but to continue to seek in this area a continuing and effective source of pressure requires great faith indeed. Apart from this, it is not clear that pressure from the political system is sufficient of itself. For example, while successive Irish governments since 1969 have not been consumed by a burning fury to implement the main Devlin proposals they have, in fact, taken all the necessary decisions, promoted the necessary legislation, and, with some exceptions, put significant weight behind the implementation of the decisions taken. Yet, this political input has clearly not been enough to get real progress. Much the same has been true in Britain.

Perhaps what is required is not so much the exogenous force of 'reform' as the endogenous process of 'development'–institutional development? Was it a failure to think this through that led both Fulton and Devlin each to recommend an agency–within the public service, it is true, but external to all public bodies themselves–to implement their proposals? This solution was weighted on the side of reform from outside rather than on development from within. Whatever the reason–and probably there have been many reasons (but which are the crucial ones?)–the instrument has, in both countries, proved inadequate to its task.

Reform, as has been pointed out, suggests the sharp transition from one state or condition to another caused by some external force. But the increasing pace of change in the size and the pervasiveness of government, in the perceptions of the demands of the citizen, and the increasing complexity of the tasks of the government itself–these require some built-in system, within and between the institutions, for orderly but ready acceptance of change according to some general principles, that is, of development, institutional development. Such development needs a dynamic. This may be sparked off by external pressures, but to achieve a self sustaining level, it must rely on an internal dynamic. Perhaps the main thrust for institutional development may have to come within the institutions themselves, as a perceptive comment on Devlin has suggested (Chapman, 1975). This poses formidable problems as to how such development can be effective not only within the institutions but also as between them and within the structures and systems that comprise them.

Can we, in consequence, identify some internal dynamics–endogenous factors–that can be harnessed to ensure that a steady, continuous momentum will be available to enable the system of government and administration to develop along orderly, principled lines so that a high level of efficiency can be extracted from the whole vastly complicated and expensive apparatus?

This problem of the exogenous and endogenous factors in the process of administrative development is one of the most baffling in the study of public administration. It poses major issues for the administrative profession itself, which we consider in the last chapter of this book. For now, let us look at the example of the trade union movement. Many of us have ideas about what ought to be done about the system of industrial relations. Yet, the failures of exogenous solutions there seem to underline the point that sustained development will come only out of the guts of the industrial relations system itself. Could this also be true of the Irish administrative system?

Chapter 4: Personnel

1. Personnel Management

Up to this we have been considering the consensus that gives its validation to public administration, and the great variety of structures and systems that rest on that consensus. These structures will not be effective unless they consist of well-motivated people, adequately organised to produce policies and to carry them through to the satisfaction of the public. For these to operate effectively there arises the issue of consensus *within* the system itself and its relationship with the consensus outside. There are two activities here, in a famous distinction.[1] First, the considering as to what *ought* to be done, and secondly, the doing of that which *must* be done. In military parlance, *staff* duties are concerned with the 'oughts' and *line* duties are concerned with the 'musts'. This distinction has been taken up by business administration and is now slowly finding its way back into public administration from which the military men originally borrowed it.

Our concern in the next two chapters will be with the 'staff' aspect of public administration, that part of it that is concerned with the 'oughts'; that is, the part that deals with the formulation, the review, and the reformulation, of policy. If we follow the Devlin analysis there are four of these staff functions common to public organisations (and, almost certainly, large private organisations as well). These are the functions that are concerned with *personnel, organisation, finance* and *planning*. In addition there is a staff function in each organisation concerned with the special tasks of that organisation. If the task of the organisation relates to health services there will be a special staff function concerned with health. If it relates to transport, there will be a special staff function related to transport. And so on. Here, we will confine ourselves to the four general ones of personnel, organisation, finance, and planning.

We have been discussing what are, in many ways, abstractions. Big

---

[1] Trevelyan's analysis of his reform of the civil services: 'It was based throughout on the positive idea of government, upon the idea that government must be carried on by men who think as to what ought to be done instead of merely doing that which must be done.' Quoted in Frankfurter (1930) p. 141.

organisational structures, or individual organisations, are nothing apart from people. It is the men and women who staff them that give them their reality, their vitality, and their dynamism. We have seen what a large investment there is of people in Irish public administration. The successful operation of our public organisations depends on how well the potential contributions of these people are evoked.

The first of our general staff services is the personnel function. The public service was one of the first organisations to develop this function. The civil service did so after World War I. A number of other bodies, notably Aer Lingus, developed an effective personnel function after World War II. In recent years the health boards and the local authorities as well as the other state-sponsored bodies, have been developing the function. However, overall, one can say that it is still not well-developed in the public service. Personnel is another of those ideas, regarded as 'good things', that are maintained, if not wholly for ornament, then not really for use either.

The basic proposition is that the human being is highly dynamic. Some are so dynamic that they create their own conditions. But the majority tend to respond to external conditions rather than create them. If these conditions tend to evoke creative energy, then people as individuals and in combination become capable of very remarkable responses. If, on the other hand, these conditions force people to be 'cribbed, cabined and confined', then their vigour and capacity for creative co-operation, at least so far as the organisation is concerned, become stunted (Crozier, 1964). The higher the quality of these people, and the greater, in a realistic sense, their apprehension of their own capabilities, the more serious are the effects of this stunting. It leads to bad morale, cynicism, and discontent. The public service has had a specially large ration of able recruits, partly for lack of other outlets for them, partly because it has always gone to a good deal of trouble to seek them out. This natural advantage poses a severe challenge to ensure that the quality of the recruits is matched by the quality of personnel management in the public service. This challenge has been met with varying degrees of success. Overall, there is a nagging fear that greater returns could be achieved for the country, and more meaningful and satisfying jobs achieved for public servants, if the general level of personnel management in the public service were better.

But let us begin at the beginning.

Apart from subordinate staff on the one hand and highly specialised staff on the other, recruitment to the public service is substantially con-fined to two educational levels – either from those, the vast majority, who have, with distinct success, finished a secondary education, or from those who, with comparable success, have finished a university education.

For those who are recruited at university level the problem arises as to what courses of study intending recruits to the public service should follow. This is relatively easy if they intend to be engineers or doctors or follow some other profession within the public service, but there is considerable controversy about recruitment of generalists. There is a school that says that it doesn't matter what subjects are followed, provided the recruit has a sound character and a good analytical brain.

This tends to be the official British approach, but the practice seems to be that these qualities have tended, for more than a century, to be found most frequently amongst those who have studied classics in the two oldest English universities, a conscious pattern, set in the middle of the last century, that keeps repeating itself. Even now, after the Fulton reforms, something like half the recruits at this level are Oxbridge graduates (Expenditure Committee, 1977). Fulton, from their analysis of the work of the higher civil service, broke it into two kinds, economic work and work relating to the social services. They recommended that recruitment should have relevance to these two kinds of work (paras 71–81); but this is the one major Fulton recommendation that was not accepted.

In continental Europe for a very long time, and still to a very great extent, the study of law has been regarded as the most promising preparation for the public service. It might be said here that law is studied to a very much higher level of sophistication there than it is in this country. However, economics is now establishing itself strongly in a number of these countries with, in particular in such countries as Holland, sociology.

Public administration as a subject has really only established itself in the United States where there are many university schools preparing young people for entry to the public service. For a long time these concentrated on such subjects as budgeting and personnel, but in recent years they have become policy oriented. At present there is a major enquiry going on in the United States to find out what it is exactly that senior public servants do, and what intellectual preparation would enable them to do it more easily or better. This empirical approach comes as a breath of fresh air amid the clash of special academic interests, but it is still at an early stage (Engelbert, 1975).

In this country there is no clear bias towards any special discipline, but as a matter of observation a high proportion of those recruited at university level have studied economics, history and/or politics. Perhaps this is because they chose these subjects with an eye to the public service in the first place.

The issue of post-entry *education* (as distinct from training) is more complicated. The most spectacular example of this is the French École Nationale d'Administration. Its students are those selected for the highest grades in the French civil service. They are given an intense preparation over almost three years. The course is a balance between practical training on the job, practical administrative problem-solving, and academic work. Similarly, young people selected for the higher reaches of the German civil service have a comparable training period, mainly concerned with practice, but also with an academic content. The higher reaches of the public service in these two countries constitute an élite profession that has no counterpart in Ireland (B. Chapman, 1959, p. 93).

So far as Ireland is concerned, the major provision for post-entry education, as distinct from training, is that provided by the Diploma in Administrative Science offered by the Institute of Public Administration, given after four years of part-time study. This attempts to give public servants who follow the course an insight into the intellectual background of their way of life. Recently, Trinity College has offered a bachelor's degree to holders of the Diploma after a further year's study in the College. The Institute, at its School of Public Administration, also offers a year's post-entry education for young, selected serving public servants, mainly civil servants. University College, Dublin has had for a number of years a two years' masters programme in Public Administration, essentially for practising public servants. It has now introduced a four year bachelor's degree also geared to the needs of practising public servants. The National Institute of Higher Education at Limerick is at a comparable stage of development in this field.

The first step in the regularisation of a branch of the public service is to get the system of recruitment properly established, so that recruits are selected according to their ability, and not according to various forms of patronage. The big breakthrough in this connection in the British civil service—and consequently in our own—was the establishment of the Civil Service Commission in 1855. For our own local government service the comparable advance, so far as the senior posts and all the professional ones were concerned, was the establishment of the Local Appointments Commission in 1926, believed to be, at that time, unique in the world. Since then there has been a general realisation that recruitment to the public service should be based on ability. A number of public bodies now conduct their own recruitment systems, but according to the standards comparable to those set by the public service commissions.

Methods of selection have varied over the years. The Chinese in ancient times placed great reliance on written competitive examinations and this was the method adopted by the British Civil Service Commission in the last century, by our own Civil Service Commission when it was set up in 1924 and, in principle, by the Local Appointments Commission of 1926. This is still the method of selection for the more junior posts.

However, for the more senior posts the system of interview by an interview board—that is, by normally three to five interviewers—is usual. There has been a good deal of discussion as to the efficiency of interview boards and various suggestions have been made to improve their reliability—successive interviews of likely candidates, supplementing the competition by means of intelligence, personality and aptitude tests, as well as developing higher levels of skill amongst interviewers themselves (Barrington, 1964; Ó Nualláin, 1971). Suggestions of this kind have been substantially incorporated into the methods used by the British Civil Service Commission for recruitment to the higher ranges of the British civil service but they have, so far, made limited impact on practices in this country.

Systems of fair and objective assessment of candidates have made a great improvement in the quality of those appointed to the public service. Whatever criticisms may be made in detail about the precise methods used, the overall effect has given general satisfaction, both to employers and to recruits.

Apart from the United States, and countries that have been under British influence, a civil service, or public service, commission is not a usual feature of recruitment in, for example, European countries. There the actual recruitment tends to be done by the individual agencies themselves, operating, of course, to generally accepted standards. That is the position in relation to recruitment by state-sponsored bodies in this country, and of local authorities and health boards for the less senior posts.

By 'placement' is meant putting the new recruit in a job that squares in some way with his interests and qualifications, at least at the initial stages. Further placement is intended to help him to develop his qualities and the sorts of skills that he will need to practise his career. In this country the Civil Service Commission now try to arrange that new recruits will be placed in the department of their choice. Once within the department—this applies also to recruitment to the state-sponsored bodies—it becomes the task of the personnel unit to ensure that the recruit is moved around the organisation in such a way as to broaden his knowledge and experience of the work. This has been carried to very remarkable lengths in the British civil service, and the investigators for the Fulton committee criticised the frequency with which officials were moved from job to job before they could get a good grasp of any one job (Fulton, Vol. II, pp. 19–23).

Ideally, this paternalistic interest by the personnel unit should be supplemented by creating opportunities for the young official to make his own career according to his developing knowledge and interests. This calls for a policy in relation to mobility, especially self-sparking mobility, that will be referred to later.

There has been a big improvement in recent years in providing opportunities for recruits to get what is called *induction training*. The purpose of this is to explain to the recruit the objectives and methods of working of the organisation, the relationships of the various parts of the organisation to one another, and the sorts of skills that he or she should develop. This last is built up from the *training survey* which tries to examine the work of the various grades and officers within the agency and to identify the special skills and knowledge that are appropriate at each level of the organisation.

This has begun, in Ireland, notably in the local government and the health services.

This type of information is built into the *staff appraisal system*, which is now beginning to be more widely adopted in this country. That sets out, on the one hand, the skills, knowledge and experience that an officer should have in relation to his job, and on the other, sets out annually those specific areas where he is weak, where special effort is needed on his part and where he can be helped by various kinds of experience and training.

Some of this training relates to the technical skills required of his job. The most immediate, and the most continuing, area of such skills is in relation to communications—how to write clearly, how to read speedily, how to speak well, how to perform in relation to the media, how to handle meetings and so on. Other specialised skills are, of course, also necessary. These may be special to the subject matter of the work of the agency—in the health area in relation to health administration, in the transport area in relation to transport administration, and so on. They may also relate to specialised functions within each agency that are common to them all— namely, skills in relation to personnel, in relation to organisation, in relation to planning, in relation to public finance, or in relation to such things as the preparation of legislation. Other types of skills relate to the use of computers, mathematical and statistical skills, and so on. A number of these techniques themselves develop over the years, and some training provision is necessary to ensure that the skills that have been learned are renewed and brought up to date.

There is a special problem in relation to those recruited because of professional knowledge or skill. In these times of the 'wasting degree' (supposedly with a half-life of perhaps seven years) it is essential that such people remain up-to-date and that there be regular systems for facilitating and ensuring this. In a number of fields—agricultural science, for example —opportunities are made available for study abroad and for general up-dating; but the problem, as a general problem, has not adequately been tackled.

The sheer weight of large organisations, and the necessarily limited range of experience of even the most active member of the organisation, means that there is a constant problem of developing knowledge, personality, self-confidence and social adroitness as an officer moves up through the organisation. This leads to a whole area of what is called 'management development' where understanding of the organisation's work, of how to plan and operate a service, of how to learn from experience, of how to communicate and co-operate with other people, of how to think clearly and reflectively—all these need to be developed and fostered in the staff in the interests of the overall efficiency of the organisation. In addition, facilities and opportunities for study and for contributions to the advance of knowledge in relation to the operation of the agency need to be made available.

The basic task of the personnel unit in this area is to stimulate and help people to realise their full potentialities, not only in order to make them better and happier people but also to make them more productive and useful servants of the state.

The problem overall is, of course, the perennial one of how much can be spared for activities of this kind. This is, in fact, the problem of saving and investment so as to yield greater returns. Up to this, investment in *people* has been pitifully small in the Irish public service.

The pay of public servants is a major personnel problem. This is because so many conflicting forces operate here. The public service aims to be a good employer but not a leader in terms of pay, especially. Basically, pay at the lower levels normally tends to be as good as that obtainable in the private sector. At the top levels the rewards do not compare with the rewards at the top levels of business or the professions. This compression tends to be a feature of public service everywhere. Indeed, in Israel the attempt was made to have very little difference between the top and the bottom of pay in the civil service (a 50 per cent differential at one time); but this kind of egalitarianism – where it is not part of the pay structure as a whole – poses all sorts of problems. In this country the general aim of pay policy is to keep the pay of the public service more or less in line with the general levels of pay in the community. In some countries, notably the United States and Britain, there are elaborate means for keeping up-to-date on pay levels in the community generally. In this country this is more difficult because – apart from the special case of national pay rounds – adequate comparison is difficult to make because there are so few comparable big employers.

Public service pay tends to show up the weaknesses in incomes policy that rely on national pay agreements, pay 'norms', and the rest. In the vast majority of enterprises in the private sector these agreements are modified by local circumstances: if trading conditions are good various additional benefits are available, if they are bad there is, usually, a willingness to wait until times get better. In this way the market smooths the rough edges of agreements both for employees and employers. This sort of adaptation to prevailing circumstances is available only exceptionally in the public sector. There, public employers are expected to adhere strictly to the norm, and a formidable apparatus in the Department of the Public Service exists to ensure that they do. So, former comparabilities between public and private sector pay levels come to an end. Normally – but this is by no means universal – public sector employees, although strongly unionised, are not particularly militant, and there has been a long tradition of patiently waiting for justice to be done to them. But, especially in times of growing affluence, when private sector employees are drifting ahead, patience in the public sector suddenly wears thin, and widespread unrest occurs. Given the existence of restraints to which government, at least, must adhere, the room for meaningful negotiation in such circumstances is severely limited, so leading to strike action and gradual erosion of that spirit of the primacy of service to the public that has been one of the best features of the public service.

The result, apart from the disruption of the public services, is either a major breach of the pay policy — perhaps thinly disguised as a so-called 'productivity' agreement — or else a smouldering discontent, bad morale and a decline in the level of service to the public. It is not easy to see what solutions there can be to this problem of public sector pay, unless some independent means of public service productivity can be put in place of former comparabilities. But here, too, the difficulties are formidable.

Problems also arise at the top end of the scale, in attempting to arrive at suitable levels of pay for the most senior officers of the state — ministers and members of the Oireachtas, the judiciary, chief executives of state-sponsored bodies and the most senior civil servants and local authority officers. In 1969 a Review Body on Higher Remuneration in the Public Sector was set up, under the chairmanship of Dr Liam St. J. Devlin, to act, primarily, as a standing adviser to the government from time to time on general levels of remuneration for such officers. So far it has published two major reports (1972, 1978). A perusal of these reports shows what an extremely difficult task has to be discharged by this body. There are, obviously, very considerable difficulties in devising reliable principles for putting a money value on work at this level. An objective index of this may well be the degree of loss to the public service of some of the limited number of senior officers in relation to whom there are meaningful market forces.

One of the troubles about the growing size of the public service, the degree to which public bodies have become self-recruiting to their higher posts, and the self-confidence of public sector pay policies, is the increasing rigidification of the whole and the declining influence of market forces. One way by which the market could assist in the perplexities of public pay at the higher levels would be to move towards the creation of a market for talent both on the supply and the demand side rather than, overall, to drift away from the concept of a market as is the present overall tendency.

Apart from the special case of national pay rounds and 'incomes policies', there are two influences on public service pay from outside the public service. The first of these is changes in the pay of specially strong unionised groups, skilled workers being a notable example at one end of the scale. Their fellows in the public service seek to maintain the comparisons with their opposite numbers in private employment. The second influence is similar, namely the pay levels of professional groups outside the public service which rapidly spill over into the public service itself. Once a spillover occurs, from either or both of these causes, a great deal of internal movement occurs based on comparability on the one hand and the maintenance of traditional differentials on the other. Elaborate negotiation procedures are in continual operation, attempting to cope fairly with these problems.

Many of the problems of industrial relations in this country arise in the public service. There are, no doubt, many reasons for this, but one is clearly that the sophistication of personnel management in this country often fails to match the, relatively, great size of public bodies so that grievances are permitted to fester and to break out in what may appear to be irrational behaviour. These outbreaks are often exacerbated by structural weakness in trade unions, by the abuse of power by handfuls of key workers, and by various other causes; but problems of this kind are the raw material for good personnel management.

The other main part of compensation relates to superannuation. As a general rule, persons who join the public service spend their lifetimes in it. They are usually required to retire between the ages of sixty and sixty-five, and it is normal for those who have spent a lifetime of service in the public service to have a pension of half their retiring rate of pay, in addition to a single cash payment or 'lump sum'. As a general rule, nowadays, pensions are adjusted for cost of living reasons in much the same way as salaries and wages. An extraordinary accumulation of mumbo-jumbo has attached itself to superannuation questions and, even as between the public bodies, the failure to achieve simple and compatible linkages between superannuation schemes is a major impediment to mobility and, thus, to the quality of the public service as a whole.

The tenure of public servants tends to vary with their status, but overall the aim is to provide security and, for officials who are well-behaved, a steady job until the retiring age is reached. Redundancy is very rare, and dismissal for offences other than dishonesty tends to be a last resort.

On the whole there are not many perquisites of office in the public service – indeed there are rigid rules against the acceptance of perquisites and gifts from outsiders, practices that are often tolerated in the business world. But for those who reach a reasonable degree of seniority there is the substantial perquisite of opportunities for a great deal of foreign travel on official business and, for those who are well-regarded by their organisations the non-material, but significant, reward of assignment to the most interesting, if most demanding, work.

The public service is highly unionised, with the unions substantially stratified according to grades. In many countries there was a long struggle for unions to be accepted, especially in the civil service proper; but that battle has been won by the unions, and in Ireland virtually the whole public service – with the exception of a very small number of senior posts at the very top – is unionised.

Elaborate systems for negotiation procedures and the redress of grievances exist in the public service (McGinley, 1976). The usual pattern is direct negotiation between the union and the personnel or industrial relations side of the agency, reference of unresolved disputes to a conciliation procedure, or to the Labour Court, and, in many areas, finally to a more or less binding arbitration procedure. It is a matter of observation that machinery of this kind has not been sufficient to allay discontent. In recent years there have been major upheavals in the Electricity Supply Board (ESB), CIE and the Post Office where there have been clashes between workers who have expressed forcefully their dissatisfaction with employers, negotiating procedures, and union leaders. In many other instances such clashes have been only narrowly avoided. There are considerable problems of industrial relations in the Irish public service.

At the level of office workers, as distinct from the industrial workers, the situation is seldom so acute. Here the problems are more often those of morale and of motivation.

2. Personnel Dynamics
The purpose of public service pay policy and of the special conditions of employment offered to the public service, is, within limits, to give them the security and the freedom from acute financial strain that will permit them during working hours to give their full attention to their jobs. However, there is more to human needs than reasonably good pay and security. Indeed, these things having been achieved, those other human needs bulk perhaps even larger (Herzberg, 1966).

It is inevitable in large organisations—and many Irish public organisations are, relatively, very large—that there should be a good deal of impersonality, fairly rigid rules, and consequential constraints on the display of initiative and imagination. The neglect, over large areas of the public service, of the skills of management, and the existence of long hierarchies stretching into clouds of unknowing, accentuate the impersonality of the whole and make little or no provision for personal leadership and charisma. The long lines of communication dilute information about, and explanation of, changes of practice that may be made. They also impede the flow of information to the top that, if received, might greatly alter decisions about changes. This makes for bewilderment. The nature of the work often relates to very long cycles indeed—imagine someone concerned with forestry where the cycle is perhaps as long as his own lifetime—so one very seldom sees a final result of one's work. Where the cycle is short—as it seldom is in the public service—this can be a considerable source of job satisfaction. The absence of the cruel discipline of the profit and loss account and balance sheet means that some practices can be carried on long after their reason for existence has passed. So some people may, inadvertently, be condemned to carry on useless tasks. Decisions may have to be taken for political reasons that may make nonsense of work into which one has put the best years of one's life (Oliver, 1978).

There is no way of life without its frustrations, and the public service can offer some very considerable compensations indeed if one's motivation relates to the service of one's country and the bringing into being of substantial operations to contribute to that service. But sometimes it is not easy to see how what one is doing *is* contributing to the common good in this way. Other forms of occupation provide extraneous compensations, such as public recognition, special perquisites, tangible expressions of gratitude for good work; but this is unusual in the public service. One contribution to a solution is 'participation', the election of employees to the controlling board, where there is one. This is now provided for in relation to seven of the largest state-sponsored bodies by the Worker Participation (State Enterprises) Act, 1977. But this, to make a real contribution, must run right through the organisation so that at all the significant levels of authority there is provision for representation of, and consultation with, the staff. There is very little of this in the Irish public service.

In the Federal Republic of Germany, where there has been long and successful operation of a genuine system of worker participation, the comprehensive systems of participation run from the hard graft on the shop floor to the policy level of the supervisory board (Biendenkopff, 1976). Problems of industrial relations frequently arise from unsolved problems of shop floor. To provide a system of 'participation' only at the top of the enterprise is, in the absence of a comprehensive system throughout, not much more than a cosmetic exercise, quite inadequate to the real problems of the, perhaps increasing, alienation of the ordinary worker from his employing enterprise. The real purpose of 'participation' is to tackle this problem of alienation by giving the worker a share in the decisions that most affect his working life from day to day, that is, to enable him to be a responsible, even creative, participant in the working of the organisation.

With other outlets for monetary or psychological reward almost entirely closed, and given what may be called the 'forced draught' of long hierarchical systems, there develops an intense concern in the public service for promotion, for climbing up this long ladder. But here again the opportunities for personal self-realisation can be closed off, especially where, as is normal, one has to wait one's turn for promotion, a promotion that often depends on age distribution within the organisation. Where there is no promotion system that transcends individual organisations of the public service one can have gross anomalies here – very rapid promotion at times where the age distribution facilitates this, very slow promotion at other times. It is a matter of observation that some people of considerable ability get caught in these age traps and, by the time their turn comes, most of the vitality has been drained from them. Conversely, others of much less ability may have the fortune to be wafted into high office.

What we see here is a system that has, in an absent-minded way, the effect of devitalising human beings. Unfortunately the personnel function, over large areas of the public service, has not sufficiently concerned itself with this major problem. This austere world, where ambition and self-realisation must so often be put aside and the ideal of abnegation tacitly put in their place, may be suitable for those who have chosen the monastic life; but it makes little sense for those who have to make their way in the world. The result is that acute problems of morale exist from place to place. In consequence, there is a sort of generalised frustration, made all the more provoking because there is no individual to blame, no 'bloated capitalist boss', to spit at. For many this frustration is usually – but perhaps to a decreasing extent amongst the young – tempered by a strong sense of public service.

There are really two problems here. The first is that a good deal of discontent arises from unrealistic expectations. If advancement is to any considerable extent a matter of chance then everyone, unless he is manifestly unsuitable, can expect that there will be a possibility that the chance will come his way. The second problem arises because, for a variety of reasons, all sorts of barriers have been erected both within organisations and between them to make it difficult for people to make their own careers. There is a striking contrast here between the local government and health services on the one hand and the civil service and the services of the state-sponsored bodies on the other. In the local government and health services advancement is almost entirely a matter for oneself. Most of the senior posts are filled through the Local Appointments Commission and it is up to any individual who wishes advancement to secure one of these. But for civil servants and people who work in state-sponsored bodies this sort of option is only exceptionally open within and as between their own services.

One of the tasks of personnel management is, therefore, to try to get some such self-sparking mechanism operating for individuals by making provision for free mobility as between public bodies (IPA, 1960). This can be achieved by, on the one hand, removing artificial barriers to movement, such as incompatible pensions schemes, and restrictive practices of one kind and another, and on the other by providing positive opportunities for movement through the advertising of the more important vacancies for competition, such as happens in the local and health services, and to some extent with the state-sponsored bodies, and is now beginning modestly in the civil service.

A contribution can also be made by giving an officer greater freedom to control his own working day. Under the flexi-time scheme, now being introduced, an officer must be at his desk during core hours of the day but his starting or finishing time is a matter for himself, provided, overall, he works for the required number of weekly, monthly or yearly hours.

A significant barrier to the best deployment of talent is the so-called 'dual structure' by which many professional officers (engineers, doctors, etc.) especially in the civil service, are restricted to being 'advisers' to administrative class officers who are directly involved in decision-making, with direct access to ministers. Because administrative class skill and experience is considered basic for the highest posts, professional officers are, in practice, normally debarred from reaching them. Not all professional men wish to forsake their profession in this way, but a number do. Others may find themselves obliged to operate decisions taken by those who lack a full grasp of the technical issues. Both Fulton and Devlin recommended the ending of this system. Some progress has been made in the United Kingdom, but very little in this country.

The problems we have been discussing arise, one way or another, from the *size* of public bodies, the very considerable size compared with all but exceptional private enterprise in this country. Are there compensating advantages? A large, personnel-intensive body can offer advantages over a small one in variety of work, in security, in giving specialist knowledge, in career patterns, in salary ranges, in opportunities for exercising special skills and for travel, and in the psychological support of a strong, corporate entity. For the individual these can be formidable advantages, although a number of them will be available only to some members of the staff. In a trade-off between individual gain and loss some individuals, therefore, will feel they have gained by size, others that they have lost. From the viewpoint of the larger organisation a similar trade-off may be made between the remoteness, the heavy overheads, the staff relations problems, the organisational inefficiencies, the problems of communication, on the one hand, against the ability to develop specialist skills, to deploy negotiating muscle, to command resources, on the other. Where the organisation is capital-intensive—as few are in the public service—the choice is clear: the economies of scale outweigh the personnel diseconomies. But where the organisation is personnel-intensive, then there can be an optimum size. This optimum may be relatively high or relatively low depending on whether the quality of corporate management (including, most decisively, personnel management) is of a high or a low order (Clarke, 1971, pp. 17–26).

Public servants have to be especially careful how they go about their jobs. They must, of course, be strictly honest in their dealings. They must, in their private and their official lives leave no reasonable ground for suspicion that they are motivated by anything other than the public interest. For that reason they must be especially careful in engaging in private business activities or, if they belong to professional groups, in professional activities. They must go to great pains to take care that nothing in their private lives will give ground for suspicion that their discharge of their office can be improperly influenced. Especially they will be careful to ensure that no question of a conflict of interest between their public duty and their private activities can arise.

The special moral quality associated with the public service is that of justice. By the conditions of *commutative justice* they, like others, are required to give a strictly fair return to their employer. By the requirements of *distributive justice* they are required to be strictly fair as between clients and applicants – not to favour one, even for the best of reasons, over another where conditions are equal. They are bound by the conditions of *natural justice* – and the courts are increasingly ensuring that they will be – by ensuring that in dealing with claims, in hearing appeals, etc., they will provide the applicant or claimant with all the safeguards of a thoroughly fair procedure. Finally they are bound by what is called *general justice*, that is, positively to seek out means by which the general welfare can be enhanced and developed (O'Doherty, 1958).

Many people engage in politics for precisely this reason but a certain reserve, in our public service traditions, is expected of the public servants in this regard, especially civil servants. So far as the more junior ranks are concerned there is little restriction on the political activities of public servants. At the more senior levels, where they are expected to give, and are accepted as giving, impartial advice to ministers, they are to eschew politics. This requirement has not applied to officers of local authorities nor to officers of state-sponsored bodies. These may take leave of absence to pursue political careers. A number of the European countries do not expect their senior civil servants to be de-politicised.

Part of the task of supervisors and managers is to ensure that order and discipline are maintained in their parts of the organisation. Where it is proposed that action should be taken against an officer for a breach of written or unwritten rules, whether by way of omission or commission, the personnel function becomes involved. It is required to ensure that procedures, in conformity with natural justice, are properly followed before a penalty, or a proposal for dismissal, is decided upon. Usually provision is made for an appeal to a minister, to a tribunal, or outside the organisation to the Labour Court if the officer feels he is being unfairly treated. Usually his union will advise and assist him in this matter, and negotiate with the personnel people about the mitigation or abandonment of a proposed penalty. Whatever the formal position – civil servants, for example, hold their positions at the will of the government – there are now so many legal and customary conventions governing removal from office that this course is seldom decided upon except as a last resort.

Normally officials are expected to retire, where they can draw a pension, between the ages of sixty and sixty-five. It is not clear whether any serious study has ever been undertaken as to whether that is or is not the appropriate age. (For certain officers, such as those in the police, the fire service and the psychiatric services retirement at 55 is possible). The argument for a compulsory retirement age is that as people get older they get less able to cope with the stress of duties. They become less amenable to new ideas and less flexible in their approach to problems generally. Very often those in high office reach it fairly late in life and thus may have difficulty in displaying all the qualities, including creative energy, that such offices demand. If there were no age limit, or a very advanced one, movement at the top would be very slow, there would be a good deal of stagnation down the line, and officers would tend to achieve high office very late in life. In these circumstances the chances of having dynamic leadership in the public service would be much reduced.

It is a matter for observation that most people in their sixties have lost the capacity for speedy action. There are, of course, notable exceptions. On the other hand, a career in the public service often results in the accumulation of a great deal of knowledge and wisdom about public affairs. A fixed retiring age tends to deprive the public service of some active workers and a good deal of experience. Ideally, some degree of flexibility would be desirable, but is very difficult to achieve in practice. There is probably considerable scope for the re-employment on a casual or part-time basis of certain pensioned officers who have, and are willing to continue to give, the benefit of special degrees of experience and knowledge. This calls for some sophisticated operations by the personnel people.

There is a good deal of misunderstanding about the ageing process. The expectation of life *at birth* of men and women in this country, and in many others, has been steadily lengthening. However, expectation of life at age sixty has tended, over the past couple of generations, to fall slightly. More people live to be sixty now, but those who reach sixty have less chance of living quite so long as in the past. In some countries, because of dramatic falls in birth rates, there may be need to continue to employ people beyond what we have been accustomed to regard as the normal retiring age. In this country, however, the situation is, so far, otherwise and the task is to find employment for the young and the active.

One of the tasks of personnel people is, for those who will be retiring, to take steps well in advance to prepare them for retirement. This tends to be a traumatic experience for those who have not prepared themselves for it. Personnel officers have been slow, as a general rule—though there have been exceptions—to deal with this question.

On the whole, women in the Irish public service have been the victims of a good deal of discrimination. The public service—unlike the private sector—did not discriminate too much in terms of pay; but there was very severe discrimination in terms of career patterns. This arose, basically, from the belief that the Constitution substantially required women to spend their lives in their husbands' homes, hence the marriage bar— the requirement that they must retire on marriage. For this reason most girls taking up public employment did not expect to make lifetime careers in their jobs. Hence, they did not, save exceptionally, go for the jobs with the best openings. For some of them, by the time it was clear that they would not marry, they were far behind in the race. The result of all this is that there are extraordinarily few women in senior positions in the public service.

The removal of the marriage bar, the establishment of equal pay, and the legal prohibitions against discrimination against women – this last under the Employment Equality Act, 1977 – will mean substantial changes in this regard in the coming years. It is to be expected that very many women, where they marry, will wish to continue with their careers. Presumably, then, they will begin to take their fair share of the higher jobs. A number, however, will wish to look after their children either wholetime or part-time so long as the children are small. This will pose problems for personnel units. Either they will have to make provision for much more part-time service, at least for part of a woman's career, or, should she decide to withdraw for some years, provide for her later re-recruitment, and retraining. This will call for a much more active and positive role on the part of personnel units.

Inevitably in any organisation there will be members of the organisation who will run into trouble of one kind or another. It is part of the task of the personnel unit to know about such troubles and, where it is not an unacceptable intrusion on privacy, to help in whatever way is possible. This may call for quite a deal of flexibility and imagination. On the whole, this tends to be one of the best traditions of the public service, notwithstanding its overall rather absent-minded air.

Other welfare activities, such as the provision of canteens, crèches and assistance with transfers are also required.

In Britain, but not to anything like the same extent in Ireland, personnel people, often indirectly through unions and staff associations, assist in relation to sporting, educational, and recreational activities, especially those of young public servants.

The tasks of the personnel unit can be seen, therefore, to be very extensive. Its responsibilities are very great. Somehow, it has to create the climate within the individual organisations, and throughout the public service, where the human personality will be encouraged to develop its potentialities, and get the maximum job satisfaction that the circumstances will permit. It must ensure that the service is equipped with the very high level of specialised knowledge and skills that present-day administration requires. It must foster the intellectual and reflective qualities that are needed for the overall management of highly complex affairs. Above all, its task is to create a market for talent, so that creativity will be developed and opportunities for its exercise made available: in a literal sense, it is a question of laisser faire, laisser passer. The conditions for the maximum personal dynamism need to be created. At the same time the personnel function must be concerned that those less gifted will get assistance to develop such gifts as they may have. Finally, it is concerned to look after in a just and humane way those who, for one reason or another, need special care, attention and sympathy (Northcott, 1960).

Chapter 5: Policies

1. Organisation

A major consequence of the growth in the role of the state has been the centralisation of so much of the decision-making process. In a relatively simple, entrepreneurial state a great part of decision-making is done by individual enterprises. However important these decisions may be to the future success or failure of those enterprises the issues themselves, on which a decision has to be made, present themselves as being relatively simple and straightforward. It is quite otherwise when decisions get clustered at the heart of government. There, every proposed decision tends to affect a large number of bodies so there must be a good deal of consultation, negotiation, and compromise before eventually – sometimes after a very long delay – a decision is reached or refused. It is part of the task of the organisation function in the public sector to bring about the conditions that will enable this admittedly complex process to be carried out as speedily and as creatively as possible. As the volume of business grows, and as its complexity increases, this becomes an ever more daunting task.

The purpose of people in coming together in an organisation is to pool their abilities in such a way that, collectively, they can achieve tasks beyond their individual, separate abilities. But the effective operation of a group means concerted effort so that each member of the group does the required thing at the appropriate time. An orchestra, for example, where each member did his own thing at the time that suited him best would not attract much applause. It is inherent, therefore, in an organisation that there should be fairly considerable constraints on the initiative and the enterprise of the individual members. In the orchestra the individual players must not only follow the score and keep to the tempo, but also rise to the conductor's interpretation of the piece. Where the organisation becomes very large there may be no clearly defined score, no system for keeping time, and no apparent conductor. This is the basic problem of any organisation beyond a certain size: how to realise its potentialities. If an orchestra, or a football team, fails to do this it will cease to attract audiences and financial support and will, most likely, disappear. Public organisations are not so vulnerable to the withdrawal of public support, at least in the short run. They may be able to carry on for a very long time failing to realise their potentialities, being, in the engineering sense which we have already discussed in a previous Chapter, inefficient. That is, they will give an output quite incommensurate with the resources they have at their disposal.

Yet the whole purpose of an organisation is to yield a plus value, as it were, a surplus, the sort of synergy that four players achieve when they produce a memorable performance of a Mozart quartet. As Mary Follett put it: 'organisation is what separates mediocre endeavour from high endeavour' (1940, p. 144).

This is precisely the result that the 'organisation function', as it is called, has to aim to produce in public organisations. It has, on the one hand, to try to remove the obstacles that impede high-level performance and to put in their place the positive inspiration and inducements that will extract the best from the players. The recognition of this as a specialised task is relatively new in the Irish public service and has not yet been fully grasped in significant parts of it, notably the civil service. One of the recommendations of the Devlin group was that every public body of significant size should have a separate organisation unit (PSORG 14.2.3; 14.6.3). This recommendation has been adopted in practice in only a very few instances.

The constituent units of organisations are not inanimate objects, but people. For that reason there must be a very close relationship between the organisation and the personnel functions. Indeed, in the civil service, they were both formerly grouped under a single 'establishments' function. This was not well developed even on the personnel side; on the organisation side it was almost wholly undeveloped. As of now, because the organisation side is still so undeveloped, it is not easy to draw a line between the two functions. Moreover, one must continually remember that, even when one is talking in organisational abstractions, one is talking basically about people, and their human dynamism is the basic motive power on which all organisations must rely for effective performance.

It is inherent in the notion of organisation that there should be differentiation of tasks. If one thinks of a simple, temporary organisation that is formed when a group of people turn out to deal with a house on fire in a rural place, one can see this in operation. One group will concern themselves to get water to put out the fire, another group will concern themselves to rescue the inhabitants and the contents, and a third group, perhaps one or two persons, will be concerned to see that the various efforts are co-ordinated, that no undue risks are run, and so forth.

Here we see the elements of organisation—two main operational tasks carried out by the bulk of the helpers on a horizontal differentiation, and a vertical differentiation, as between the person or persons in command

and the other helpers. We see here the pattern on which even very large organisations are composed – the horizontal differentiation into *classes*, and the vertical differentiation into *grades*.

Basically the purpose of operational classes is to provide for specialisation, for example in engineering work, tax collection, legal work, and the like. There tend to be impermeable vertical barriers between the classes, so giving rise to the sorts of problems that, as we have seen, are inherent in the so-called 'dual structure'. The purpose of grades is to provide a filtering system so that each kind of work will be dealt with at its appropriate level, according to its inherent difficulty. If it is the routine application of known rules to straightforward cases, it can be dealt with at the lowest grades. If it involves the interpretation of rules and their application to fresh types of cases, it can be dealt with at the middle grades. If it involves work for which there are no rules or which demands the elaboration of new rules it will be dealt with at the highest grades. Grades also exist to exercise control over the grades below, to ensure that work is being done according to the rules, that targets are being met, etc. The grades build up like a pyramid to a single point at the top, and this facilitates overall command. In this way the grading system constitutes a hierarchy.

Wherever in nature complex material has to be organised we find these two kinds of differentiation, the horizontal and the vertical. But in public organisations (and, no doubt, in private ones) of any size very considerable defects can be seen in the way these differentiations work out in practice. For example, so far as the operational classes are concerned, there is a constant drive towards more specialisation. This is reasonably controlled within the existing professional groups, but at the sub-professional levels new groups are constantly establishing specialisms of their own and seeking exclusive recognition for that specialism. The result is a great proliferation of classes, the erecting of barriers between one sub-class and another, and, inevitably, isolation from the main stream of decision-making leading to frustration and discontent.

So far as the grades are concerned, the higher the hierarchy the more a 'forced draught', as with a tall chimney, is created. For a variety of reasons we have considered in relation to the personnel function, the public service does not have, especially at the lower levels, much opportunity for self-realisation.

As a consequence of these forces, there develop great personal drives towards promotion, which gives increased status and job satisfaction. The more grades there are, the more branches there are on the tree, the more self-realisation calls for a continuous climb to the top. For this reason there is a constant temptation to encourage the growth of more branches, to proliferate grades in order to, as the saying goes, 'increase promotion opportunities'. In consequence there develop very long vertical lines that inhibit communication, control and command. As the number of grades tends to exceed the possible genuine differentiations of the work itself, the duties of the grades overlap and become confused. The very system that was intended to facilitate the organisation of complex material tends to impede it. So, responsibilities become confused, discretion is limited, and a great deal of unnecessary work gets done and re-done. There comes about the situation where 'work is marginally improved, at disproportionate cost'—that is, when it is not positively disimproved by, for example, the resulting dissipation of responsibility and accountability.

Again, schemes get started for good or bad reasons and are carried on many years after their usefulness has expired, but cannot, without great trouble, be dropped because vested interests, both within and outside the organisation, will bitterly resist their abandonment.

The result of all this needless proliferation and the survival of ineffective services is to reduce job satisfaction still further, to make for confusion of purpose, and, generally, for the decline of morale. Responsibility gets dispersed because so many hands are involved in any operation. This is strikingly illustrated when something goes wrong: so many people have made marginal, or only nominal, contributions to the defective decision that usually it is impossible to pin responsibility on any individual. In addition, the breakdown of the notion of a clear-cut hierarchy, and of significant jumps in the nature of the work done at each level of the hierarchy, as well as the failure, in consequence, to define unambiguous responsibilities, accentuate the problems caused by the centripetal forces in Irish administration that suck so much detailed work to the centre. For these reasons the most senior officers are overwhelmed with detailed work while many of those at the middle and lower levels may not have their abilities effectively used.

The task of the organisation function is to tackle this sort of problem at two levels. The first is to remove, so far as possible, the obstacles to better operation. The second is to lay on the services that will facilitate more effective management.

The first obstacle to remove is the tendency to proliferation, and the consequences of past proliferation. This involves a programme of simplification, of role-definition, and of concentration of responsibility. The Devlin Report pointed out that there were over a thousand grades in the Irish civil service (PSORG 7.3.1). The situation has improved somewhat since then. The Federal Civil Service of the United States seems to be able to get by with about twenty scales. Something similar is true of the great international organisations, all of them many times larger and more complex than our civil service. This is an elementary example of the case for simplification. Another is the extraordinary variety of administrative areas used by different agencies and, indeed, by different parts of single agencies (IPA, 1973, App. IV and maps; Roche, 1973; NESC 22). But there are innumerable examples of failure to stand back from the day-to-day press of business and from the consequences of hurried, ad hoc solutions. Complexity tends to become more complex, and confusion and waste are enhanced. Often the concern to simplify, the time to take the perhaps single high level decision that would cut through all this complexity, are smothered by the press of day to day problems.

Secondly, a vast programme of role definition is required. The Devlin aireacht – agency differentiation was intended to tackle that problem at the top, but within the agencies the tasks appropriate to individual grades, and the responsibilities of officers within these grades, need to be defined with some degree of precision. For example, ranges of discretion need to be defined so that there will be concentration of responsibility for various kinds of decisions at the appropriate levels and in appropriate office holders.

It is part of the administrative process to try to define standards and to achieve reasonable degrees of uniformity. It is the task of the organisation function to marry this with the need for discretion and responsible management. Cast-iron standards and leaden uniformity are the death of responsibility and adaptability. Ill-defined standards lead to muddle and confusion.

Sometimes – and this is particularly true of the civil service – responsibility and effective operation are frustrated by the non-operation of well-meaning 'common services'. A scheme may be much delayed in getting off the ground because some other organisation, which has urgent priorities of its own, may fail to supply the necessary accommodation or staff, or equipment, or whatever. 'Common services' may be justified by the economies they achieve, but these may be more than outweighed by the cost and delays inherent in fragmented responsibility and overall drift. It is the task of the organisation function to stand back from these inherited practices – that grew up under very different circumstances – and to get them adapted to modern conditions and problems. Moreover, its duty is to assess the overall consequences of individual decisions and practices that, in their own contexts, make sense but in the aggregate raise serious obstacles to the effective conduct of public business.

The second main task of the organisation function is to facilitate the effective management of the organisation over and above the removal of difficulties. If there is adequate definition of the duties of grades, and concentration of responsibility, then the big problem of delegation of responsibility and authority will be substantially solved. A giving of discretion and some degree of autonomy to individuals and the groups within the organisation and in related organisations will involve some abdication of judgment on the part of people in higher grades. They will find it hard to accept the principle that the man on the job should be allowed to use his judgment unless he is clearly wrong in some matter of real substance. But the chances of mistakes and delays are much reduced if the man on the job is clearly and solely responsible for his decisions.

The second way of assisting is to ensure that the necessary specialised skills are available and are adequately used. One of the most important of these skills, often overlooked, is administrative skill itself. The skilled administrator shows his quality by having taken general, high-level decisions that obviate the need for vast quantities of low-level decisions. The organisation function is concerned to ensure that this occurs, that individual points are generalised into broad rules, regulations and legislation and are made known to all concerned so that what has been decided in the past does not need to be decided again, until the time comes for a review of what has been generalised. In the same way minimum, or acceptable, standards of performance need to be built up for individual decisions, generalised, and publicised.

Part of the function of organisation relates to the assisting of management by the provision of adequate management services. These are concerned to ensure that the output for which any manager is responsible is adequate in quantity and quality. Nothing like enough work has yet been done on the measurement of the quantity of the output of administrative units and of unit costs (Cogan, 1978; NESC 43). If a manager's performance were to be assessed in the public sector not only by what he managed to get done, but also by the cost of doing it, there would be good reason to believe that fair output would be achieved and the dangers of overstaffing and waste of human talents would be much reduced.

It is more difficult to measure the quality of output but a good deal can be done by, for example, assessing the extent to which individual decisions have been assimilated into published policy and the level of the individual decisions that remain. 'A man is known by the dilemmas he keeps' (Follett, 1940, p. 35).

Of course, a great deal can be done to facilitate management by the introduction of machinery. On the whole, office work is still very much in the pre-machine age. Even the typewriter is still relatively scarce in many public offices. At the other end of the scale the development in computer technology, especially of micro-computers, makes possible the accessibility of wide varieties of information at widely dispersed centres. That is, if we had a good telephone service!

The organisation function has the task of making other kinds of information and skills readily available to decision-makers. This is by 'buying in' knowledge by way of research and skills, by way of consultancy. It is no inconsiderable organisational skill to know how to use such outside bodies effectively. In recent years there has been a great growth in the size of university departments and in specialised research institutes. There is here a very substantial resource waiting to be exploited. On the whole, public bodies tend to regard their own staffs as possessing all the skills, and their files to contain all the knowledge, necessary for the formulation of policy. It is the task of the organisation function to see whether this is so or not; more often, the specialised skills of the body are best deployed *after* the research body has made its input.

There are, of course, other sources of information that can be exploited for appropriate problems. There are various methods, such as the use of working parties or commissions, by which light can be thrown on problems that have already received a certain amount of study.

The organisation function can facilitate management by helping to create the conditions in which the staff generally are well-motivated and where leadership can be expected and evoked.

The organisation function has significant tasks as between its own organisation and both subordinate organisations and controlling ones. Perhaps the first task is to tackle that of sanction. Most controls are operated by way of individual sanctions. Over a period of time application for sanction, and sanctions themselves, fall into clusters. From these patterns can be derived, and general sanctions, that obviate correspondence between the two bodies, worked out. Sometimes this can be done by way of an agreed procedure. At other times, discretion within specified financial limits can be decided upon. Here again there is the task of defining areas of discretion for 'the man on the job'. Sometimes it can be agreed that prior sanction will not be required but that the facts will be reported in due course, or the decisions can be left to scrutiny at audit.

One of the major defects of our system of administration is the lack of a free flow of information, and adequate consultation, between bodies engaged in co-operative activities. This, also, is a task for the organisation function.

Nearly every public body is engaged in some activities that impinge on the activities of other public bodies where there is no question of a controlling relationship. Where there is a comprehensive planning system a good deal of this co-ordination will be taken care of. But, otherwise, use must be made of special instruments, such as inter-departmental committees or working parties. These can be efficient if the basic decision on the policy to be pursued has been taken and the task of the group is, within a given time, to work out how to implement the policy. But, usually, when the task is the *what* of policy, what overall decision to take, then the process is usually highly inefficient.[1]

Interdepartmental committees are inefficient partly because there is no

---

[1] This is a matter of observation, but is seldom documented. See, however, NIEC report no 3 on manpower policy, the negative conclusions of the Interdepartmental Committee (1965), p. 49, the feline comments of NIEC no 9, and the subsequent decisions to set up the Department of Labour (1966) and An Comhairle Oiliúna (AnCO) (1967). For the general background, see FitzGerald (1968). Research conducted for the Royal Commission on (Australian) Government Administration reveals a similar state of affairs (Vol. IV, pp. 289–339). See also Schon (1973), p. 156, on the US federal civil service use of such committees.

clear definition of the role of the members—are they there simply to voice the viewpoints of their organisations? Or are they there to pool their special knowledge and experience, and in particular their judgment, to find the best solution overall? In practice, the first of these courses is the normal one, so inhibiting the processes of face-to-face bargaining, compromise and mutual accommodation by which positive decisions get taken. Because of this the committees tend, where the issue is important and contentious between the parties, to produce solutions that are at the lowest level of agreement and that seldom or ever represent a creative solution to the problem. Sometimes a better solution can be produced as the result of a piece of independent research, or as a result of the labours of a commission consisting of detached, but informed, persons.

It is the task of the organisation function to know which of these instruments to use where a difficult co-ordination has to be achieved, and to ensure that the work of the appropriate body is so organised that the most that can be achieved, rather than the least, will be recommended for action.

Finally, the organisation function is concerned with the client groups of the body. Sometimes these are highly organised themselves and are well able to take care of their access, consultation, information and negotiating needs. But very often the client groups are not so well organised, and some orderly way by which they can have reasonable access to the body, and reasonable consultation, requires to be devised. For both groups, a good deal more information may have to be made available so that there will be an informed public opinion about the activities of the body, and so that client groups will find themselves constrained to act responsibly within roles that public opinion will accept as reasonable. There has been, in a number of cases, a great falling-off—especially as compared with nineteenth-century practice—in the quantity and quality of information given to the public by way of informative annual reports, occasional explanatory booklets, and other *factual* publications.

Where individual clients are concerned it is important to ensure that, so far as possible, the services provided by the body are as clear-cut and as simple as possible. There is great scope for the more orderly relating together of distinct services that are directed at easing different social *symptoms* displayed by individuals, families and communities under stress. A big part of the organisation unit's task is therefore to make things easy for the individual client. It does this by providing as many of its services as near as possible to him in a single, reasonably agreeable, and accessible location and by having them staffed by people who have the knowledge and sympathy to give him the necessary and appropriate advice (Andersen; see also Royal Commission (Coombs, 1976, pp. 161–3) for a parallel, the 'one-stop shop'). In any event, it sets out to simplify the service, and the related services, as much as possible by achieving as much unity and flexibility as can be, by clarifying rules about eligibility, and by providing for prompt, delegated decision-making. In particular it goes to pains to give him information, both orally and in written form, that is clear, simple, and helpful.

We see, therefore, that the role of the organisation function is rather like that of the doctor. His task is not only to cure the disease but also to provide advice and assistance for positive health. The diseases to which organisations are very prone are proliferation, woolliness and complexity. Their positive needs relate to the removal of the obstacles to effective performance, and the underpinning of effective management. So far as relations with other bodies are concerned, the organisation function is concerned to improve the quality of day to day management, to ensure that there is adequate consultation, and to achieve forms of co-ordination that will raise the collective conduct of business to the highest level. So far as client groups are concerned the organisation function busies itself with improving access to its information, negotiation procedures and benefits. It strains itself to bring its services close to individual clients and to simplify and clarify them. It makes a special effort to ensure that the body is informative and helpful.

2. Finance

In early times, when trade was by barter, it must have been difficult to fix the price of any commodity or service with anything like precision. In later, feudal times, when so many relationships were fixed by obligation and contract, the same sort of problem was evident. Eventually, in the eighteenth and nineteenth centuries, when the management of money was taken in hand, it looked for a while as if a common measure, the price system, could be found for all goods and all obligations. If this were so, we should all be caught up in a single network, an economic system where everything and everyone would have its or his price. In such a system, decision-making would be relatively straightforward and we should all be governed by the relative return on any proposed decision. Had this been possible, virtually the whole of public administration would in fact have been financial administration and all sorts of goods, rights, duties, and values would have been reduced to a single price-list. There are still some people, mainly economists, who hanker after this consummation.

It was towards the end of the last century that Oscar Wilde made the gibe about the cynic who knew the price of everything and the value of nothing. It is clear that there are many values on which a price cannot be put and this has greatly complicated the problems of financial management. In very many ways people are prepared to behave totally contrary to their economic and financial interests. Nonetheless, a great part of the original conception remains. One has only to look through the book of estimates for the public services to realise, for all the fragmented and confusing information it contains, the extraordinary range of activities and services that *can* be and are, reduced to the common terms of money. Adam Smith conceded that 'defence is more than opulence'; but at least we can now measure in money terms just how much defence costs. The same applies to education or health or charity to one's neighbour. They all have their price set down in that book. What is more, their relative values to any society from time to time are also set down there.

One of the oldest and most important features of government in modern times has been the handling of public finance. The balancing of income and expenditure, the prudent management of resources, careful accounting and the rooting out of dishonesty – these have contributed to the rise of many great powers, and their absence to their decline, century after century. For example, one of the reasons given for the collapse of the ancien régime in France in the eighteenth century was the irremediable weakness of the system of public finance. The task is to collect what can be collected without undue strain and with reasonable equity, to live within that income, and to spend it prudently and economically. It was in this spirit that Gladstone, a great Chancellor of the Exchequer, said that one of the tasks of the Treasury was 'the saving of candle ends'.

As kings ceased to be absolute, there grew up a separation between their private spending and the public finances. Gradually it became possible to prevent them bestowing sources of public revenue on their favourites and some control began to be exercised on the access of energetic persons to well-paid public sinecures. Castlereagh is reported to have said, in paying out large sums to establish the Union at the end of the eighteenth century, that the task of government was 'to buy out the fee-simple of Irish corruption'. Gradually, in the latter part of the nineteenth century in Britain and consequently in Ireland an elaborate system was established for ensuring that money voted by parliament was spent on the purposes for which it was voted and that those who spent it did so honestly and kept a careful account of their spending. Under the Exchequer and Audit Act, 1866 the general financial mechanism that we still operate was codified.

The financial year in this country now coincides with the calendar year. Each summer government departments prepare their proposals for spending, on current and capital account, for the year beginning the following January. These proposals are discussed in detail, and haggled over, with the Department of Finance during the autumn months. Eventually, when the aggregate of the proposals for current expenditure has been reduced to something like what is expected to be the yield of taxation in the ensuing year, and the aggregate of capital expenditure has similarly been reduced to what can feasibly be borrowed in that year, the proposed expenditures are published in detail in the month of January. The Minister for Finance then produces his budget in the Dáil showing how he proposes to raise the money on both capital and current accounts.

As current expenditure usually involves some changes in taxation, the precise proposals are incorporated in a Finance Bill which is enacted during the early months of the year. The detailed proposals for expenditure on current account are then discussed in detail in the Dáil, and eventually incorporated in an Appropriations Bill which is enacted, usually, during the latter part of the year. In the meantime, there is a standing statutory authorisation, within certain limits, to enable the various existing services to be maintained until consideration of the estimates has been completed.

At the end of the year the departments prepare their accounts as to how they have spent the money voted for them, under fairly detailed headings. These accounts are then audited by the Comptroller and Auditor General and his staff. These accounts, known as the appropriation accounts, with the comments of the Comptroller and Auditor General, are then published. A committee of the Dáil, the Public Accounts Committee, examines the accounts in detail in the light of the comments of the Comptroller and Auditor General, discusses the accounts with the accounting officer – usually the secretary – of each department and makes a report to the Dáil. From time to time, the Committee raises special points either with the department concerned, or the Department of Finance. The chairman of the committee is always an opposition deputy. This completes the cycle. It is described in detail in Finance: *Outline* (1976).

It can be seen, therefore, that there is a very elaborate system of parliamentary control in relation to public finance. However, it is very largely a formal system, concerned with regularity, and has very little to do with *financial* problems of present-day government (Clarke, 1971, pp. 10–13).

First of all, for reasons that will be explained later, the budget is substantially concerned with overall economic and social policy. Very long debates tend to occur on the budget but these tend to have little or no relevance to *financial* as distinct from general policy issues. Similarly, endless debates occur on many of the financial estimates for the departments but again, almost invariably, they tend to be about the details of day-to-day administration of the departments. The work of the Comptroller and Auditor-General is to ensure that the money has been spent, without formal wastefulness, on the headings that have been authorised by the Dáil. The comments he raises, which tend to be the raw material of the deliberations of the Public Accounts Committee, are nearly always about minutiae of procedure. The comments of the Committee are of the same order. The fact is, that over the century since this procedure was established, departments have become very careful about their *procedures* for spending and accounting for money so that very little is left over for useful comment by the Comptroller and Auditor-General and the Committee. There are, of course, major problems about the effective control of public expenditure in other than an accounting sense; but these are almost totally ignored by the elaborate, and elaborately out-of-date, system of parliamentary control of public expenditure. This out-of-dateness is substantially the result of its own success and its subsequent failure to recognise this fact. In a number of European countries, and in the United States, the audit system has been concerning itself with efficiency as well as regularity, but, so far, there has been little development along these lines in this country.

For a long time it was believed, even for a considerable period after the independence of this country, that the role of the state was to get out of the way of private enterprise, to keep public expenditure at the lowest possible level, so that private enterprise could take off spontaneously. If the state had to invest, and to borrow money for that purpose, it should do so only for projects that would directly repay the borrowing. Thus it was justifiable to borrow for the Shannon Scheme, on which the ESB was founded, because eventually this money would be repaid by electricity consumers. However, other problems raised their grisly heads. In the 1930s, for example, something had to be done about the housing stock of the country. As houses were scarce because people could not afford to pay an economic rent for them, it was necessary to subsidise them. Because the economic system did not provide the houses, it was necessary for public authorities to do so. This involved raising large sums on capital account that, by definition, were not self-liquidating. Thus was born the terrifying monster of the 1930s, Dead Weight Debt. This monster haunts the pages of the Banking Commission Majority Report of 1938. Here was a clear conflict between social (and political) imperatives and orthodox finance.

However already in 1936 Keynes's great book, *The General Theory of Employment, Interest and Money* had been published, in which he outlined a new role for the system of public finance as the general overseer of the economy, quick to intervene to restore equilibrium wherever it seemed to be disturbed. This was, of course, a by-product of the great depression that had set in from 1929. This provided a theoretical justification, particularly in times of slump, for an active investment policy by the state. Eventually in Ireland, in 1950, there began to be adopted the Swedish idea of a separate capital budget, as distinct from the current budget, concerned with the overall development of the economy. There followed a good deal of discussion in the 1950s as to the economic spinoff from social capital expenditure, especially in the three reports of the Capital Investment Advisory Committee of 1957–8. This culminated in Dr T. K. Whitaker's famous paper, *Economic Development*, which produced a scheme for an integrated investment programme in the interests of economic development. There followed the first programme for economic expansion of 1958. In this way a planning system was born in this country. This will be discussed in the next section of this Chapter.

One of Keynes's ideas was that where total demand fell below capacity it was the duty of public expenditure to fill the gap. He argued that public expenditure had a 'multiplier effect'–that is, a more than proportionate effect–in getting economic activity going. So, for example, expenditure on social needs need not necessarily be limited by existing resources–it could actually increase them. Accordingly, there was not necessarily a conflict between social policy and financial policy. The adoption of Keynesian ideas in the period 1950 to 1970 led to unprecedented growth in the western world and this was accompanied by unprecedented growth in public expenditures. (The subsequent high inflation, coupled with stagnation–known as 'stagflation'–has shown that there are certain limits to this beneficent cycle.) Keynes argued that restraint in booms was as necessary as action in slumps and he underlined the destabilising effects of the arbitrary and inequitable distribution of wealth and income; but ideas, in becoming popular, lose most of their sophistication, so these warnings went largely unheeded.

Indeed, already from the 1960s there was mounting anxiety about the increasing cost of the public services. One school held with the views of the Australian economist Colin Clark (1964) that once state expenditure exceeded 25 per cent of net national income there would be inflation. Now state expenditure in western countries is heading towards 50 per cent of gross domestic product–the 1974–6 average for *all* OECD countries was just over 40 per cent (OECD, 1978). At the same time, they have all been suffering from serious inflation. So there may be further empirical support for his views.

The growth of 'free', or nearly 'free', social services has meant that the financial constraints on consumers have been removed. They accordingly make insatiable demands for such services as health and education. There have developed in consequence, acute problems for the management of the public finances (NESC 20, 21 and 31). From the 1960s, therefore, there has been an increasing preoccupation with trying to ensure that, so far as public expenditure is concerned, there is what has come to be called 'value for money'.

Existing systems of public expenditure control have put a strong accent on historical headings of expenditure. It is always easier for a department to get an increase in its allocation for an existing service than to introduce a new one. Many existing services were introduced to meet specific problems that over the years have been, or ought to have been, solved; but expenditure on them continues. Similarly, schemes are introduced to tackle problems, which have had little success; nonetheless, expenditure continues. Existing patterns of expenditure become rigid and are supported by a variety of vested interests. For all these reasons, there is very little pressure to meet the cost of new services by winding up expenditure on the less successful ones (*Public Expenditure* (Plowden) 1961).

In consequence of all this there has arisen a good deal of interest in new techniques of financial control. One objective has been to try to build up a more analytical approach to the broad areas of public expenditure. If one stands back from the rather bewildering details of present-day systems of financial control, can one discern broad programmes, analyse how far various kinds of financial expenditures within those programmes are earning their keep, and how far financial expenditures in other programmes are conflicting with them? Secondly, is it possible to arrive at some way of calculating what is called 'cost-effectiveness'? That is to say, can one lay out one's expenditure even within single services that will give the most return for the expenditure of, say, the last million pounds? For example, in every country the health services are increasing their financial demands at an insatiable rate. Within the health services the hospital services are the great spenders. Is it possible to moderate the growth in the cost of hospitals by spending more money on health prevention, especially in moderating people's life styles so as to come to grips with such problems as atherosclerosis, cancer, and accidents, now the main causes of premature death?

The problem can be oversimplified by saying that under traditional methods of financial control, the hardheads were in the controlling department – the Department of Finance, the Treasury, the Bureau of the Budget – and the softhearts were in the spending departments. In recent years efforts have been made to synthesise the various techniques of financial analysis and control into orderly systems – programming, planning, budgeting (PPBS) (substantially borrowed from the United States) in Ireland (O'Mahony, 1971, 1972), and in a number of other countries; programme analysis and review (PAR) in Britain; rationality in budgetary allocation (RCB) in France; and so on. The idea was to have established within each spending department a unit of this kind which would consistently analyse existing patterns of expenditure and try to ensure that they were kept some way under control so that a fairly equal return could be obtained from each. Hitherto finance units in government departments and in local authorities, as well as non-commercial state-sponsored bodies, have been substantially concerned with the careful accounting of approved expenditures. It was hoped that these would be developed into ·fully-fledged finance units, capable of providing management throughout the organisation with up-to-date management accounts and with the appropriate skills for evaluating the financial effects of various kinds of investments. Progress on this front has, nearly everywhere, disappointed expectations. This has been partly because the techniques were not strong enough to bear the loads imposed on them. Nonetheless, there is general agreement that the analytical approaches they provide for considering public expenditure are extremely valuable. In Ireland these too, after a promising start, have largely fallen victims to the blight that affects so many initiatives for the development of our systems of public administration.

A good deal of this work has been overtaken by the inflation crisis that has afflicted western countries in recent years. The problems of the control of expenditure in such conditions have become almost insuperable (Wright, 1977). Because a great part of the work done by public bodies is done by people, and because pay has tended to rise at least as fast as inflation and often, initially, faster, a big part of the problems of public finance has related to public service pay and the attempt to keep it under control. In Britain, where the problems have been on a scale so much greater than in Ireland, a powerful weapon has been the imposition of 'cash limits', namely limits on spending that remain, in principle, unchanged throughout the year, irrespective of what happens to costs. Other weapons against inflation that also have been applied in Ireland are limits, often suggested by outside bodies – the European Commission, the International Monetary Fund, the OECD – on the amount of public sector borrowing, and on the supply of money in the economy. But even if the fever of inflation does manage to abate the other problems of the effective control of public expenditure – to ensure that value is received for all that is spent – will remain.

One of the main and continuing problems of public finance is, of course, taxation. How can enough taxes be levied to pay for all the services that people want? One of the features of modern society is that where direct payment for services such as education, health, transport, is removed or reduced, people demand more and more of these services; but a recent phenomenon is that they become increasingly reluctant to pay for the cost of them in taxation. If, to pay for increased social services, take-home pay is reduced, there is strong pressure to increase pay and, in times like the present, thus to fuel inflation, because overall demand then becomes greater than current resources. To make a perhaps unfair comparison, we moderate our demands on electricity supply, which is a public service, because we have to pay directly for what we use; but no such direct discipline is exercised on us in making demands on the health services. This is now a major problem of public finance.

Basically, taxes have to give secure and substantial yields, to be economical to collect, and to lie with reasonable equity on all classes of taxpayers. Moreover, they should be progressive – that is, better-off people should pay proportionately more tax than worse-off people – and not regressive, which is the contrary situation. Taxes fall, very broadly, into three classes – income, expenditure, and wealth.

In Ireland the main tax on income is, of course, income tax which is levied on salaries and wages under PAYE before these are paid. This is, overall, a progressive tax. Another tax levied on income is social security contributions. These are now beginning to be related to income, and are therefore mainly neutral; but in so far as they continue to be flat rate contributions they are heavily regressive, and therefore regarded as inequitable. Moreover, as the employer also pays a contribution for each employee, they are a tax on labour intensive, as opposed to capital intensive, employment.

The main expenditure tax is Value Added Tax (which can be mildly progressive in that high rates are charged on luxury goods), which is levied on the value added at each stage of the production process. Another expenditure tax is excise, levied mainly on alcohol, tobacco and oil.

Taxes levied on wealth have been estate duties – on the estates, beyond a certain value, of those who die; wealth tax, which was levied – and is in a number of countries – on the current value of a person's wealth beyond a certain limit; and property rates levied by local authorities. Estate duties, wealth tax, and rates on domestic dwellings have all recently been abolished in Ireland. The main capital taxations that now remain are the capital gains tax, levied on capital gains realised within a period of twenty-one years, and succession tax in place of estate duty.

Overall the taxation system exhibits many of the features of public administration generally – the piling of ad hoc solutions on top of one another, and the occasional standing back to try to rationalise the system, as happened in relation to income tax levied under PAYE. Nonetheless, the system is riddled with anomalies. Some of these come from the attempt to moderate the effects, especially, of progressive taxation. Sometimes this produces remarkable anomalies, as when a person paying the highest rate of tax can get reliefs amounting, at current rates, to almost £1,500 a year for a mortgage on a house, greater than the subsidy given to many a poor person. Similarly, he gets tax relief for keeping a child at university long after poor people have had, perforce, to lose their children's allowances. In addition, given the fact that subsidies for university education vastly exceed, per head, the subsidy for primary and secondary education, the better off one is the more one can extract really substantial benefits from the state. Similar anomalies arise in relation to tax relief for medical insurance.

All of this, and a great deal more, comes from the muddling of three separate activities in one – taxation, social policy, and the financing of major public services, such as education, health and transport and the failure to think through the effects. At the same time, there is the failure to link the system of payments under social security with the income tax system. One result of this is the famous 'poverty trap' where a person on social security who gets a job may find his increased income, in effect, taxed at 100 per cent. A good deal of thought has been given in other countries to linking the two systems by means of negative income tax or otherwise but no satisfactory solution seems to have emerged. Apart from this, there is the stage army effect of the 'circular transfer', where people pay high rates of marginal tax – which tend to have a strong disincentive effect – and then receive, perhaps disguised as in the university case, very substantial benefits. There is a strong case for simplifying the system so as to reduce this give-and-take effect (NESC 37).

Apart from these technical questions, financial administration has very strong policy orientations. One of the major ones is *monetary* policy which is carried on between the Department of Finance, the Central Bank, and, through their command of the financial situation, the other financial institutions of the country. The first task is to try to keep the supply of money neither greater than current needs, nor less. Effective management requires frequent and flexible adjustment to circumstances that sometimes change with startling speed. There is the problem of the relationship of the currency with other currencies – in the Irish case, this hitherto has been simple enough in that we have been so closely linked with the £ sterling; but with our membership of the European Monetary System, this may not always be so. Then there are the questions of the management of the country's external reserves, and the effects on them of changes in the balance of payments.

Usually, all these involve a great deal of international consultation and the governors of the European Central Banks tend to meet together at least once a month. On a world scale, the ministers for finance and the governors are heavily concerned with the operations of the World Bank and of the International Monetary Fund.

Since the time of Keynes overall financial management has had a profound effect on the economic life of the community. Nowadays, only a part of the national budget is concerned with normal financial house-keeping. Its main task is to try to achieve the maximum rate of economic growth that is possible within certain major constraints. These are, first of all, to try to achieve a reasonable balance between public income and expenditure. Secondly, to achieve a balance between the amount of investment in the community as a whole, and the amount of savings available both from inside and outside the country. Thirdly, to ensure that the balance of payments between the country and all other countries, both on capital and current account, is in reasonable equilibrium. Fourthly, to ensure that the amount of effective demand within the country closely matches the amount of resources that can be made readily available. Given the inherent uncertainties in all of this, especially in times of economic upheaval, the task is extraordinarily difficult.

In order to try to bring more stability into this situation most countries now are devoting a good deal of attention to the problems of increasing the efficiency of forecasting what is likely to be occurring in the short and the middle terms. Similarly, by means of planning, they endeavour to influence the longer term forces.

One of the crucial problems here has been to try to relate closely the annual budgeting system to the four to five year planning system. It is recognised that the economic and social decisions taken each year in the budget are, or ought to be, the motive force for giving realistic effect to what is in the plans. On the whole, techniques for doing this have not been satisfactorily worked out.

The budget, as we have seen, is closely tied to an annual cycle, but most of the expenditure is already committed on a continuing basis for salaries, for interest charges, subsidies, etc. so that the room for discretion from year to year in shifting the direction of expenditure is marginal in the extreme. Significant financial changes can be brought about only over a period of years. The implication of an *annual* budget is grossly misleading. So far as capital works are concerned the actual period of construction seldom falls within a single year and may extend over several years. Moreover, certain works involve long forward commitments to providing capital sums some years ahead.

A simple distinction, therefore, between the finance function that is concerned with the short-term and the planning function that is concerned with the medium and long-term, cannot be made. There are also, as well as annual financial cycles, medium-term *financial* cycles and long-term *financial* cycles. But the obsolescent clinging to the annual budgetary cycle has let this point go by default.

It was because of such linkings and parallels as these that Devlin recommended (PSORG 20.3.2) that overall, the finance function and the planning function both be maintained within the same Department of Finance. Now that the decision has been taken the other way, there may be clearer thinking about the development of the finance function not only in the Department of Finance but in all the other spending bodies, departments and agencies as well. It may also help to sharpen minds as to the real distinctions, as well as the similarities, between the two functions.

A further problem for financial management has been the increasing importance, in all countries, of social policies. Very simply, the economic system, usually with a good deal of stimulus from the state, is reasonably good at increasing the resources available within the country. But, left to itself, it does not distribute fairly those increased resources. It is necessary to have some state intervention to ensure that the weak members of the community, for example, share in the increased affluence. Moreover, part of the well-being of the community as a whole involves the provision of better public services. Better educational and health services, for example, are essential to overall well-being and, indeed, to further economic advance. Apart from the social problems we have already referred to, what sort of overall principles ought to guide the Minister for Finance in deciding each year how much of the resources of the country should be given to social needs? Given that it is only possible to distribute what has been produced—though there are complexities here that we shall consider later in this Chapter—is the need for growth so pressing that there should be some, relative, decline in social expenditure? Or should the rise in social expenditure equal the economic growth rate? Or, given that there are still substantial areas of social backwardness, should the growth in social expenditure exceed the growth rate of the community as a whole? These are major problems of overall policy that are, perhaps, best considered in the context of an overall planning system. But how far is it possible, in practice, given the realities of political life, to divorce them from the feverish discipline of the annual budget?

Overall, therefore, it is clear that the task of financial management is of great importance. For that reason the Minister of Finance is usually one of the most senior ministers in the government and his department plays a senior co-ordinating role. However, to an increasing extent in a number of countries, as well as in Ireland, this role is now being shared with a Department of Economic Affairs—in our case, the new Department of Economic Planning and Development—as part of an overall planning system. In addition, it becomes increasingly important for the task of financial management and control to be shared with the 'line' or operating departments. For example, the Departments of Education, of Health, of Social Welfare, are each, now, spending in real terms more money than the total budget of the state fifty years ago. The health boards, the local authorities, the state-sponsored bodies collectively and sometimes individually spend vast sums of money. There is urgent need for the development within all of them of a strong, sophisticated finance function.

3. National Planning

The general reason for planning is to be able to take the comprehensive and the long look. What is happening at present? Given the various forces that one can identify now, what is likely to be happening over a period of years? Given the long gestation period of certain schemes, what ought one to be doing now, or next year, to ensure that there will be a well-timed response to major occurrences in the future? The two special qualities required for planning are overview and foresight.

This is all very well until one gets into the hurly-burly of day-to-day and week-to-week activities and until one has some experience of the sheer unpredictability of the political, the administrative, and the economic world. For that reason, public servants have long accepted such admonitions as 'let us not cross that bridge until we come to it'. Nonetheless, not everything in the future is unpredictable. For example, if there has been a substantial rise, or fall, in the birth rate in the past two or three years, it is quite predictable that in a few years' time there will be a substantial rise, or fall, in the number of children beginning at school. This has all sorts of implications for school building, training of teachers, etc. Other early warning signs also exist in education (Tussing, 1978).

Moreover, if one looks around at the great volume of present-day state activities, nearly all of which have grown up in an ad hoc, unplanned way, it is inevitable that there will be contradictions as between them, that one will be undoing, or impeding, in whole or in part, with the left hand what another is doing with the right.[1] So, there is scope for exercising higher degrees of rationality both in place and in time.

The purpose of planning, therefore, is both to raise the overall effectiveness of current activities and to reduce the opportunities for being surprised by events (and so having to engage in policy-making by crisis). Major demographic changes—where people decide to live, the age they choose to marry at, the number and spacing of their children, the periods they will live after they cease work—all these have profound effects on the business of government. So timely warning of major demographic changes, and properly phased reactions to them, are essential to good administration. In the same way, it is prudent to look, for example, at the likely growth in the cost of public services, and to see whether the continuance of existing trends will add up to an aggregate demand on the community greater than it is likely to be willing to meet (e.g. NESC 20, 21 and 31). Early attempts to control such growth are likely to be less painful all round than if the situation is allowed to drift.

The task of planning is, primarily, one of definition. First of all, to try to define the objectives of the society and of government within those objectives, at least over a period of some years ahead. Secondly, as has been indicated, it is to forecast what is likely to happen if existing trends continue as at present. Thirdly, it is to try to identify what are the constraints on action—whether shortage of resources, skills, freedom of manoeuvre—or whether there are physical obstacles that either cannot be removed or that can be removed only over a considerable period of time. Fourthly, there is the question of concertation—to ensure that what is done in space and in time is coherent and that, so far as possible, the various operations of government at least do not impede, and hopefully contribute to, the successful achievement of the objectives decided upon. Fifthly, it is necessary to have policies to achieve those objectives, policies that settle *what* is to be done, *how* it is to be done, *when* it is to be done, and *by whom* it is to be done. These policies have to be broken down into consistent *programmes* and these programmes have to achieve certain *targets* within certain specified periods of *time*. Finally, into the system must be built methods of review at regular intervals to test how far assumptions have worked out in practice, how far policies are achieving what is expected of them, and what adjustments have to be made in consequence of shortfalls. These shortfalls are then subject to intensive analyses to find out

---

[1]'The wiser a man is the less he is prone to unrelated decisions, and the more comprehensive and connected are his views. Each particular decision is conceived in relation to all other decisions, to the end that their integration may be the best possible.' Leibniz: *Nouveaux Essais sur l'Entendement*, quoted by de Jouvenel (1957) p. 208.

what improvements need to be made. Then the whole process begins again.

Many years ago the distinction was drawn between two kinds of planning – crustacean planning and vertebrate planning (Franks, 1947, p. 40). A crustacean is an animal with a hard impervious shell containing a soft gooey mass. A vertebrate animal has a firm backbone but on the outside has a soft, flexible, sensitive skin. There is an old Latin tag about being suaviter in modo, fortiter in re, which means flexible in the means but firm on principle. It is a mark of bad administration to have crustacean planning, or to get those Latin adverbs mixed up, so that one is soft on principle but firm on details. It is a mark of good administration to have vertebrate planning, firm principles and flexible means of operation.

A further feature of planning is the 'planning period'. Some operations take a long time. For example, if one is in the forestry business the cycle is at best forty to fifty years. Hitherto in this country, it has taken thirty years to achieve a large general hospital. A major sewer development may last twenty years before an additional sewer may be needed. An electricity generating station takes about eight years to bring into being. And so on. Planning, therefore, has a number of different 'natural' periods, ranging from the few months that elapse between sowing and reaping a grain crop, to a generation or more. The degree of precision of a plan will, therefore, vary with the time-span involved. What must be done in the near future will be seen with great clarity. What will be the shape of things twenty or thirty years hence will emerge only in very broad outline indeed. This latter is called 'horizon planning'. In between, there are various other planning periods, with different degrees of precision. If, for example, one were to think of a developing country without a medical school, then, from the first day the first medical students begin their studies, it will be seven years at least before there are qualified doctors available. But before that there must be qualified teachers, and these must be attracted from other countries in the short term and suitable buildings, etc. must be provided. Finally, the native students must be given opportunities for post-graduate studies so that they themselves may take on the task of teaching in the medical school. If one adds these planning periods together one finds that the whole process will take some fifteen to twenty years. The task of planning is to think through the various steps that must be taken, to bring about amongst them as many overlaps as possible and, thus, to reduce to a minimum the length of the total cycle. But there is a certain minimum period that cannot be reduced. It is the task of planning to ensure that the actual operations come as close to this minimum period as possible.

The chart on page 127, given by Andren (1976, p. 348) to illustrate defence planning for weapons systems, shows the general process. In addition, it brings in the further factor of obsolescence which is of crucial importance for defence planning, and is inherent in all planning.

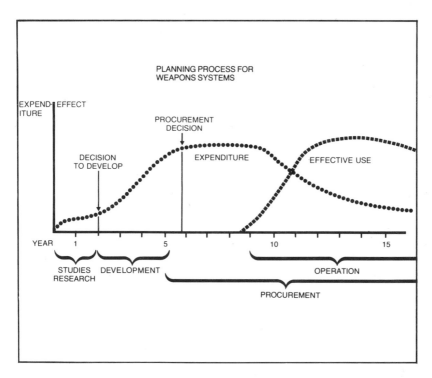

This sounds very complicated. It is. One reason for the lack of success of so many plans is failure to recognise this complicatedness and to cope with it.

Modern planning has diverse origins. Perhaps the first origin is as a by product of physical, environmental, or, as we shall call it, infrastructural planning. This arose from the attempts of engineers and architects to concert their efforts in such a way that various infrastructural services – water supply, sewers, roads, houses, domestic services, communications – would be related together in some form of time scale, so that various services would be provided at or about the appropriate time. This is much the same process as when various groups of tradesmen are programmed to make their appropriate contributions in housebuilding. This sort of thinking became a feature of military activity in the First World War.

These two traditions were married in the author of the world's first national plan, an army surveyor and engineer, Brigadier Sir Gordon Guggisberg, governor of the Gold Coast (now Ghana) from 1919 to 1927. He presented his *ten year development programme* in 1919. The purpose of this was to speed the economic development of Ghana by establishing a harbour, a railway system, 'feeder' roads to the railheads, and the beginnings of a system of trunk roads throughout the colony. This had a dramatic effect on the production and transport costs of cocoa, the main cash crop of the colony. Other expenditure was on hydroelectric work, drainage, water supplies and posts and telegraphs. Infrastructural development planning of this kind had the effect of accelerating economic development. Economic development was to provide the means to a programme of educational development—secondary schools, trade schools, specialist schools, and an embryo university—and these in turn were to provide the trained manpower and womanpower for economic development. The point is that the productive and dynamic interrelationships of planned development for infrastructural services, economic development, and cultural development were, from the outset, grasped by this planner (Wraith, 1967).

However, the fruits of this innovation were not generally gathered, and the innovation itself became overwhelmed by the dramatic impact of socialist planning in the Soviet Union. Originally, socialist thinking had no place for the market as a system for allocating resources. It was necessary, therefore, for the state to take on this responsibility and, given the enormous problems of modernising the Soviet Union, organising the forced march towards the objectives of military strength and consumer plenty. This origin, and the gross abuses associated with it, closed the minds of many people in democratic countries to understanding the usefulness of planning as a political and administrative instrument. This understanding did not begin to occur until after the end of World War II.

Already in Sweden it had been appreciated during the 1930s that capital investment by government could play a significant role in economic and in other kinds of development, and the Swedes began to do this in a planned way. In France from 1945 the Monnet plan—named after the first French planner and the founder of the European Movement—concentrated on capital investment in six basic sectors—coal, electricity, cement, steel, agricultural machinery and transport (Massé, 1962; Monnet, 1978, Chs 9–10). This was the foundation of French planning which was to become a significant influence on Irish planning.

By now, planning in the western world had become an enthusiasm of the economists. They substantially appropriated it, and had very considerable success in increasing rates of economic growth. A severe price was paid for this success, because it seemed to so many that planning for economic development could be dealt with in isolation from social and political development, as in the dramatic example of success followed by failure in post-independence Pakistan, or in the more recent example of Iran.[1]

[1]Thus the former American Secretary of State, H. Kissinger, interviewed by *The Economist*, 10 February 1979: 'The fashionable "progressive" view for decades has been that economic development would more or less automatically produce political stability, that a rising standard of living would reduce discontent. The enlightened view was that there was a sort of automatic stabilising factor in economic development. That has turned out to be clearly wrong. It would probably have been wiser for the Shah to concentrate explicitly on a political evolution to be more commensurate with Iran's economic evolution'.

In the years after World War II the statistical techniques of measuring national income became widespread and, so far as the western world was concerned, the OECD disseminated the information on growth rates in each of its member countries. In this way each country could measure how it was doing in the growth league. So far as Ireland was concerned it became possible to measure our performance as compared with other countries, and by the later 1950s it was clear that we were lagging far behind (Fanning, 1978, Ch. 11). This, coupled with a severe economic and psychological slump at that time, led to the adoption, from 1959, of a system of planning (or 'programming', as it was called), the first Programme for Economic Expansion. This programme, on the Swedish and early French models, was basically a system for ensuring that capital investment by the state was directed towards economic growth in a coherent and consistent manner. This was based on the study, *Economic Development*, by the newly-appointed secretary of the Department of Finance, Dr T. K. Whitaker.

As the planning system developed in this country during the 1960s the French influence was stronger and some of the French jargon of planning was adopted, especially in the second programme. On the model of grammar, two 'moods' of planning could be identified, the imperative mood, in the socialist countries, where what was laid down in the plan became a duty on those affected, and the indicative mood, as in France, where the planners, following their analyses of the best way for the market to develop, would 'indicate' what would be profitable lines of action for private enterprise. In this country, indicative planning seemed to be the answer to relating the thoughts of the planners to the actions in a market place; more recent thinking has been questioning the validity of this analysis (Katsiouni, 1978). However, what was largely overlooked was the point, referred to in the Devlin Report 1969 (PSORG, 9.1.4), that in a mixed society the two kinds of planning should march hand-in-hand. If a large proportion of the activity in the society was carried out by the state itself, then, *for public bodies*, imperative planning was the appropriate discipline. This is because indicative planning cannot affect such bodies because they are substantially independent of market incentives and disciplines and so can afford for long periods to ignore them (Bristow, 1964–5). So far as the private sector is concerned, the indication of where profit may be made should be a sufficient inducement to fit in with the broad outlines of the plan. In the event, this distinction between the disciplines of the public and the private sectors was not made and the firm commitment of public bodies to devise and implement policies that would represent their expected contribution to the plan was not achieved (NIEC 24).

A second weakness was the failure to grasp – as Guggisberg had grasped – the interrelationships between the various aspects of public activity.

Although the third programme (1969) was called a programme for economic and *social* development, its social (and infrastructural) sides were not so much plans as assorted shopping lists from the appropriate departments. This, in turn, came from the big gap between the sophistication of the thinking by economists, and the relatively underdeveloped planning skills in the social and infrastructural areas.

A third weakness was the virtual ignoring of the need to create a sufficient administrative structure to operate the planning process. Over the years a full division of the Department of Finance had been built up to devise a planning system from the centre and much econometric work and model building was done there, in the newly established Economic Research Institute (it later broadened its remit to cover social research), and in the Central Bank. In addition a monitoring representative council, the National Industrial Economic Council (NIEC)–later the National Economic and Social Council (NESC)–was established. But at the grass-roots–especially in the operating Departments–virtually nothing was done to develop the necessary administrative skills. The third programme, when it was published in 1969, just ten years after planning began, announced (pp. 231–2) that the departments would be equipped with development (or planning) units. This statement has many times since been repeated but very little has yet been done. The formal reason for the delay has been the difficulty of deciding about where the planning function begins and the finance function leaves off. So, generally speaking, over the past decade nothing has been done about either!

In 1963 a powerful Local Government (Planning and Development) Act was passed, concerned to involve local authorities in the environmental part of infrastructural and regional planning and to exercise discipline over private environmental developers; but this was never effectively integrated into infrastructural planning as a whole, much less into the overall planning system. Some of the state-sponsored bodies, notably the ESB (Roche, 1978) and Aer Lingus, developed sophisticated project, operational and corporate planning systems, but these were not matched in the supervising departments.

We have, in part, individual pieces of a public sector planning process, but these pieces have not been built into a *system* that encompasses not only the public sector relationships across the board, horizontally as it were–political, economic, social or other–but also co-ordinates and integrates the various vertical relationships, so that the numerous planning sub-systems that exist would fit together into a smoothly operating set of structures.

For example, we have in the ESB, apart from the actual planning of individual *projects* themselves, a good *operational* planning sub-system concerned with the planning of future generating stations, transmission systems and so on. These are integrated into a sophisticated *corporate* planning sub-system concerned with the overall role of the ESB in supply-ing the energy needs of the country. The ESB is only one body concerned with energy, but at this level we lack a planning system concerned with co-ordinating the plans of all such bodies together into a *functional* plan for energy. Within the Department of Industry, Commerce and Energy we lack a planning sub-system to co-ordinate the problems of energy into a whole *sectoral* plan for industrial development. We have no specific means of integrating the sectoral industrial plan into a *facet* plan for economic development. Only at the top do we now have a means for integrated *national* planning.

For example, in CIE there is planning for moving more freight and for clarifying the role of CIE in transport generally. But we are only now beginning to achieve a means of co-ordinating functional planning for transport into the sectoral planning of communications. We are still far from integrating the sectoral plans into facet infrastructural planning, and from working out the place of that in national planning.

There is another dimension to all of this. Operational planning of transmission lines and public transport systems relates to people and emerges as individual projects in places where people live and move. Individual projects are particularly the concern of *local* planning bodies – county councils or other – which, as it happens, have little direct relation-ship to such important locational decisions. Local plans themselves contribute to, or may conflict with, *regional* plans; but there are inadequate means for tackling this problem. Regional plans should find their way into *national* plans but, again, we lack any clear cut means of doing this.

Finally, while much thought went into what ought to be in the plans much less went into the task of ensuring that what was in the plans was actually carried out, that there was effective planning management. This is a common failing that can be blamed for much of the disappointment that planning nearly everywhere has evoked.[1] In the socialist countries one device for tackling this problem is the *contract*. This has also become a feature of French planning. By this means state bodies, local authorities and others contract to carry out certain provisions of the plan within appropriate periods. In principle, they are free not to enter into the contract, but, once having done so, they are bound by its terms. In this way the indicative mood is freely transformed into the imperative. There are significant problems in relation to such contracts (e.g. their legal status) but they do offer a means by which those on whom the carrying out of the plan's provisions depend can be mobilised for the task.

In the circumstances, therefore, the Irish experience of national planning

---

[1]"There is little point in planning when there are no policies to ensure that the plan will be implemented. Planning in future should be concerned as much with how things should be done as with what should be done'. – K. A. Kennedy in *Management*, May 1974, p. 60.

has been largely confined to the economic area, and the results have been mixed. The first programme ran from 1959 to 1963 and aimed at a growth rate of 2 per cent a year, a substantial rise on the then existing situation. In fact, double that rate of growth was achieved. The second programme, adopted in 1964, was intended to run until 1970, but was abandoned in 1968. The formal reason for this was that the programme had been built on the assumption that Ireland would have been a member of the European Economic Community before 1970, and this was clearly not going to be achieved. However, this was only one reason for the failure of the programme. The third programme, for economic and social development, was intended to cover the four years 1969–72 but it, too, was abandoned before the final date. The occasion for this abandonment was the disturbance to the economy caused by the disorder in Northern Ireland.

Whatever the full reasons for the non-completion of the second and third programmes – and I think there were a complex of reasons – many of the objectives of Irish economic policy were achieved. Overall the 1960s represented a period of unprecedented growth in the Irish economy (Kennedy and Dowling, 1975). The great social evil of emigration gradually died away and was replaced for a time in the 1970s by net immigration. Very severe problems arose as to the distribution of the increased affluence (McCarthy, 1973).

The local depression brought on by the troubles in Northern Ireland, added to the deepening depression in western Europe and exacerbated by the steep rise in the price of energy, led to a number of problems in the 1970s – the shake-out of older industry, unemployment and, of course, severe inflation. This caused acute problems of public finance and, notwithstanding a number of promises from the government, it did not become possible to produce a plan during this period.

The first programme arose from the preoccupations in the Department of Finance with the state's capital programme. However, as the years went by this close connection between the planning system and the budgetary system became obscured. This was notwithstanding the fact that the planning system and the budgetary system were working side by side within a single department, the Department of Finance. By the time the third programme had been abandoned it had become quite clear that the annual budget was the basic engine for giving effect to the state's side of the planning system. However, as we have seen, the extreme severity of both the depression and the inflation required that all hands had to be mobilised to try to get the system of public finance once more under control.

A number of people, including the author of the planning system himself, Dr T. K. Whitaker (1977), argued that it was precisely in times of economic danger that one should clarify one's objectives and try to achieve consensus on a system of priorities, such as would be features of a good plan. When the Fianna Fáil government returned to office in 1977 they were convinced of the importance of this point and set about re-establishing the planning machinery. Notwithstanding what had been learned, however, through bitter experience as to the crucial linkage between the planning system and the budgetary system, planning was taken away from the Department of Finance and given to a new department, that of Economic Planning and Development. The argument was that planning was so important that it required the full concentration of a minister and a department and to be protected from the danger of being subordinated to purely financial considerations. The remit of the new department covers economic, social and regional planning in the medium and long term. The Department of Finance concentrates on short-term planning, that is over the budgetary cycle of about eighteen months.

One of the remarkable features of the planning system that operated for virtually fourteen years was that it almost totally bypassed the legislature. This is in striking contrast to the tedious mumbo-jumbo that goes on in the Dáil in relation to the annual debate on the budget.

The public, and representative, input into the planning system came from a nominated body, representing what have come to be called the 'social partners'. The first of these bodies was the National Industrial Economic Council (NIEC) on which were representatives of trade unions, industrialists, employers, government departments, as well as a number of economists. NIEC was under the chairmanship of Dr Whitaker, and published a number of reports about the state of the economy and played a significant part in informing public opinion about economic problems. In 1972 it was decided to reconstitute it by adding to its members representatives of agriculture. As if to underline the difference between vocational representation and representation through the political system, deadlock was reached because one of the trade union representatives proposed was a member of the Seanad (which is supposed to be a substantially vocational body!), and the Minister for Finance was not prepared to have any member of the Houses of the Oireachtas on the Council. However, when the government changed in 1973 and the new Council was constituted, the trade union representatives included a senator and the government representatives included, amongst the independent members, not only economists but also persons experienced in social questions. The Government's direct nominees now include two senators.

The new Council, the National Economic and Social Council (NESC), was under the chairmanship of Professor W.J.L. Ryan up to March 1978. Professor Ryan had played a big part in drawing up the second programme and in the work of NIEC. NESC is now under the chairmanship of the secretary of the new Department of Economic Planning and Development, Dr Noel Whelan. NESC has three sub-committees – for economic policy, for social policy, and for regional policy. In its first four years of existence it published some thirty-five reports, twenty mainly about economic policy, ten mainly about social policy and four about regional policy, as well as a general one surveying its work and methods of operation. On the whole, it has made a most distinguished contribution to public awareness of economic, social, and, to a much lesser extent, regional problems.

Perhaps the most remarkable of these contributions has been the grasping of the crucial importance to a planning system of demography, namely the likely size, age distribution, and geographical distribution of the population for some ten or fifteen years ahead. Very great demographic changes are occurring in the society and it is essential that planning at all levels should be fully informed of these changes.

We have seen that, by a process of trial and error, some of the technical nature of a planning system has been identified. There was, first, the close connection between it and the state capital programme. There was the problem of distinguishing the correct areas for indicative and imperative planning. There was the problem of equipping the various state agencies, especially the government departments, to make an effective input into the planning process. There was the importance of using the annual budget as the basic engine for operating the plan. There was the problem of consultation with, and commitment to agreed courses by, the social partners. There was the crucial importance of insuring that there was overall political commitment to what was contained in the plan, and effective administrative means and policies to implement what was in the plan. There has been the need to build up technical, econometric models of the economy so as to have reasonably reliable means of forecasting the likely behaviour of the economy under different conditions. There has been the need to keep the plan for a relatively short period – Dr Whitaker (1977) has suggested the term of office of a government between elections. There has been the slowly rising realisation that, instead of having separate plans for fixed periods, there ought to be adopted the system of 'rolling plans'. If, for example, four years is regarded as an appropriate duration for the next plan, then, after one year another year is added at the end, so that there is always in being a four year plan, subject to adjustment each year.

Perhaps the most important lesson, which is still possibly not fully accepted in practice, is that it is inherent in a planning system to look at the whole society and not simply at sectors of it. It is not just enough to plan for the growth of resources. The very existence of increased resources raises problems as to how these resources can best be distributed, how much ploughed back into investment, public and private, how much made available as reward for enterprise and labour, how much made available for various forms of social and cultural development. There is, of course, room for fierce debate as between the various claims under each of these headings, but the great political task is to try to achieve a consensus on a prudent and fair distribution as between the competing claims.

The real task in human affairs, as Baron von Hugel pointed out early in this century in relation to theological debate. is 'not aut......aut...... but et......et'. That is to say the situation is seldom an *either–or* one, but a *both–and* one, and this insight is crucial to the whole notion of growth and development. For example, increased public investment in roads and communications may be essential to increased economic activity. If it does not take place, that activity will be impeded. Again, economic growth depends on increasing the number of educated and skilled people within the society. If sufficient money does not go into education and training, economic activity will be impeded. Again, good social services can only be afforded if there is sufficient economic growth. If there is rapid economic growth and the social services do not get a reasonable share of the increased resources, there will be discontent and, conceivably, the consensus on which the whole operation depends may break down, and the corresponding discontent may have serious political and economic consequences. And so it goes on. The task of planning is, somehow, to strike such a balance between all these considerations that each makes its optimum contribution to overall development and that the level of public satisfaction is as high as can, from time to time, be achieved so that no group is left with a sense of real grievance.

This poses a daunting challenge to the clear-headedness, the compassion and the sophistication of the system of public administration as a whole.

4. Social Planning

It is a commonplace of present-day discussion that the economy of any particular country is seen to grow, or is expected to grow, at a certain percentage rate each year—2½ per cent, 3 per cent, 5 per cent or whatever. We talk in these terms because of two revolutions. One is the revolution in thinking implied in the word 'development'. We expect our societies to be developing, that is, to be in a situation where the amount of resources available each year grows at some recognisable rate. The second revolution is that we now have means for measuring this growth in gross national product (GNP). One may have some doubts about the precision of this measuring, but it is undoubted that we have some means of knowing, with reasonable accuracy, what is the change from year to year in the resources of any given community.

But 'development' as we shall be seeing later, means something much more than the simple accumulation of additional resources. How are these resources being distributed within the community? The economic system is effective in increasing the resources, and in distributing them to those who can be classed as 'producers'. But there are many people in the community—the young, the old, the handicapped—who are not 'producers' in this sense, or else whose current production is relatively small. Unless there is some system within the society for distributing the increased resources fairly as between the 'producers' and the 'non-producers' there will be social inequity and, sooner or later, political instability. Three NESC reports (40, 41, 42) show the startling gap that has opened, with affluence, between economically strong and economically weak rural dwellers. Because there is no automatic mechanism for tackling this problem, one of the major functions of the state is to engage in such redistributive activity. For example, in 1978 expenditure classified as 'social' on capital and current accounts was just half the state's budgeted expenditure (*National Development*, 1978, Tables 2.1 and 2.2). This is the main part of what we call social policy, and one of the most important instruments for effective social policy is social planning.

The second weakness, so far as social policy is concerned, is that there is no generally acceptable criterion – such as growth in GNP is for economic policy – which will say how effective, or otherwise, social policy is in tackling its problems. For that reason those who are concerned about social policy have been trying to develop what are called 'social indicators' which attempt to give some pointers as to whether the quality of life in one society is high or low as compared with another – for example, expectation of life, housing space, schooling – and, as compared with one period and another, is rising or falling. On the basis of such comparative information it should be possible to produce, periodically, a 'social report' which would provide information about the development of social wellbeing in much the same way as the annual figures for GNP indicate economic wellbeing. However, this kind of study is still at a very early stage, and does not, so far, produce much in the way of firm guidance for social policy and social planning.

The National Economic and Social Council in report no. 25 have made a beginning here; their report draws together statistics and policy developments in a number of selected fields, divided into eight sections. These are *population* trends, national and regional; structure of *employment*; trends in *incomes*; trends in *health*; in *education*; in *housing*; in *social welfare* services; and changes in *crime* rates. The periods covered are mainly the previous fifteen years or so. The document does not attempt to evaluate the efficiency and the effectiveness of the relevant services. Nonetheless, it does give some idea of the range of the problems of social policy and of the sort of methodology that is necessary for judging how well social policy does its job.

While the analysis of social issues has made remarkable progress under NESC, this advance had not been matched at the administrative level. The high point was reached with the third programme which at least discussed social issues with some degree of sophistication. Nonetheless, although it was called Programme for Economic and Social Development in fact it worked out no system of social *planning*. It devoted less than 10 per cent of its space to social questions and little to evaluate, interrelate or put in priority the projects prepared by the various social departments.

The Green Paper, *Economic and Social Development 1976–1980*, discusses problems of economic policy in some detail, but is extremely cursory in relation to social policy. The same can be said about two recent white papers, *National Development 1977–1980* and *Programme for National Development 1978–1981*. The state of social policy and planning as it appears from these documents is not well developed. As we have seen, it is precisely the overall look, both in space and in time, that is the special feature of planning. Because of the importance of social planning to the whole administrative system, on the one hand, and its present state of intellectual neglect, on the other, it is worth spelling out some of the most obvious of the issues that arise.

The light that beckons through the darkness and confusion of social policy is the value of equality. In social policy one is concerned with the redistribution of the resources of the community to reduce, and if possible remove, hardship and suffering and to give those who are less privileged a better opportunity for achieving a contented life. One can approach this problem from several standpoints – for example, the authors of the Poor Law in the last century believed that the least that could possibly be done for the poor was the best for everyone in the long run. More recently, social policy was more empirical, and was concerned to identify gaps in the social structure through which unfortunate people could fall, and to attempt to close those gaps, or to provide some cushions to soften the fall. In more recent times there has been the growth in the so-called 'free' social services or in heavily subsidised ones – education is the classic case – which *may* have been intended to help the poor, but in practice are chiefly of benefit to those already reasonably well off (see NESC 12 and 16; Kennedy, 1975). Where – as in the housing system – we have a combination of these two approaches, ad hoc solutions combined with heavy subsidies and other interventions, we end up with the sort of overall situation described by two recent writers: 'Unfairness appears to be endemic and to have increased rather than diminished with the flow of public money into the system'. They go on to speak of removing from the housing system 'some of its more glaring anomalies, inconsistencies and abuses' (Baker and O'Brien, 1979, pp. 251–2, 255).

The great discipline of planning for social development means that one must get one's value system in this area clear and specific. Overall, it is hard to see what ought to be the final or overriding value, other than the attempt to enable society to achieve a higher degree of equality, by the removal of the causes of gross inequality within it. In consequence, one can aim at progress to a closer and more real community. The immediate objectives, accordingly, are to try to bring about a caring society and, in consequence of this, a more cohesive one.

If we approach the problems of social planning with these objectives and values in mind, we get some idea of the opportunities and the constraints that are inherent in social planning. The degree of concertation inherent in planning has two advantages. First of all, it enables an overall view to be taken about priorities – where are the needs greatest? Secondly, it enables a view to be taken of what is going on at present, where there is over-lapping, or the undoing by one hand of what is done by the other, or simple waste. Given that resources are always too scarce, this kind of concertation means that the savings that come from a tighter grip of social policy as a whole can be directed to the places where needs are greatest.

There are seven main arguments that support the case for an effective system of social planning.[1]

The first of these is the management argument. From a managerial point of view, the very size, scale and dynamism of the social services and their increasing share of public expenditure make planning in this area impera-tive. To achieve efficiency in the delivery of the services and to ensure that the resources allocated to them are well spent it is necessary to examine the rationale underlying existing services and to evaluate continually their success in realising their particular objectives, and their contribution towards the achievement of overall objectives – as is done in e.g. NESC 37 and 38.

The second argument is that of coherence. Social planning is necessary in order to direct the various state interventions in the most effective and coherent way, so that what is done is directed to mutually consistent social objectives, that adequate resources are committed to achieving those objectives, and that what is done in consequence is well done.

The third argument is that, as there will always be a scarcity of resources in relation to needs and wants, it is essential that there be overall objectives and clear-cut *policies* for whatever can be spent in the social area.

The fourth argument is that of linkages. Economic and social develop-ment are not distinct entities. They inter-penetrate as part of planning for national development as a whole. If this linkage is recognised and acted upon each will contribute to the other; if it is neglected, both will suffer. Some examples may help to clarify this. Decisions in relation to economic development involve deciding on objectives and priorities that, necessarily, also have social and political facets. Social expenditure is a major part of public expenditure, the levels and distribution of which have a significant effect on economic activity. Social expenditure, properly planned, can be a net contributor to the process of economic development; unplanned it can hinder it – for example the provision, or lack of provision, of houses, schools and amenities in an industrialising area. Education and training

[1] What follows relies heavily on Council of Social Welfare (1976).

policies have an important role in easing skill bottlenecks, so alleviating unemployment and raising productivity. Where economic development requires changes in work methods and flexibility of employment, they can be introduced with less resistance if there are appropriate social services to meet the special needs of those most likely to be affected by such changes. Measures to meet the particular social problems of elderly and solitary persons living in rural areas can possibly be devised so that at the same time they make a substantial contribution to agricultural restructuring, and thus to agricultural production (NESC 41, Ch. 5).

There is another form of linkage. While economic development provides the resources for social development, it also provides problems for social policy, for example, the remarkable parallel between rising wealth and rising delinquency.

The fifth argument for social planning is based on the fact of redistribution. There is an inescapable redistributive component in all governmental activity. In his NESC paper (no. 8, p. 30), Professor David Donnison clearly establishes that it is not only those government departments that deal with the social services that have a redistributive role, but that all governmental activity may 'deliberately or accidentally affect the distribution of resources, status, opportunities, and life chances among social groups and categories within the country'. It is highly desirable that this redistributive process should be directed towards defined objectives. In order to ensure that it is, planning will be required: not only must the social services themselves be planned more carefully in order to achieve social policy objectives, but, since other departments also contribute towards the shaping of social policy, they must take into account the redistributional consequences of their policies, and consider if these are contributing towards, or hindering, the achievement of defined objectives.

The sixth argument is that social planning is needed to help the poorest; Donnison also points out that the social services themselves may not in fact benefit most those who are poorest. Even when they do, their effects may be negated by the unanticipated redistributional consequences of the activities of other government departments (NESC 8, p. 28). If the redistributive process is to achieve a greater degree of equity, specific planning towards this aim is required.

The seventh argument is that social planning is needed in order to improve *political consensus*. Underlying all planning is the political fact that any planning system is subject to the major constraint of the willingness of the public to co-operate with it. If one believes in a society of free-for-all and sauve qui peut the role of politics becomes one of reconciling the conflicts of interests; but if one believes that economic and social problems can be eased or solved by the orderly process of planning, then it is essential to an effective planning process to bring about a public acceptance of the idea that co-operation and self-discipline in setting limits to individual and group selfishness can contribute to the overall wellbeing. Thus political consensus is both a condition and a product of successful social planning. One way of achieving this consensus is by making it clear that the system involves, in turn for a fair allocation of sacrifices, a fair allocation of benefits (Whitaker, 1977, p. 294).

At the present time it is generally recognised that perhaps the biggest single social reform that could be achieved in this country would be to have good employment opportunities for all those seeking work. It would remove a good deal of poverty, relieve a great deal of personal frustration, reduce social tensions, and create a climate of optimism and growth that itself would contribute to a more healthy society. So, this might well be the first objective of social policy—as of course, economic policy—at this time: but for the formidable problems that arise see Walsh, 1978a.

A second objective might be to give priority to the care of those that are worst off in the community. No matter how efficient the economic system is in providing well paid employment, experience shows that it does not give adequate care to the weakest members of the community—the handicapped, the old, the chronically sick, and their children. Apart from this, much of the activity in the social services—especially in relation to housing, education, and taxation—does not benefit those most in need: to a very considerable extent it, as has been pointed out above, benefits those who are already reasonably well off and who have the ability to make full use of the services provided. So a major thrust of policy might be to direct resources, existing and growing, in the first place to those who suffer severe privation.

A third objective might be to remove inequalities of access and opportunity. Very many people are in a position of 'multiple deprivation': because they are poor they do not have sufficient educational opportunities, and because they are not well educated, even when they have plenty of natural ability, they cannot hope to get the better paid and more secure jobs. There are also regional inequalities in access to service and opportunities: being born in a deprived place may lead to as much deprivation as being born in a deprived family.

Objectives have to be linked on the one hand to values and on the other to systems of implementation. This is done by means of operational principles. Let us take, for illustration, four of these. They are:

1. the principle of minimising inequalities;
2. the principle of alleviating greatest need;
3. the principle of positive discrimination; and
4. the principle of integration.

What do we mean by these principles?

First, the principle of *minimising inequalities*. We have seen that an increasing degree of equality is inherent in the whole business of social policy and planning. Steps to make available increased equality in access to opportunity and to public services and benefits, are of high social and economic value because they permit human resources to be fully utilised and not wasted. They remove social and other barriers, enable those with ability to develop their potentialities and remove the physical and geographical disabilities suffered by various members of the community. By increasing the quantity of usable resources of the community they illustrate once more the concordance between the needs of social and economic development.

Secondly, the principle of *alleviating greatest need*. At least so far as *new* expenditures are concerned, this principle would give priority to those in greatest need, rather than, for example in education and health, as at present, giving as much or more to those who are less, or not at all, disadvantaged.

Thirdly, the principle of *positive discrimination*. The normal drive of a democracy is towards distributing benefits equally, so that the widest number may benefit from them. But, unless resources are very plentiful, social objectives and priorities to be meaningful must call for *inequality* in the distribution of the social dividend and *inequality* in favour of those whose needs are greatest or whose handicaps are most severe.

Fourthly, the principle of *integration*. Most social ills have been diagnosed in isolation and many social remedies are therefore problem or symptom oriented, rather than person oriented, or family oriented, or community oriented. The principle of integration would require overall social policy to be person, family, and community oriented and not fragmented as at present (Barrington, 1975, pp. 116–8; Andersen; NESC 41).

So far as the machinery of social planning is concerned, there are problems at three levels, the sectoral, the facet, and the integrative or national.

At the *sectoral* or departmental level there are three broad classes of planning problems. The first problem area is to get the departments and the major agencies concerned with the provision of social services to adopt the sort of planning disciplines that we have been considering.

The second problem area is to get this done, in a social context, even by those bodies that are not mainly concerned with social questions at all. This is because of the redistributive effect of their activities which we have been considering. Just as there is an economic dimension to the social services, so also is there a social dimension to economic and other services, and adequate machinery for social planning must take this into account.

Thirdly, at a higher level of generality there are problems of thinking through thoroughly the means by which social services are paid for, and the redistributive effects of taxation.

Secondly, *facet* planning, as the Dutch call it. They have separate bodies concerned with economic planning, with infrastructural planning, and with social planning, in all aspects. It will not be possible to have good social planning unless all the social aspects of the sectoral plans are pulled together and some form of social priorities, cutting across the institutional boundaries, established (Roes, 1976).

Finally, there is integrative, or national, planning, when all the facet plans are integrated into one overall plan for national development. This is, of course, the work of the new Department of Economic Planning and Development.

5. Infrastructural and Regional Planning

A number of these issues arise in another form of planning, infrastructural planning. At first sight this is surprising because, at the project stage, planning is an accepted discipline for the provision of roads, housing schemes and the rest. The problems begin at the operational level, as witness these spasmodic approaches to the development of major roads, the backlog on telephone development for many years and, most recently, the underspending of the annual capital allocations.[1] Symptoms of this sort show the need for better operational planning.

However, the big problems are at the sectoral, the facet and the integrative levels. This is because of the multiplicity of the agencies concerned and the difficulties of achieving effective co-ordination between them. We have seen the problems that arose in relation to Rossaveal harbour. On a more spectacular level is the mis-match between the ready capital availability for factories and industrial estates contrasted with the shortages of capital for the corresponding water, sewerage and road services or the shortages of administrative capabilities in relation to telecommunications. There is a clear lack here of means of effecting high level co-ordination of infrastructural development at the sectoral, facet and integrative levels.

The point is that 'planning' is a method that has to adapt its disciplines to the facet in hand—economic, social, or infrastructural. For the last-named, the problems are not mainly intellectual—as with social planning—but are principally problems of co-ordination and management.

In a very special way infrastructural planning causes something to happen in a given *place* and there ought to be, therefore, some local or geographical system of co-ordination in relation to what happens in that place to ensure that all the things to be done are neatly dovetailed there. In a sense this is what *local* and *regional* planning ought to be about. In practice, however, things do not always work out this way. Under the Local Government (Planning and Development) Act, 1963, there are strong 'imperative' powers to be applied to the private sector but government departments and 'statutory undertakers' are mainly exempt even

[1]Telephone capital provision and expenditure: 1975—provided £45m, spent £45m; 1976—provided £50m, spent £46m; 1977—provided £55m, spent £48m (Posts & Telegraphs Review Group, 1978–9, p. 34).

though they are responsible for some significant infrastructural planning. This comes, in part at least, from an extraordinary application of the notion of state sovereignty – an organ of central government could not be expected to subject itself to the rulings of a local authority! There are certain informal practices to get around this curious problem, but they work with indifferent success. So, there are significant loopholes in this basic form of co-ordination.

Some efforts have been made to tackle the problems of infrastructural planning at the regional level, but, as we shall see, with indifferent commitment and, consequently, success.

Regional planning is the attempt to achieve an integrative plan for a sub-national level or region. It thus partakes of the nature of national, integrative planning. It operates through co-ordinating the relevant *geographical* features of agency plans and projects, of functional plans, and of sectoral plans. Regional planning, therefore, although closely concerned with agency and departmental planning, as well as with facet planning, is distinct from any of these. Its main role is co-ordinative, as is departmental planning, but on its own distinctive plane.

Its purpose is to try to achieve reasonable degrees of equality and of income and of opportunity between the various regions of the country. It aims to tackle the problems of the underdevelopment of some regions and the overdevelopment of others. It claims to pay its way by bringing into use resources that would be overlooked in a purely national development plan.

Most Irish people are familiar with the argument that the peripheral regions of the European Community are disadvantaged as compared with what is known as the 'golden triangle' in the heartland of the Community. Thus, the gross national product per head in the Hamburg area has recently been calculated to be six times that of the west of Ireland or the south of Italy, and the GNP in the Paris area to be five times as great. These disproportions tend to increase, if anything (European Development Fund Report, 1975; Barrington, 1976, p. 353). Given the operation of compound interest, very considerable efforts would be needed to prevent these gaps from increasing, and, unless something extraordinary occurs, there is very little likelihood that they will ever be closed. Even within this country, there are disparities. Income in the eastern, that is, the Dublin, region is about 50 per cent more than income per head in the north west (NESC 30, p. 15).

Regional planning in Ireland exists only in an embryonic form. It began in the mid-west region, following a study of infrastructural planning problems in the Limerick area. This was taken up by local initiative and a voluntary regional development organisation was established for the region, consisting of representatives of the main local government and administrative bodies operating in the region. A good deal of useful work has been done, but on a mainly voluntary basis. This idea was taken up for the other eight physical planning regions in the country, with varying degrees of success, but, notwithstanding the sponsorship of the Department of Local Government, following the same voluntary, amateur-type operational style.

Also in the mid-west the existence of the Shannon Free Airport Development Company (SFADCo), as an agency for economic development first in the Shannon area, and then throughout the region, has been a powerful dynamic force. In the Gaeltacht areas, Gaeltarra Éireann has had the task of developing the cultural, social, and economic areas of the Gaeltacht. The Gaeltacht areas, of course, cut across county and regional boundaries. In addition, a number of the national bodies have some embryonic regional structures – the Industrial Development Authority (IDA), the National Manpower Service, An Comhairle Oiliuna (AnCO). These, some central departments, and some of the state-sponsored bodies, co-operate, to a greater or lesser extent, with the regional development organisations, insofar as these have proved effective. But overall, if regional development depends on the disaggregation of national statistics, the study of expected demographic changes within the region, the establishment of a distinctive regional dimension and linkages between the economic, the cultural, the social, and the infrastructural bodies operating within the region – even, as we have been considering, effective co-ordination in the region between the various infrastructural bodies themselves – then, one can say that, so far, regional planning in this country is still very underdeveloped indeed (NESC 22, pp. 14–15; Barrington, 1976, pp. 360–64).

At the sub-regional level of the counties there has existed since the 1960s in the western counties, and in the other counties more recently, systems for promoting county development. These are aimed primarily at stimulating and at facilitating industrial development and community development. But, on both fronts, major role problems arise. So far as industrial development is concerned, the main thrust lies with such major central bodies as the Industrial Development Authority (IDA). So far as community development is concerned comparable problems arise. One of the features of present-day Ireland has been the growth of community groups, in a sense a form of political development; but, as we have seen, there are significant barricades here, arising from the political system itself.

Development in Ireland has overwhelmingly been seen as the question of providing factories and jobs. A long-standing feature of industrial development has been the dispersal of such jobs throughout the country. It has been the task of the Industrial Development Authority to stimulate and encourage industrial development in as many places throughout the country as possible, and in this it has had very considerable success. It was believed that the growth of the Dublin area, in population and in wealth, did not require any such underpinning and one of the tasks of the IDA was to divert industrial work away from that area. By Irish standards the Dublin area had achieved a level of self-sustaining growth and no further promotion of it was needed.

However, the recent recession has shown that the issues are nothing like so simple. Because the Dublin area achieved some degree of industrialisation at an earlier stage than the rest of the country, a lot of its industry was obsolescent and, accordingly, suffered severely in the recession. Apart from this, Dublin has been suffering from one of the typical diseases of overdeveloped areas, namely decay at its heart, economic decay, social decay, cultural decay. This has been, and is still being, overlooked. However, the IDA have now adjusted their policies to take into account the special industrial problems of Dublin (IDA Plan, 1977–80).

At the same time, the Dublin area continues to grow at a significant rate. In particular, higher-order white-collar employment (i.e. professional, technical, administrative and managerial work) is increasingly concentrated in the East (i.e. the Dublin) Region (NESC 28, p. 11). These, of course, attract the best-educated people from the country as a whole. So, we have had the striking situation that many of the sorts of industrial jobs that people in the decaying central areas of Dublin could perform were diverted elsewhere; and a great part of the jobs that well-educated young people in other parts of the country could hope to aspire to were being created in Dublin. Here was a double mis-match. The role of government here was quite ambivalent. On the one hand it was responsible for the policy of the dispersal of industry. On the other hand, it was, either directly or indirectly, the main employer of office workers in Dublin. Moreover, by reason of the intense centralisation of governmental decision-making in Dublin, the headquarters of a high proportion of the other main office employers were concentrated there.

So we see a double failure in relation to regional planning and development. In the first place no adequate instruments were created within these regions to get going the preconditions for effective regional take-off. On the other hand, regional policy, as administered from the centre, suffers from this very lack of an overview which is at the heart of the planning approach to development.

A full public sector planning *system* would look something like chart 5 overleaf. Two general points should be made about this. First, the chart does not attempt to portray the relationships between the public and private sectors in this matter, partly because this would make the chart too complex and partly because this would bring us outside our present purpose which is to explain the system of Irish public administration; but it must at all times be remembered that public sector planning is not carried on in a vacuum and is primarily concerned not with itself but with its impact on society as a whole. Nonetheless, the burden of the present argument is that its impact would be greater if it were more conscious of,

THE PUBLIC SECTOR PLANNING SYSTEM

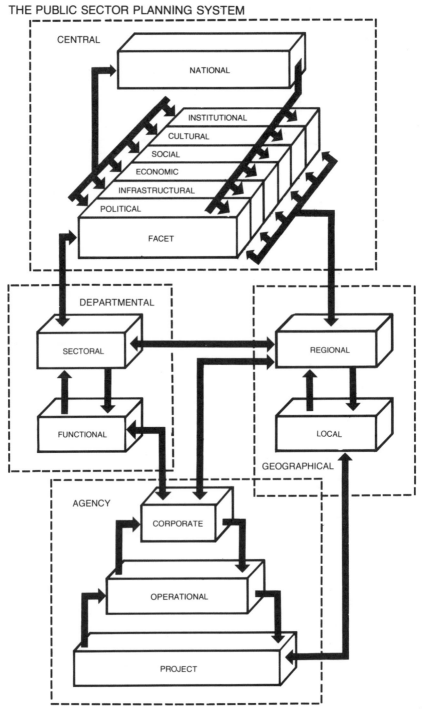

and more active in tackling, its own problems.

The second general point is that two processes can, or ought to, be seen working through the system as a whole. The first runs down through the system defining, after some degree of iteration, the parameters and the overall priorities for the operation of the system as a whole. The second runs from the bottom up, pulling together the detailed projects, identifying gaps to be filled, and setting goals and targets for implementation. These two processes, by their mutual interactions, relate needs to feasibilities.

The system, as portrayed, is divided into four sub-systems marked off by the dotted rectangles of the chart. These are, from the bottom up:

1. *Agency planning:* This is the primary planning sub-system. It comprises, in relation to each public body, its own planning at the project, operational, and corporate levels.

2. *Geographical Planning:* This is a second-level sub-system concerned with the *co-ordinating* of the plans of the individual agencies at the geographical level. Locally it is mainly concerned with infrastructural problems; regionally it is concerned (hopefully) to match projects and operational plans to regional needs and to overall feasibilities.

3. *Departmental Planning:* This is also a second-level sub-system concerned with the *co-ordination* of the plans of the individual agencies in relation to specific *functions* of the relevant department (e.g. energy by the Department of Industry, Commerce & Energy, hospitals by the Department of Health), of these in relation to the *sectoral* responsibilities of the department as a whole, as well as matching these to overall needs and feasibilities as defined at the national planning level.

4. *Central Planning:* This is a third-level planning sub-system concerned, on the one hand, to *integrate* the various sectoral and regional plans into facet plans and these into a coherent national plan, and, on the other, to view the planning system as a whole so as to match overall needs to overall feasibilities.

The system as a whole works through, as we have seen, two main processes – the stream of information about needs and possibilities that descends through it from the top, and the flow of detailed plans that rise up through it from the bottom. But as well as these, there is, especially at the co-ordinative level, a great deal of horizontal to-ing and fro-ing. Not every product of the system will have to go through the processes portrayed but, taking the system as a whole, a great number of its products will have been through all or most of these stages.

Overall, the system, as portrayed even in this simplified form, looks complicated. It is complicated; but it is not half as complicated or difficult to work as to attempt to work a system where several essential parts are missing and others have not been geared for effective operation. A complicated system will work simply if it is open to free movement of power and information through *all* its essential parts. One does not simplify a system by losing some of those parts or by allowing them to be clogged up. Simplification of a complicated system is not the same as a simple system, just as the simplification of the modern motor vehicle still leaves it a complicated system quite different from, say, the simplicity of a bicycle. Similarly the task of planning is to simplify extremely complicated material; the sophistication of the planning system must match the difficulty of the task if that task is to be successfully accomplished.

Examples of how two current projects work through the system are given in chart 6 opposite. These are the proposal to build a nuclear energy station at Carnsore, Co. Wexford, and the present project for building a new county hospital at Tralee, Co. Kerry.

It cannot be stressed too strongly, or frequently, that planning is about coherence: coherence over time, and coherence in place, that is the concertation of the various activities that are engaged in at any one time and as they occur or manifest themselves in any one place. Whether the immediate task is political development, or infrastructural development, or economic development, or social development, or cultural development, or development for the institutions for achieving these other kinds of development, clear-cut objectives, consistent priorities, coherent and concerted operations are the heart of the matter. If planning is indeed to be for bringing about more comprehensive and more speedy national development, then there is no choice but to operate it according to its own inherent logic. Unfortunately, although many brave initiatives have been made, this logic has not been followed in the four crucial areas of economic, social, infrastructural and regional planning.

There is (so far at least) no final, technically perfect form of planning. As fresh insights are gained and circumstances change, new technical problems arise. For example, French planning is in a constant state of evolution. Planning in the Soviet Union is still encumbered with technical administrative problems. There is in this world no final state of rest where no technical problems remain to be solved.

INTEGRATED PUBLIC SECTOR PLANNING: 2 EXAMPLES
1. CARNSORE NUCLEAR STATION
2. TRALEE COUNTY HOSPITAL

CENTRAL PLANNING

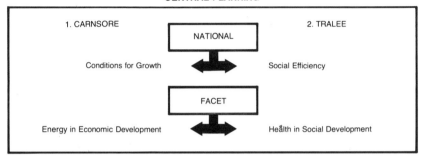

DEPARTMENTAL PLANNING

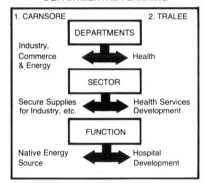

GEOGRAPHICAL PLANNING

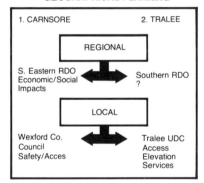

AGENCY PLANNING

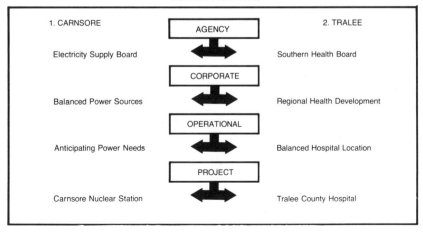

Chapter 6: Implementing Policy

1. National Development

We have been considering the various ways by which policy is formulated, that is to say, how the governmental system decides *what* it is to do. But, of course, the great bulk of activity in the administrative system is in fact carrying out policy, implementing the decisions taken overall, and is, therefore, concerned with the *how* of action. The best policies are no good unless they are carried into effect, and they can totally fail to have their expected effects if they are badly carried out. Concern with the *how* of policy implementation is thus crucial to the success of governmental activity.

There are two dimensions to this. The first is, given the extraordinarily wide range of government and the complexity of the various activities to be engaged in, how to identify an overall objective that will permeate all the activities and give them a basic unity and, if possible, simplicity. The second is, given this overall objective, how to manage the implementation process effectively and efficiently. For now, let us confine ourselves to the question of overall objectives.

In newly independent countries it has been fashionable, for some years past, to draw a distinction between traditional administration, which contented itself with preserving the status quo under the former colonial government, and development administration, which was concerned to use the freedom that had been won to tackle the problems of the society and to bring about economic and other kinds of development. The expression 'development administration' is a tautology. The task of government, where a colonial power is trying to hold down a subject nation, is wholly artificial, especially in the unlikely event that no change will occur within that nation. This is, in effect, non-government. But otherwise the task of government is to cope with those changes that arise within the society, and the corresponding changes that are caused by changes from without, as well as to initiate certain changes itself. This is what government, so far as its justification is the public interest, is there for. This coping with change, if it is done in a random way, is likely to be self-defeating. Hence the concept of 'development' where one attempts to use the dynamism of external and internal forces to achieve a speedy and inter-related growth of the various services that contribute to the 'progress' of the community, whatever that may be held to mean from place to place and from time to time.

One can say, therefore, that the objective of government is 'development'. But what ought to be the role of government, or of the state, in striving for development?

If one is thinking of a totally socialised society, then there are no great conceptual difficulties in determining what the state ought to be doing: it ought to be doing everything. Though even within the socialist societies there is debate as to the use which the market system can be put, and poets and other artists are a constant problem, as Plato recognised. In a pluralistic, open-market, democratic society there are considerable conceptual difficulties and thus room for intense debate as to the role of the state. However, if we look at the actual operations of the state in such societies in a detached and empirical way, we can discern six main forces that tend to define the broad outline of the role of the state and its functions.

The first of these, historically and logically, is the factor of *intervention*. This means that it is inherent in the role of the state to create the conditions in which an organised society can exist at all – to preserve internal and external security, to create the basic conditions in which economic and other activity can be carried on. It is perhaps no accident that the oldest surviving statute of an Irish parliament, dating from the end of the thirteenth century, is an act to define weights and measures – such definition is absolutely basic to the development of economic activity. The old Gaelic custom of using the cumal, or female slave, as the unit of value, related (depending on the current rate of inflation) to three, four or five cows, obviously made for appreciable difficulties in the development of trade.

It follows from the principle of intervention that the role of the state is to facilitate activity by other groups and persons within the community but not to supersede these if they are working with reasonable effectiveness. This is the principle of *subsidiarity*, affirmed in two papal encyclicals (1931, 1963) but hardly anywhere discussed in depth. However, one can see that this principle is inherent in the notion of a free society – that the individual and the individual group have the right of initiative and the right to pursue legitimate interests at least up to the point where there is a conflict between those interests and the overall interests of the state.

However, where there is a gap between the sum total of the activities of the subsidiary bodies and the overall needs of the society, then the objective of development requires that somebody be responsible for doing something about the slack. In the last analysis, this responsibility falls on the state, as a sort of residuary legatee of responsibility for the community as a whole. This is the burden of Keynes's essay 'The End of Laissez Faire' (1926) and is explicit in de Jouvenel: 'The sovereign authority . . . is the residual legatee of all problems' (1957, p. 80). This factor, therefore, we can call that of *residuary responsibility*.

The economic system is, on the whole, good at increasing wealth and at distributing it amongst the wealth producers. It is not good at distributing some of it to the non-producers – the old, the handicapped, children, the sick. So a major part of the task of modern states is to transfer resources to these less advantaged people and to build up services for health, education, and the like that will help to remove some of their disabilities in relation to the more fortunate members of the community. The principle that governs this is that of *social justice* and is the burden of a series of papal encyclicals (1891; 1931; 1961; 1963; 1967).

As economic growth continues people are enabled to buy many more goods and services. Some of these make demands on the infrastructure that require 'lumpy' capital investment, such as major sewers, that cannot hope to pay for themselves except over a very long term. Unless these sewers are laid down, the desire of people to have new houses, for which they are willing to pay, will be frustrated. Similarly, their buying of motor-cars will be ultimately self-defeating unless there is some system of roads and of traffic engineering backed by statutory powers. So, the free exercise of decision by individuals to buy houses and motor-cars necessarily involves the state in providing the physical and legal infrastructure to enable these decisions to be fully realised. The principle that operates on the state here is that of *social balance*. The expression comes from Galbraith (1969, Chs 18, 19).

All these ad hoc interventions by the state need, from time to time, to be rationalised and harmonised. Otherwise, as we have seen, what is done with the left hand may frustrate that which is done by the right. This is the principle of *planning* elucidated by Myrdal (1960). It attempts to arrive at an overview of the effects of the operation of the five other principles we have been discussing.

When these six principles are added together they come to constitute a coherent role for the state as the active instrument in giving effect to the duties of the 'responsible society', an expression popularised by the World Council of Churches in the 1960s. In a modern western society this means that the state, through one or other of its organs, becomes responsible for perhaps half the activity in the community and, because of the importance of some of the state's functions – for example, in trying to keep the economy on an even keel – for what may be, qualitatively, often the more important half.

The responsible society gives effect to its task through various *sectoral* activities. These sectoral activities can be seen to be the responsibilities discharged by the members of the government, amongst whom the various tasks of government are parcelled out. Basically, in the Irish system, they are divided amongst eighteen government departments and, leaving aside a number of minor activities, three major offices. So, at the operational or sectoral level the task of government can be seen to be, for example, agricultural development, the development of the health services, the development of the infrastructural services, and so on, through the twenty-one major organisations concerned, supplemented by the large number of state-sponsored bodies, local authorities, regional bodies, etc. that feed into these twenty-one.

However, it is possible to classify analytically the work that concerns these twenty-one bodies, though not without considerable difficulty. If we follow a practice from the biological sciences we can distinguish within each of the twenty-one bodies a dominant purpose and one or more less significant ones. So, we can think of the Department of Agriculture as having primarily an economic function, but it also has a very extensive social or redistributive function, as well as an educational and scientific one, and, especially in relation to the European Community, a political one. If we classify the twenty-one major bodies – the eighteen government departments and the three major offices – by major purpose we arrive at something like the table below.

Classification of Departments

Purpose	Facet	Departments	Offices
Order	Political	Taoiseach, Defence, Foreign Affairs, Justice	
Infrastructure	Infrastructural	Environment, Posts & Telegraphs, Tourism & Transport	Public Works
Production	Economic	Agriculture, Economic Planning & Development, Finance, Fisheries & Forestry, Industry, Commerce & Energy, Labour	
Redistribution	Social	Health, Social Welfare	Land Commission, Revenue
Culture	Cultural	Education, Gaeltacht	
Cohesion	Administrative	Public Service	

We can see that the major common purpose of the Departments in the first column is that of order, that of the bodies in the second column infrastructure, that of those in the third column production, of the fourth column redistribution, of the fifth column culture and of the sixth cohesion. If we take each of these as a *facet* of the whole we might think of the first as a political facet, the second an infrastructural one, the third an economic one, the fourth a social one, the fifth a cultural one and the sixth an institutional and administrative one.

These six facets, taken together, give us another insight into the nature of the role of modern government. We have the developmental role of the individual bodies, feeding into the developmental responsibilities of the individual ministers and members of the government, and falling into six developmental headings – political development, infrastructural development, economic development, social development, cultural development and administrative development. These, taken together, add up to a single responsibility of national development.

However, there are a number of complexities in all of this. If we think of national development as covering all the activities of government in a modern western society, then how much of the 'mix' that constitutes national development is to be made up, from time to time, from each of these ingredients?

It is clear that the function of political development is basic to all else – if society breaks down from internal disruption or external aggression everything suffers. Apart from this, the effects of the other forms of development raise new problems for political development; for example, there seems to be a close relationship between social cohesion and political stability, between the rise of affluence and the rise in delinquency.

Once political order is established the first task of government is communications and other infrastructural services – roads, ports, houses, water supplies, etc. Until these are established economic development becomes impossible, and they are also essential for maintaining political control.

Economic development is possible only on a basis of internal and external order and of certain basic infrastructural services. It provides means of extending these, and also provides the resources for social and cultural development, as well as new problems for these.

Economic advance calls for social change. If this is withheld, economic development is impeded. Economic development itself poses the issues of the socially just distribution of its product. Unfair social provision leads to disorder.

National purpose and understanding come from educational and cultural unity and continuity. Trained and alert minds lead to social responsibility. Cultural unity is basic to political consensus. Education and training are big factors in economic growth. Cultural development is impeded by political, economic, and social weakness. It gives meaning to a more peaceful, affluent and leisurely life.

Government must be carried on by institutions. These do not readily or coherently adapt themselves to change. Any government may need some special agency to do this, and many have; in Ireland we have recently required one. This is concerned with coherent administrative structures and the allocation to them of the appropriate human resources.

So, the task of national development involves striking a balance between the contributions of these six forms of facet development, now a bit more from one and a bit less from another, at other times a somewhat different set of priorities. What is important, however, is that, always, all of them have some contribution to make if the overall process of national development is to proceed at the optimum rate.

The second major complexity arises from the existence, within each sector and facet, of purposes other than the dominant one, sometimes one of the lesser purposes, sometimes several. So, for example, the work of the Department of Justice is primarily concerned with the maintenance of internal order. But the diagnosis and treatment of problems of delinquency cut right into the social facet. Again, education has its own cultural end, but it has been found to have a profound effect on economic development (OECD, 1965, 1966), as well as in contributing to the solution of a number of social problems. The major purpose of the Department of Labour is economic, but its social purpose is nearly as important. The primary purpose of the Department of Economic Planning and Development is economic, yet it has specifically social and regional roles and, generally, a most significant cohesive and institutional one.

This feature of the many-faceted nature of national development as a whole, and of the multiple purposes of individual sectoral development, poses problems of very considerable sophistication. Just as an individual body cannot ignore its minor purposes in pursuing its major purpose so the individual facets – economic, social or other – cannot be considered without their impact on the other facets. The point is that national development, if it is to be effective, requires that its many-faceted nature be taken fully into account in day-to-day operations and the various interrelations fully grasped. In the strictly economic sphere we have input-output models to assess the interrelations of the various economic forces in the community. We need a similar conceptual approach to the interrelations of the various facets of national development.

This is a point that is not readily grasped, and we have been slow to learn the consequential lessons. Not unnaturally, the first programme for economic expansion put a heavy emphasis on the economic facet, and almost entirely avoided the problems of the other facets of the developmental process. Less explicably, the second programme made the same error and one of the reasons for its non-completion was its ignoring of the problems of redistribution inherent in the social facet of development. The third programme was explicitly concerned with economic and *social* development, but on the social side was not more than a shopping list, and it largely ignored the other facets of national development. Perhaps not surprisingly, it too did not stay the course. Yet in 1978 the White Paper explicitly labelled 'Programme for National Development', seems (e.g. at para 7.1) to hark back to the less sophisticated thinking of the first programme. So, while over the twenty years since the first programme in 1958 there has been, overall, reasonable success with economic growth, no comparable sophistication has been applied to the other five facets of national development.

It is of the nature of things to change, not always for the better. One of the major activities of government is to bring about progress towards ever better development, and often this is successfully done. In the same way, individuals and groups continually struggle for improvement. Nonetheless, the efforts of government and of individuals and groups can be overwhelmed by bouts of regression, as, for example, when there is a war, or a great economic slump. Apart from this, the effect of development itself forces the need for change and for consequential development. For example, the success on the economic development front in this country over the past twenty years led to the ceasing of long-standing emigration. This, combined with other factors, has meant that we now have a very young population, about half of it under thirty. This forces the need to enlarge educational facilities, job creation programmes, and, as these young people get married, house building, and the other infrastructural services that this calls for.

The point is that the task of government is never-ending even though it may be relatively larger or smaller at any given time. But it does remain very extensive, and comprehensive. Whatever may be the different composition of its units from time to time there is no stage at which one can say that national development has been reached, or that some aspect of it cannot be subverted by some further change, or that human wants and demands will ever be satiated. For this reason new and revised policies will always be necessary, the whole system must be kept under constant review, and new and more effective systems of policy implementation devised to keep up with the changing circumstances. National development involves continuity with the past, constant maintenance in the present, and ready innovation for the future.

2. Administrative Management
We have seen that the concept of a single overall objective of national development, however complex it may be, is a sort of guiding light which the national convoy can follow in its never-ending voyage. The second method by which the immensely complex mass of public affairs can be led

along is by means of public management, effective and efficient.

There is a good deal of discussion as to whether management and administration are not basically the same thing. If a distinction is to be drawn between them – usually management is related to business operations, administration to operations of government – which is the more comprehensive? If one approaches the problem from the standpoint of business, then 'administration' in a business context has a fairly limited meaning, usually those responsibilities that come under the company secretary; that is, secretarial work generally, accounting, and, occasionally, personnel.

On the other hand, if one approaches the problem from that of public administration, public management or administrative management tends to be seen as part of the whole. Whatever the rights and wrongs of this debate – and I think it is not a very fruitful one – I propose to use 'management' in the sense of the means of implementing policies that have already been devised and agreed upon and to distinguish from business management by using the American term 'administrative management'. This need not prevent one from freely admitting that 'management' in the private sector covers not only implementation but formulation as well.

If we think of administrative management as concerned to implement policies, to make things happen in accordance with desires and decisions, then we are discussing a most important part of the whole. On this reading policy is related to administration, namely what ought to be done. Management is related to implementing the resulting decisions. This is a distinction, whatever the nomenclature used, that runs through all forms of organisation.

In military organisation there is a clear distinction between the line and the staff, staff concerned basically with planning, line concerned with implementing the plans. This is a distinction that has been carried over also into business administration.

Similarly, in the classical distinction in the civil service between the administrative and the executive work, the administrators are concerned with 'policy' and the executive classes concerned with the carrying out of policies.

Nonetheless, when we look at work in actual operation, it is not possible in real terms to make so sharp a distinction. There are two main reasons for this. The first is that both policy formulation and policy implementation are two related aspects of a single administrative cycle. There is no clear cut-off point between them, as we shall see in Chapter 8. The second reason comes from the meaning of the word 'policy' itself.

Policy is, essentially, a decision to deal with similar recurrent events according to some consistent line. These events may be of great general significance, or they may be of local application. For example, one can think of, on the one hand, policy in relation to a major economic slump and, on the other, a policy that typists in a given organisation will take two carbon copies of all letters. In between there can be a great variety of recurring cycles that require policies. It is a useful shorthand, for example, to say that, under the Devlin proposals, an aireacht will be concerned with policy, and an office or agency concerned with implementation. In fact, if one thinks of bodies the size of Córas Iompair Éireann, the Electricity Supply Board, the Dublin Corporation, the Eastern Health Board, one realises that within each of these organisations a very considerable amount of policy-making occurs. The distinction that is intended to be made in the aireacht/agency dichotomy is that policies that are intended to have wide general application, outside the range of operations of individual executive agencies, would be matters for the aireacht and that policies that would have their main application within the agency would, naturally, be matters for the agency itself: the distinction is between agency, or corporate, policies on the one hand, and departmental, or sectoral, policies on the other.

When we talk of the agency as an implementing body we think of it as being concerned not only with making and implementing its own policies, but also implementing policies that are substantially determined outside it, however considerable its own input into the formulation process of that external policy may be.

Administrative management is, therefore, on the meaning given above, substantially concerned with the task of implementing policies, no matter where they are made. If one looks at the public service as a whole we see that, quantitatively, this implementing work is the overwhelming part of the work done by the public service. Hence, administrative management is of great importance in all day-to-day operations.

There are two broad areas of administrative management, introducing the new service, or *innovating*, and carrying on an existing service, or *maintaining*. Each has its special characteristics.

Let us take as a simple example of innovation a new Act that has been passed to set up a scheme to provide some sort of benefits to the public. This requires fresh action under a number of headings.

The first thing is to determine what sort of organisation will be needed to ensure that the scheme is successfully implemented. Will it be carried out directly or through some form of agency? If the latter, what sort of extra resources does it need to do a good job? Is it clear what its function will be, and how it will relate to the 'parent' body? Generally, the more policy-oriented the body is, the wider the range of its responsibilities, the more it should seek to mobilise the implementing skills of the more executive-oriented agencies—functional, geographical or private—because in the day-to-day stress of implementing work policy work is nearly always the loser: the urgent almost invariably drives out the important. It is the negation of the role of a policy-oriented body to encumber itself with implementing work that could be performed by another body or bodies and so to impede or inhibit its 'special' duty of policy formulation.

If the job is to be carried out directly it is necessary to determine what the probable flow of work will be; what kind of staff, both in numbers and in experience, will be required; what sort of training they will need for the new duties; what is to be done to get appropriate accommodation, office machinery, and so on.

While this is going on it will be necessary to try to envisage what the day-to-day work will be like under the new scheme. What sort of snags are likely to crop up, and how might they be tackled? It may be necessary to draw up some sort of statutory regulations under the new act, and essential to work out, as clearly as possible, the rules that should govern the operations of the staff in relation to all foreseen eventualities. It will be clear that some of these will not, in fact, be foreseen, so it will be necessary to put in a system of monitoring the operations so that the unexpected will be rapidly brought to light and receive appropriate treatment. Apart from this it will be necessary to have an effective feedback system, to ensure that the scheme is, in fact, operating according to the intentions of the legislature, that the estimates of likely expenditure are being borne out in practice, that the original estimates of staff, accommodation, and other requirements were neither too small nor too great.

All of this work will be done by a small nucleus group recruited well in advance of the date by which the scheme has to begin. They will have a substantial leadership task which will first manifest itself in relation to good project planning. That is to say they will try to give operational significance to the general objectives set out in the legislation, so that there will be clear objectives at each level of operation, from the objectives of the organisation as a whole, down to the objectives of various sections within it. There will be defined, also, probably as a result of a long process of negotiation, the standards of service that will be provided under the scheme – whether first class, second class or third class, depending on the resources, especially the financial resources, that can be recruited for the scheme. The task of trying to define what these resources should be, and of negotiating with the Department of Finance to get them, and, perhaps, some redefinition of the standards of the scheme when it is known what resources will be made available, will occupy the attention of the most senior members of the group. Given the objectives defined, given the standards that can feasibly be worked to, certain target dates must then be established.

At the next level it is necessary to build in appropriate controls, especially financial ones, to ensure that expenditure is running as planned, or that significant deviations of performance from plan are immediately brought to notice, that there are all the necessary safeguards against waste and abuse. In the same way it would be necessary to have controls to ensure that performance is in accordance with the standards that have been set, that these standards are realistic in all the circumstances, and that the whole operation is reasonably immune to justifiable criticism, with enough information available to rebut such criticisms that may be made, or else to remedy speedily those failings that have led to sustainable criticism.

Apart from these conceptual forms of leadership, there is also the need for one directly aimed at the morale of the staff. There is the need to establish the right atmosphere in the organisation, which is likely to determine its temper for many years to come. This might, possibly, be described as one of cheerful dedication. This calls for clarity of mind, and clear definitions, the setting of time-tables and firmness in seeing that realistic time-tables are met, and that unrealistic ones are suitably amended. This calls for considerable firmness in relation to principle but reasonable flexibility in relation to details. The staff must feel that, in the inevitable upsets and confusion of the early days of the operation of the scheme, they have the trust and support of their leaders and that, in industrial relations matters, reasonable complaints will be speedily and effectively attended to.

A further stage arises in determining and applying principles of action for the staff at the various levels. So far as can be foreseen, and certainly in the early stages, certain routines should be laid down for the most junior staff, and they should be trained to these so that the great bulk of work can be disposed of quickly and regularly. Where the staff have to come in contact with the public then they should be trained in their demeanour, and provided with the necessary facilities, so that members of the public can feel reasonably at home in their relationships, and that the organisation exists, so far as possible, to serve them.

Inevitably, there will be snags and exceptions to whatever routines are laid down and it will be necessary to have a system to bring these clearly and speedily to light. At this level of operation there must be a system by which those exceptions that can be dealt with, either by an alteration of the rules or the statutory regulations, will get the necessary high-level attention, and those exceptions that cannot be dealt with, either because they are contrary to the statute, or because they would call for expenditures beyond the available resources, or for some other general reason of this kind, are also identified and good reasons for not meeting them are clearly elucidated. At the higher levels it will be necessary to ensure that issues of this kind are submitted and considered, not only in relation to themselves, but in relation to other issues to which they may relate, or by which they may be affected, so that, when necessary, proposals for amending legislation, or for persuading other bodies to change in some way, are speedily put in hand.

This leads on to the tasks of administrative management at the highest levels. These involve devising methods, and operating them, to achieve a continual critical overview of the operations of the organisation as a whole, and where it fits into some larger picture. Part of the task of top-level management of this kind is to ensure that the organisation has the capability for continual self-scrutiny, in an objective way, and that it can and will prepare new and better projects where existing deficiencies have been found, as well as where gaps may exist between the operations of one organisation and some related one. This involves a built-in system of analysis to consider legal, economic, financial, political, and other constraints on the effective operation of the organisation as a whole.

At this level, analysis of what needs to be done is followed by perhaps very long periods of persuasion and negotiation, both within the organisation and as between it and related organisations, so that acceptance of new projects, or of projects as amended in the light of further discussion, can be secured. On the whole, day-to-day administration in Ireland is carried on on the basis of persuasion and one of the most important management skills is that of winning acceptance from other people for the projects of one's organisation. This involves achieving, wherever that is possible, an easy relationship, specially one of trust, with the other interests concerned, skill in committee work and in negotiation generally, articulateness, and other social skills.

Inevitably, there will be conflict with other interests, and it is essential to handle this conflict in a skilful and creative way so that an overall solution is achieved that, where at all possible, will incorporate the essential interests of all parties. And, moreover, that does not leave behind sentiments or bitterness that will impede further such negotiations.

Sometimes this, as in the case of industrial relations, means the willingness to establish procedures for the resolution of conflict and the willingness to engage in bona fide negotiation and discretion about the solution of the problems that emerge. But even outside the industrial relations field, it may mean the establishment of some standing committee or body or channel of communication where fresh projects can be thrashed out and conflicting interests reconciled in a spirit of reasonable accommodation. It may also be necessary to establish, either on a regular or on an ad hoc basis, procedures for consulting, and being seen to give serious consideration to, the views of persons and groups who may have interests in the area concerned.

Of course, consultation and discussion can, like everything else, be abused. This can occur in two main ways. The first is where the body itself is reluctant to take on the responsibility for what it wants to do and is anxious to involve as many more people as possible in the ultimate decision so that, should it go wrong, nobody can be blamed. Those in charge of organisations who are motivated to behave in this way are unfit to hold their positions.

The other limitation is where a conflicting interest is not prepared to arrive at a reasonable accommodation and authority must be invoked to get the matter settled one way or the other. This, also, is a case for the effective discharge of responsibility.

If the problem is important and a solution to it is necessary, and all reasonable methods of accommodation have failed, then it is the duty of the sponsoring organisation to press the point to that of ultimate decision. This, in the system of public administration, is, of course, the government itself. This regularly happens in interdepartmental conflicts, where it is not possible to reconcile differences of view between two government departments. The matter is then normally referred to the government for decision. A great part of the standing of a minister within his department depends on how effective he is in getting what the department would regard as the 'right' decision in these circumstances.

The position is more difficult for other bodies in the public service outside the departments directly under ministers but, here again, some method of achieving ministerial backing is part of the management skill of the organisation concerned. This is usually done by achieving very good methods of communication, largely on an informal basis, between the body and the appropriate department and minister. Good management is often said to be nothing more than good communication. A mark of a good public manager at this level is in fact the system of communications he has been able to establish.

We have been discussing the problems, basically, of innovation because these are the most characteristic of management in the public sector, especially at the highest level. However, it must be repeated that the great part of activity within the public service is in carrying on schemes and operations that have been in existence for a long time and are likely to continue so to exist. This 'maintenance' type of management makes its own demands.

One of the most important of these, and one where there is room for considerable improvement in many parts of the public service, is in the maintenance, and the lifting, of the morale of those who are operating such long-outstanding, and therefore potentially dull, schemes. This calls for a form of leadership in human terms that is not, on the whole, well developed in the public service. It involves, basically, the replacement of impersonality by a more personalised style of management oriented towards human motivation and a sense of personal responsibility.

Related to this is the question of productivity of labour. For the most part it is not easy to calculate the product of a public servant's work. The more one moves from relatively routine operations up to more policy oriented ones the more difficult the task becomes; but the difficulties are not such as to prevent *some* progress (Cogan, 1978; NESC 43). Because there is not a constant pressure on costs in large parts of the public service, so requiring continual adaptation, staffing levels may not be readily adjusted to declines in the volume of work, or to the increasing skill and experience of the workers. It is certainly true, and can constantly be seen, that, when there are increases in the volume of work, the system is sluggish in adjusting itself. Often bottlenecks in back-up services are allowed to persist. Elaborate–and in consequence futile–systems of checking and re-drafting tend to grow and grow.

The absence of a continuous, nagging, effective instrument for speedy adaptation–such as a profit and loss account tends to be in private business–tends to permit the growth of certain unrealistic attitudes in public bodies, and therefore the building up of considerable resistance to necessary change and to cost consciousness. This reluctance is often exacerbated by the degree to which certain senior officers tend to be over-whelmed by detailed day to day work, so making them 'too busy' to be worrying about such general problems. This comes from two main causes. The first is the nature of the ministerial system that we operate in this country. The second is defective management training in such senior officers themselves. The point here is that there is, by very reason of the lack of market pressures on most public bodies, a special need for manage-ment training and services that will bring about a ready adaptation to necessary change

In Britain there has been much discussion of the relevance of manage-ment and management theories to public administration. The Fulton Committee accepted the case without, perhaps, fully understanding it, or so argues one of their consultants (Garrett, 1972, e.g. p. 53) who makes an impressive plea for better management practices in civil service. However, that management skills are but a part of the skills of administration is well brought out by Keeling (1972) and·the limited relevance of much of the theory relating to organisation and management emerges from other writers (e.g. Baker, 1972; Browne, 1971; Hill, 1972).

So, when we consider administrative management in the public service we see that it falls into two broad, but closely related, categories. The first category contains the management requirements of innovation, in getting done the new thing. The primary requirement here is for *effective* manage-ment. The second category contains the management requirements of carrying on the doing of things in the most adaptive way possible. The need here is for *efficient* management, that is, the doing of what must be done with the least use of resources. This is where the widespread use of management services can play a useful part.

3. Management Services
The concern with management as a process has had a number of different origins over the past century or so (Urwick and Brech, 1945, 1946, 1948). The first was the engineering approach, which was concerned to simplify

work-methods and procedures so as to increase the output of workers, individually and collectively. This was the so-called 'scientific management' movement, the originator of which was the American, F. W. Taylor. A second source was the work of the Frenchman, Henri Fayol, about the turn of the century, who was concerned to analyse the operations carried out by senior managers. A third source, mainly American, was the attempts by group psychologists and sociologists to analyse the behaviour of working people in groups (e.g. Roethlisberger and Dickson, 1936). A fourth source, also American, began with the work of C. I. Barnard and Herbert Simon who were concerned with the processes of decision-making within organisations. Nowadays these four sources have joined into a common stream which is concerned with the ways by which management can link the desire for ever-increasing productivity with individual and group psyches (e.g. Herzberg, 1966; Argyris, 1957).

The study of management has now become extremely complex (Drucker, 1955). It is not possible to cover here more than a few significant features of it. The study began, and derived most of its nourishment from, the private sector, especially in the United States. However, the public sector was not left fully behind. Fayol had applied his talents to the French Post Office. It was not until the work of the President's Committee on Administrative Management in the United States just before World War II that management ideas made their first major onslaught on governmental procedures. After the war, a major American influence on Europe, and indeed on the rest of the world, was the idea of self-conscious and self-critical management.

The most enthusiastic responses generally to the possibilities of improving management were, initially at least, in the private sector, but the public sector did not wholly lag behind. For example, the British civil service and, following it, the Irish civil service adopted some of the earlier, and simpler, work study ideas under the odd name 'Organisation and Methods', especially so far as clerical procedures were concerned (Mundow, 1953, 1955, 1956). In Ireland, a big part of the initiative for the establishment of the Irish Management Institute in 1952 came from public bodies, notably Aer Lingus and the Electricity Supply Board. However the analysis of the work of public administration at the higher levels received nothing like the same attention. This was an objective of the Institute of Public Administration founded in 1957. The Devlin Report of 1966–9 represented a very ambitious attempt to analyse the work of public administration at the higher levels. The analysis of just why this effort has substantially failed may lead to some badly needed development of the whole study of what might be called 'Administrative Management'.

Nonetheless, some progress has been made on a number of other fronts. We have already seen that there has been a fairly constant attempt to master the problems of public finance and planning, even if success has been less than expectations. In more specific areas, also, there has been some success. For example, the internal structure of the health boards, following the legislation of 1970, was based on proposals of management analysts and this was true also of a major overhaul of the ESB in 1968–9.

The major change has occurred in relation to quantifying the work of public administration, and in establishing what have come to be known as management information systems. Finance is, of course, a major one of these systems and the attempts to improve the methods of analysis of public expenditure, and to calculate relative pay-offs for different kinds of expenditure associated with the programme, planning, budgeting innovation (PPBS), were aimed to try to give decision-makers in the public service the sort of information that their colleagues in the private sector might reasonably expect from their management accounting systems.

There is a saying that science is measurement and a major contribution towards a more scientific administration – or, if one prefers, a more management-oriented one – comes from the attempt to base policymaking and implementation to an increasing extent on facts, their measurement, their analysis, the measurement of change, the measurement of attitudes, and so on. There has been in Ireland a very long tradition of a high class statistical service dating back to the second third of the last century; but now this tradition of the collection and analysis of all the relevant facts is being supplemented by the techniques of survey, of sampling and of the measurement and monitoring of such intangibles as public attitudes. The greater concern with quantities and their analysis has led to an increasing interest in the application of mathematics to the business of administration. This has led on to the development of techniques for the balancing of probabilities, the taking of decisions under conditions of uncertainty, and so on. Allied to this has been the development of accountancy and the methods by which information, basically quantitative information, can be readily and reliably assembled, analysed, and presented in such form that the areas where action must be taken can be readily identified.

The analysis of information has been greatly facilitated by the development of computers, and these, for their effective operation, have demanded the growth of new skills, for the identification and analysis of information systems, and to the rationalisation of the result into the programmes for the, as yet, limited intelligences of the machines. In this area the civil service, both in Britain and Ireland, have been leaders. This is particularly true of our office of the Revenue Commissioners. Nonetheless, the mechanisation of office information systems has yet a long road to travel. Other quantitative skills have arisen from the development of operations research, which is basically concerned with techniques for arranging related outputs, with their different productivities and costs, in optimum patterns.

All of this is on top of the longer standing measurement techniques of organisation and methods (O & M) which is concerned with the measurement and rationalisation of clerical procedures, and with work-study, which is concerned with similar procedures under industrial conditions.

Notwithstanding these techniques we are still left with the, as yet, sadly undeveloped task of achieving methods of measuring the output of what is sometimes called 'unproductive' work, that is, work the output of which is not as easy to measure as that of industrial or agricultural activity. This area of trying to quantify the 'productivity' of the non-industrial and non-agricultural side of the public service has not received the attention it deserves. There have been work-study and O & M studies in specific areas, but no significant or comprehensive overall study on how far the productivity of the public service per head is increasing or decreasing. So, we have the widespread assumption that those who are producing boots, beer or cosmetics are 'productive', because what they produce can be counted, while those who are producing policies for implementation are not 'productive' because it is so difficult to count the results (Cogan, 1977, p. 475–9). It is possible that a number of major misconceptions about the direction of, for example, employment policy, may result from this failure of quantification.

At another level there is the question of 'common services', namely the supply of accommodation, furniture and equipment, and other goods required in day-to-day administration. These functions of 'procurement', as it is called, are carried out in several centres in the civil service – the Office of Public Works, the Stationery Office, the combined purchasing section of the Department of the Environment, the Post Office Stores Branch. Here there is a great deal of activity, but it is doubtful whether the economies achieved in bulk purchase outweigh the diseconomies in the actual service to the ultimate consumer. Much of the practice here rests on very archaic ideas of effective management, ideas perhaps appropriate to the stage of development of the society in the last century, but quite inappropriate to present-day conditions.

For example, the Office of Public Works provides an accommodation service to government departments. This has three distinctive features, all of them disappointing. There is a great deal of cancelled architectural work, because the system is not geared to getting buildings up quickly. There is gross fragmentation of policy in relation to the accommodation needs of even single departments. There is no evidence that the Government has any policy in relation to the provision of buildings as a contribution to the development even of the capital city, much less of the other cities in the country. It was for reasons such as these that the Devlin group recommended (PSORG 14.5.1-2) the dispersal of the procurement side of the Office of Public Works and the concentration of all those procurement functions that would benefit from centralisation in a special side of the proposed Department of the Public Service; but this recommendation has not been acted upon.

At a more immediate level there is much delay and confusion in the supply of normally required goods. In other places there has been a good deal of development in the skills of purchasing; but these have not been much developed in the civil service.

The overall problem is that of the fragmentation of responsibility between those who are expected to carry out services and those – sometimes several other bodies – who are expected to supply the ancillary services. A central idea in the notion of effective management is that responsibility for the carrying out of particular services should be clearly concentrated and accountability for success or failure be clear and unambiguous. Fragmentation of responsibility cuts at the root of this principle, and removes one of the great forces for effective operation. One of the strongest arguments for the setting up of state-sponsored bodies, where responsibility for operation is concentrated in the body itself, comes from this very fact.

One of the most important insights of modern management ideas is that events and operations, in all their complexity, must not be seen in isolation, but can be grouped in patterns or *systems*. The preliminary work for installing a computer requires the analysis of the linkages of information that constitute an information system within the organisation concerned, or as between a number of related organisations. In a structural sense one can think of geographical systems of government, linking traditional local government and new regional organisations and long-standing field services of central bodies into a complex of interrelated systems. This approach leads one to look, for example, at all the operations of government within a single area as possibly related in some way and to identify the relationships and interactions where they exist. A significant contribution to co-ordination comes from the concept of *place*. On another plane one thinks of the economic system or the social system, or the communications system.

This type of approach has led, in other countries to some considerable extent, to the development of analysts whose task it is to apprehend these systems and to identify the points at which they can be improved. This has happened also in a small, but growing, way in Ireland. It is fairly commonplace for good managers now to make use of analysts of this kind, as well as of the research capabilities of universities and specialised research institutes to help them in the disentangling of these complex problems and to suggest possible ways of solving them. A large number of the reports of the National Economic and Social Council illustrate very effectively the use of this approach.

It has long been known that only part of the problem of raising productivity has been to get methods and procedures right. At least as important is the need to consider the human and organisational factors involved (e.g. Brown, 1971). Individuals and groups can by good leadership be motivated to produce very good work. Conversely, an organisation that has been badly managed, or where the human factors have been neglected for some period, can produce very poor work indeed. Sometimes, but not always, poor industrial relations are a symptom, rather than a cause, of poor organisational behaviour, and especially of poor management. Sometimes, and this may well be true of organisations which, for a variety of reasons, do not erupt into open industrial disputes, poor management can result in low morale, apathy, and 'couldn't care less' attitudes. There are severe psychological and sociological problems here, and part of the requirement of a good manager is that he should have a grasp of management theory, of the significance of group dynamics, and of how these can be harnessed to organisational adaptation (Lawrence and Lorsch, 1969). He should also be capable of providing the kind of leadership needed for the special circumstances of his organisation.

There is, quite obviously from the history of a number of large Irish public organisations, very substantial room for improvement in personnel management, not only in so far as it relates to industrial relations, but more fundamentally, in showing skill in relation to the human side of the enterprise at least equal in sophistication to the skills that, in general, one expects to find in relation to the purely engineering or mechanical side of the enterprise. It is important to remember that the management of any large organisation is a two-horse coach, one horse concerned with the mechanical side of the production and the other concerned with the human side. The good manager is the skilful coachman who ensures that both of these run happily in double harness.

This twofold approach is reflected in the organisation of the Department of the Public Service, with one division concerned with personnel questions and a second division concerned with organisation and equipped with a wide range of management service skills (PSAC, 3 (1976) Appendix).

A major factor in the development of management in the private sector has been the pressure of the market place and the competitive economy. This has provided a compelling reason for seeking out newer and better ways of raising productivity and cutting unit costs. A socialist society lacks these pressures to a very great degree. For that reason the development of management techniques in eastern Europe, for example, has, to some considerable extent at least, lagged behind that of the western world. However, there has arisen in Poland an initiative that is relevant to socialist societies but is also relevant to the management of those public affairs in the western world that are also relatively immune to the pressures of the market place. This is the study of praxiology (Kotarbinski, 1965; Kiezun, 1977). This is an attempt to study the correct order of events, good practice as it were, in order to derive rules for effective and efficient behaviour. By the study of what might be called the grammar, the syntax, and the style of good administrative practice certain insights can be obtained that will help to raise future performance. The rules for Latin grammar, syntax and, to some extent, style, were drawn up some centuries after the classical period, and were based primarily on the study of the usages of Julius Caesar. If events are in process, and one can identify the rules that govern these processes—and this is, of course, inherent in the whole Marxist position—then one is in a position to draw up some specifications for good administrative usage. That remarkable manager who practised his skills in Ireland in Cromwellian times, Sir William Petty, used say 'res nolunt male administrare', that is, that it is against the grain of things for them to be badly administered. In the same way, a remarkable American woman writer, Mary Parker Follett, who flourished about fifty years ago, used to talk about discerning the 'law of the situation' and operating according to it (1940 passim). Chester Barnard (1956), with, e.g. his fascinating 'theory of opportunism', develops a similar vein. At a lower level method study is in the tradition. But a great deal of work remains to be done if these ideas are to be developed into operational form.

In the business world, in the world of the stock market, a chairman and board of directors are judged by the return they are able to secure on the capital entrusted to them. Following this line of thought several attempts have been made in Britain—most recently in *Nationalised Industries* (1978)—to determine rates of return on capital employed in the great nationalised industries, and to lay down minimum acceptable rates of such return. Great difficulties have been found, in practice, in achieving any such targets. For example, many of the industries, such as the railways, seem in modern conditions to be inherently uneconomic. Others have been, in effect, nationalised because of economic failure, such as British Leyland. Price rises needed by some industries in order to remain profitable may cause widespread secondary effects in other industries and conflict with anti-inflation policies of government.

In France attempts have been made to carry this notion much further so as to achieve a system of accountable management. Those in charge of large pieces of public business are held periodically accountable for the way they have used the resources, human and material, current and capital, entrusted to their charge over a certain period.

Similar ideas were behind the Devlin proposal that public bodies should be subject to a periodical 'administrative audit' (PSORG 14.6.6; 15.3.7).

The problems of achieving effective management within the public sector are, normally, very great. When organisations are relatively small and it is possible to put them in the charge of administrators of outstanding ability, then the difficulties are not so great. But as organisations grow too large for the effective and comprehensive impact of one man, some sort of systems of management have to be established. Because of the limited impact of market forces in the public sector and because of the very strong impact of political forces, which operate according to different principles, it is difficult to establish systems for efficient management within the public sector (Self, 1977). So, on the whole, progress has not been very heartening. An index of this has been the rapid rise and fall of different management ideas. Every few years a new solution to the problem of public service management presents itself and is hailed with delight. It makes some small contribution, and then disappears into a cloud of disillusion and cynicism. So we have a system of continuous change of management techniques and nostrums not unlike the changes in women's fashions, and as speedily seen to be dowdy and ripe for discard.

Nonetheless, just as the fashion industry is perennially creative, so new management ideas keep emerging. One can hope that, at least gradually, the most useful of these to the public sector will cohere into a reasonably effective system of public, or administrative, management in the interest of greater productivity and more effective performance in public administration.

Chapter 7: Clientele

1. Constitutional and Legal Controls

Whatever about the structures, the staffing, the policies, of the management of public institutions, they exist basically to serve the people, not only The People, but individual people and groups of people, with their own ideas, their rights, their aspirations and their personal quirks. However irksome it may be for public institutions, they have to learn to live with this limitation on their actions and on what they may consider to be the pure rationality of their institutional position. On the other side of the coin, institutions themselves are not immune from irrationality and obsessive behaviour. Their arteries can harden and they can become highly unresponsive. They can become negligent and, sometimes, even corrupt. They can become seized of their own interest – or, worse, the interests of those who staff them – at the expense of the public interest. They can engage in abuse of power or they may fail to use adequately the powers granted to them or not press ahead with tackling important problems within their area of responsibility.

Everywhere, therefore, a balance has to be struck between the need to have administrative institutions with powers and discretion wide enough to serve effectively the public interest against the need to have some forms of control that will limit the possibilities for the abuse, or the ineffective use, of the powers granted to them. The most obvious of these controls is, of course, the political system – the strength of ministers (especially in our system) vis-à-vis the administration; the significance of parliamentary controls by way of questions, motions, raising issues on votes of supply and legislation; and the extraordinary volume of representations transmitted by members of the Oireachtas to ministers. There are also, of course, the various financial and administrative controls on the behaviour of public institutions, including particularly, so far as Ireland is concerned, the very high standard of professional and ethical responsibility and commitment of public servants themselves. Nonetheless, as the size and pervasiveness of government grow there is, to an increasing extent in every country, an uneasiness that the great and extensive powers now being enjoyed by public bodies are open to opportunities for corresponding abuses. To an increasing extent the old recourse to parliament as a means of remedying grievances is felt to be inadequate. This comes, at least in part, from the increasing predominance of the executive, that is of the government, over parliament itself, and of the necessarily close working relationship between the government and the administration. So, there is an increasing tendency to look elsewhere for the redress of grievance.

Redress has now become a significant feature of Irish public administration. In particular, citizens are showing a readiness to invoke the help of the courts to establish their rights under existing law and to clarify to an increasing extent their inherent rights, especially those implicit in the Constitution. Apart from this there has been the establishment of other tribunals – for social welfare rights, redundancy rights, dismissal rights, etc. – on an ad hoc basis. This movement towards administrative tribunals is perhaps less developed in Ireland than in a number of other countries and certainly has not reached the level of sophistication achieved in France and other countries that have adopted the full conseil d'état system for the general redress of grievances. In addition, there has been some interest in the largely peripheral institution of the ombudsman for the redress of grievances that fall outside the existing systems of review. The important point is that, to an ever increasing extent, the administration is being surrounded by formal systems of appeal and review that have been deliberately taken out of the political and parliamentary system.

There are three main issues here. The first is what might be referred to as the inherent powers of the State, and their limitations. The second relates to the specific legal powers conferred on individual institutions, and their limitations. The third relates to the specific application of those powers to particular cases, and the reasonableness of the discretion so exercised. For now, we shall be dealing with the first two of these.

It is the normal practice for a constitution to establish, or provide a charter for, the major institutions of the State and to lay down limitations on the discretion of these institutions. It is usual in most modern societies to have these matters written down in a document which may be amended from time to time and, occasionally, as conditions change, replaced by a new document. In some countries these documents are changed fairly regularly, and there is a body of opinion in Ireland that this should be the position here also. In other countries, most notably in the example of the Federal Constitution of the United States, these documents have shown remarkable durability. Then there is the special position of the United Kingdom, where there is no single document that could be described as 'The Constitution'. There, exceptionally, the Constitution consists of a number of documents plus a very large number of conventions that have great and durable force. However, it would be mistaken to draw too sharp a distinction between the United Kingdom and other countries. For example, in Ireland our written Constitution is supplemented, as we shall see, by a number of other documents and conventions, that, between them all, make up the whole constitutional scene.

We are all conscious that, whatever the limitations in practice, the modern world is made up of a large number of sovereign states. But, *within the state*, where does sovereignty reside? In the early days of kings the sovereign, like everyone else, was subject to a virtually unchanging law; but in the days of the divine right of kings (and, still, in the government of the Roman Catholic church) sovereignty was held to reside in the person of the ruler, or monarch, who was nonetheless expected to adhere to the law. .Eventually sovereignty was wrested from the monarch by parliament, which, of course, could change the law, and by the executive that, to a greater or lesser extent, was responsible to parliament, so giving rise to modern absolutism (de Jouvenel, 1957, pp. 89–90). Sovereignty, and therefore prerogative antecedent to law, are thus held to reside in an entity called 'The State' and to be exercisable through its various organs. There was thus a power 'of the State' that could be called upon if need be to override the law and the conventions. This is still, except insofar as legislation of the European Community is concerned, the formal position in relation to the British Parliament which, in law-making, is claimed to be sovereign in this sense[1] but there are also vestiges of it exercised by the executive under the guise of 'royal prerogative'. In other countries, of the Roman law tradition, there exists, to a varying extent, the notion of raison d'état, a power inherent in government that, on occasion, may transcend formal law (Chapman, 1959, Ch. 1). There is also a grimmer tradition, where the forces of the state act, or are encouraged to act, as if there were no legal restraint on them.[2]

The situation in Ireland is quite different. Here sovereignty is held to be possessed only by the people of Ireland, again subject to the obligations of membership of the European Community. With this exception, sovereignty may be exercised only in accordance with the powers granted by the people through the Constitution to the various organs of the state.

[1]Thus Dicey (1961) pp. 39–40: 'The principle of Parliamentary sovereignty means neither more nor less than this, namely, that Parliament thus defined [Queen, Lords and Commons] has, under the English Constitution, the right to make or unmake any law whatsoever; and, further, that no person or body is recognized by the law of England to override or set aside the legislation of Parliament'.

[2]The following is an extract (*Observer*, 30.4.1978) from the cross-examination of the senior South African police officer at the inquest of Stephen Biko, who died while in police custody: 'Mr Kentridge (for the Biko family): 'Where do you get your authority from? Show me a piece of paper that gives you the right to keep a man in chains—or are you people above the law?' Colonel Goosen (head of the Eastern Cape Security Police): 'We have full authority. It is left to my sound discretion.' Mr Kentridge: 'Under what statutory authority?' Colonel Goosen: 'We don't work under statutory authority'.

There is, except possibly in relation to the plea of privilege, no surviving vestige of sovereignty in parliament or prerogative in government. There has been established in real form a *res publica*. These are the implications of a remarkable decision of the Supreme Court in the case of Byrne versus Ireland—which arose out of a case where a citizen claimed damages against the Post Office for leaving a hole in the road! The point of all this is that public bodies can exercise no powers except what they derive from the law and the Constitution and they can only exercise them within those limitations (Beth, 1967, pp. 20–22; Byrne, 1972; O'Sullivan, 1978, Ch. 2).

Under the Constitution three broad classes of bodies have been established, the legislative bodies, the judicial bodies and the executive bodies.

However, there are other institutions of the state that have not been provided for in the Constitution specifically. For example, the Ministers and Secretaries Act, 1924, provides (s.1) for the legal constitution and spheres of responsibility of government departments. Because it also provides (s.2) that the acts of the Department must, to be legal, be the acts of the minister (the concept of the 'corporation sole')—an interpretation upheld by the High Court (in the case *Minister for Local Government* v. *Ennis Mental Hospital*, [1939] I.R. 258) and because of the independent status of ministers in relation to one another provided for under those Acts, they determine the whole temper and modes of operation of our civil service. In other countries provision is made in the Constitution for local government bodies, but not in this country. There are also various non-statutory bodies of great constitutional significance—for example, political parties and major interest groups.

There are various conventions about the use of power. A simple example is the almost invariable practice of ministers in answering parliamentary questions, although there is no formal obligation on them to do so.

Of great interest are the relationships of the various organs established under the Constitution. For example, the courts, because of their function to determine whether legislation is in whole or in part repugnant to the Constitution, can exercise certain powers of restraint over the legislature (and through it the administration)that would not apply in Britain (Kelly, 1967). The most notable example here is the famous Sinn Féin Funds case ([1950] I.R. 67) where the courts ruled that the Oireachtas was not competent to pass legislation that prevented the citizen from having access to the courts. In a less striking way the courts can act as a stimulus to the legislature. A current case here is the McGee decision ([1974] I.R. 284) that part of the law restricting the import of contraceptives was unconstitutional, so throwing the situation under that legislation into such confusion that new legislation became necessary.

The situation of the relationship between the legislature and the executive is, in many ways, less clear-cut. In our practice the executive, and ministers individually, exercise extraordinary dominance over the legislature, in contrast – to take the extreme case – with the relationship between the executive and the legislature in the United States. One does not hear in this country, as one does in Britain that parliament is 'the supreme safeguard of liberty'. Certainly, so far as the short-term is concerned, neither in this country nor in Britain, as recent events have shown, could this be held to be true. However, in the middle and long-term the situation tends to be different. In the last analysis constitutional rights and legal and international commitments to, for example, civil liberties, depend on formal acts of the legislature. Nonetheless, as the modern development of civil rights in the United States has shown, the executive may need a very severe prod indeed from the judiciary before it will act and before it is likely to get support from the legislature.

Thirdly, there is the relationship of the executive with the judiciary. On the side of the system of public administration this is an uneasy one, largely because officials often lack comprehension of the issues. The task of the judiciary is to maintain the rule of law, and to uphold and clarify the citizen's constitutional rights. It is also to ensure that public bodies go about their business with full regard to the concept of 'natural justice' and the procedural implications of this. More particularly, it is its task to clarify the meaning of the law where there is a conflict between the citizen and the administration and to review how this conflict has been conducted under the law. The main part of this duty falls on the High Court and, for these purposes, it possesses an armoury of what are called 'prerogative' and declaratory orders.

In effect these serve to define the limitations in which the administration may act. The first of these limitations is, of course, that public bodies derive their authority from law, and from nowhere else. This law may be a statute or some form of statutory instrument made under statute. The statute or the instrument must be of course in conformity with the principles of the Constitution. Procedures that are established under the statute must be followed in the instrument and must be conformed to in practice. Policies that are followed, or individual actions taken, no matter how admirable in themselves, will be upset by the courts if they do not adhere to these conditions.

In Ireland, following the British tradition, rules for day-to-day operation of public bodies tend not to be formalised in specific regulations, as is the general European practice. But, whatever the administrative tradition may be, actions under the regulations, rules and procedures must be authorised by the law, must not go beyond what it provides, must not go against its provisions, must adhere to any procedures laid down by it, and must be in accordance with the general principles of natural justice.

There are two main rules of natural justice (see PSORG pp. 456–7). One is that the person or body deciding an issue must be unbiased, that is, ought not to be judge in his or its own cause.

The second rule is known as the audi alteram partem rule. This is that each party must know the case against it and be given an opportunity to reply. (It was for this reason that the Supreme Court annulled in 1979 the purported dismissal of Garda Commissioner Garvey). The overriding duty on the administration is to treat the citizen fairly, and all citizens, in comparable situations, alike. This whole area is being slowly opened by the Irish courts. They are increasingly reluctant to accept the attempts by the administration to preserve secrecy on the grounds of ministerial privilege. So the citizen is being put, to an increasing extent, in a position to have access to all the papers that relate to his case, to have made clear the procedures that govern the decision taken in relation to him, and the considerations that were taken into account in the use of discretion (Murphy, 1972; Geraghty, 1976; O'Sullivan, 1978). There are some major issues here, in relation to 'Open Government' that we shall discuss later. The main thing is that there is a natural tension between the desire of administrative bodies to preserve secrecy and the practice of the courts to thrash out issues in the open, so far as this is humanly possible.

The advances in constitutional law and the evolving role of the High Court as a supervisor of administrative acts, have, of course, very considerable implications for the day-to-day conduct of administration. Perhaps the first implication is that administrators should understand the evolving relationships between the administration and the courts, that they should not be too defensive about these, but should attempt to realise that they are part of the system of achieving overall consensus, less frequent, more intimidating and expensive, but nonetheless as real as the attempt to achieve, for example, interdepartmental consensus.

The second implication is that administrators should have a clear grasp of the concept of natural rights, and of how these are being increasingly defined by the courts, and of the requirements of natural justice in their procedures. These latter call for such qualities as fairness (which is overwhelmingly the norm in practice), clarity, (which is, in the Irish system, rather unusual), and openness. This latter is contrary to nearly all bureaucratic traditions but the extent to which it is being increasingly achieved in many countries, without the breakdown of the whole administration, suggests that it is a value that administration in Ireland will find increasingly difficult to resist.

Perhaps because so few lawyers are employed in Irish government – this is in extreme contrast to the practice in continental countries – the administration is slow to use the courts in an active or creative way for the purposes of clarifying the implications of important pieces of legislation. In consequence, the administration nearly always appears on the defensive and often it is being defensive on the weakest issues. But there is a large resource of interpretation and aid available to the administration that, in important cases, might more actively be availed of.

Finally, public bodies are sometimes defeated in the courts because of a *defect* in the legislation which, if it is allowed to continue, will impede important work. There is no reason why defects of this kind should not be speedily remedied by amending legislation, where there is no question of conflict with constitutional and other major rights.

It is usual following Montesquieu to talk of the *division* of powers in our Constitution. It would be more meaningful to talk about the *balance* of powers between legislature, judiciary, and executive. It is inevitable that there should be tensions between all three of these, but it is important that these should be creative tensions. In the past two decades the leadership in adopting a creative role in relation to these tensions has been taken by the judiciary. There is every reason why the other two parties should seek to maintain the balance by an equivalent degree of creativity. This would require, for administrative bodies, to change over from the defensive and the negative and to accept the legal system as a means of making a positive approach to the development of a freer, more open, more consensual society.

2. Administrative Justice and Review
Given the size and pervasiveness of modern government, it is inevitable that large numbers of citizens should, from time to time, feel aggrieved about the decisions, or non-decisions, of official bodies.

Some indication of the scale of this, and the willingness of Irish citizens to take *some* action about it, comes from the remarkable size of what are known as 'representations' to members of the Oireachtas. This, so far as can be judged, is remarkably high per head of the population as compared with most other democracies. A good part of the public standing of Irish public representatives comes from their success in acting as 'brokers' between their constituents and public bodies. A survey taken in 1974 of the representations received by deputies and senators suggested that about 140,000 representations were received by them in that year (Murray, 1975). Of course, the word 'representation' covers a variety of problems, not all of which may relate to the public service. Nonetheless, the inference is that the majority of them did relate to public service problems, problems that individuals felt would not have been dealt with as favourably for them, or with sufficient speed, had they taken them up themselves with the appropriate bodies.

Where tribunals exist for the redress of grievances, they tend to have a substantial volume of business. For example, in 1978, according to the Minister (Dáil, 21 February, 1979), in the Department of Social Welfare, over 18,000 appeals were decided. That many of these were well founded is shown by the fact that 36 per cent of them were upheld. In 1975 the Department of Local Government (which then dealt with planning appeals) received 3,709 (IPA 1976, p. 4). In 1973 the Income Tax Appeals Commissioners received 18,041 appeals, the Commissioner for Valuation received 9,664 rating appeals, and the Redundancy Appeals Tribunal received 1,035 appeals. These are, of course, the busiest of the tribunals. Several others, of the eighty or so of these tribunals received little or no appeals (Administrative Justice, 1977, p. 12). On the other hand, there are large areas of the public service for which no appellate tribunals exist, which, if they did exist, might also evoke a considerable number of appeals.

All in all, enough information exists to suggest how important a part of the system of public administration is the redress of grievances of one kind or another. These grievances tend to fall into two broad categories, the grievances of individuals or small groups, and the grievances of large groups.

Individual grievances arise because a decision, or non-decision, of a public body is not acceptable to an individual or a small group. This may come about because the individual has failed to be given an allocation of some sort – a licence is a typical example – to which he feels he should have a right. It may arise by a decision to take away from him something that he has – a piece of land, an amenity, part of his income. It may arise because the decision has been unduly delayed, or has been dealt with negligently. It may arise because of a conflict of interpretation of a statute or a regulation. It may arise about a complaint about the procedure followed in dealing with the original application.

In general, one can talk of grievances arising because of a complaint that the official body has operated in excess of its powers, in abuse of its powers, or has unreasonably used the discretion given by those powers.

Collective grievances arise most particularly in the area of industrial relations, about pay, conditions and duties. It is a feature of most industrial relations systems, nowadays, to have a grievance procedure built-in to the conditions of work and, where this breaks down, to have some national or third-party system for trying to avoid a breakdown in relations. There has grown up, in consequence, a very considerable network of systems for dealing with those problems which concern pay, conditions of work, duties and so on. Most large organisations now have, in agreement with the appropriate trade unions, a disputes procedure. In the public service there have been established elaborate systems for negotiation, conciliation and, as a last resort, arbitration. Similarly, so far as the private sector is concerned, apart from procedures that may exist within the firm, there is a substantial conciliation service under the Labour Court. Where this fails, there is provision for a hearing by the court and recommendation, and, where this is not acceptable, both sides can agree to go for arbitration by the court. A great volume of disputes gets settled peacefully by such means.

Nonetheless, it is clear that the industrial relations climate in this country is not a wholly happy one. There is general agreement on the need to improve the procedures for resolving disputes, and perhaps to develop some sort of a jurisprudence on industrial relations. There seems to be a painful struggle between the ready recourse to power as a means of solving disputes and the desire of many to reduce the need for this by the evolution of effective procedures and contract. But to follow this further would bring us too far from the systems of redress special to the study of public administration as distinct from those of labour relations generally.

If one approaches the study of public administration from the standpoint of the redress of individual grievances, one can see that there are three levels of operation. The first of these is the level of *decision*. The second is the level of *appeal*. The third is the level of *review*. A well developed system, conscious of the importance of moderating the sharp edge of grievance, and conscious of the need to maintain assent and consensus as the conditions for successful administrative operation, will have clear-cut and smoothly operating procedures at each of these levels, and for linking one level with the next. Finally, where a grievance has been established, it will have an effective system of *remedy* or, where that is not technically possible, of *compensation*.

A considerable part of the difficulties that arise in relation to grievances experienced by individual citizens comes from failure to understand what is on foot, distrust of the motives of the official body, and a sense of powerlessness and fear when the individual matches himself against the great powers possessed by the body. A big part of the remedy here is to clarify and explain what is on foot, and the procedures that exist for taking care of the rights of individuals.

A number of issues arise at the first level, that of *decision*.

The first need is to clarify to the client, as he is at this stage, the scope of the proposed decision – that is, how far it effects him, the period of time involved, the procedure that will be followed in relation to it, the information that may be required of the client. This needs to be set out in clear, plain (if careful) language that the client can understand. Secondly, when a decision seems likely to go against him he should, if possible, be given the chance to give his answer to any snag that is seen in his case and that is likely to make him fail. Thirdly, when a decision has been taken it is necessary to set out, equally clearly, the reasons why it has been taken. Fourthly, if the citizen is likely to be aggrieved by the decision, the method by which he can appeal the decision, if there is such a method, should be explained to him. Apart from its inherent merit there is a considerable psychological benefit to the individual in being made aware of the fact that his case has been dealt with strictly in accordance with procedures that are rational and fair. This removes anxiety and distrust.

All of this is made more difficult because of the variety of ways by which decisions are taken within public bodies, and the different legal fictions that govern such decisions. As we have seen, typically in a government department decisions are legally reserved to the minister himself but, in practice, they are taken at various levels within the organisation. Similarly, in some civil service organisations they are taken by the 'Commissioners' but, in fact, there may be extensive authorisation by the commissioners to take decisions in their name – as do inspectors of taxes and certain officers of the Land Commission. One may get a decision from, say, the Dublin Corporation intimating that the 'Corporation' has decided. Who is the 'Corporation' here? The City Manager? One of the assistant city managers, a delegated officer, or the City Council itself? A decision by the 'Board' from the Electricity Supply Board may leave one just as baffled as to who exactly took the decision. There is great need to clarify, and to standardise as far as possible, the decision-making levels within public organisations, much as inspectors of taxes are clearly seen to be the decision-makers in relation to income tax, or deciding officers of the Department of Social Welfare in relation to social welfare benefits administered by that department.

The second major reform at the deciding level is to ensure that every decision that issues is accompanied by the reasons why it was taken. This is contrary to a long standing tradition in the public service of 'playing it close to the chest', not giving anything away so that, if one possible ground for the decision is successfully challenged, one can always substitute another in its place.

Apart from this there is need for each agency to establish criteria by which it would operate its administrative functions. These criteria should be made known to the public by each agency. If some such general approach as this to the question of decision-making was taken – the definition of the level at which decisions are taken and its generalisation; the requirement of giving reasons for the decision actually taken; and the publication of criteria of operation – it would substantially raise the level of administration. Once some such general rules as these were laid down, failure by any agency to comply with them would constitute a prima facie case of maladministration.

It must not be assumed that, even without the safeguards that have been set out above, decision-making in public organisations is an arbitrary or capricious affair.

First of all, a great part of the tasks committed to such bodies are governed by statute, and where a statute has laid down what may be done, the conditions under which it may be done, and so on, the degree of discretion left to the decision-maker may be relatively small.

Secondly, even though the statute may leave a reasonably wide area of discretion, there are other inhibiting factors, notably administrative ones themselves. The most important of these is, of course, the financial one. It may be necessary to keep a scheme within very tight limits because the financial resources for a more generous approach may not be available. It may be necessary to keep the scheme within certain tight categories because once a breach has been made in those, the next category may be so large that to admit it would swamp the whole scheme and the resources that can be made available to it, financial, human, administrative. Again, it may be necessary to keep the scheme relatively tight so that whatever resources are available may be directed to the most needy objects or the most pressing problems. To broaden the scope may mean that the resources may have to be spread more thinly and, therefore, that those who need those resources most may get less than they might otherwise receive.

Thirdly, there are the ethical considerations that restrict administrative discretion. The most important of these here, in this context, is that of equality of treatment to those in like cases. This means that, given that the scheme has to be confined to a certain category, no individual exceptions to those outside the category should be made.

These constraints of statute, resources, and ethics much limit the scope of decision-making in this context.

At the next level are the general problems that arise in relation to *appeals* against unacceptable decisions.

Very typical of the Irish system of administration has been the ad hoc and specific development of facilities for formally appealing against the sort of decisions we are considering. The ad hoc nature of this development has meant that, on the one hand, there are a very large number of appellate tribunals in the public service and, on the other, it is difficult to discern any logic that will determine why one area will have an appellate tribunal, and another will not. For example, two of the main services conducted by the Revenue Commissioners are income tax collection and custom services. There is an appellate tribunal—the special commissioners of income tax—on the taxes side. But there is nothing of the sort on the customs side. Apart from this, there is a great variety of *forms* of appellate bodies and, again, it is hard to determine what logic there is for the adoption of one kind of body rather than another (Grogan, 1961).

The simplest form of appeal procedure is to the appropriate minister. This appeal can be one or other of two kinds—an appeal to the minister against himself, and an appeal to him to alter a decision of somebody for whose action he has some general responsibility.

The first of these derives from what is, more or less, the fiction of the 'corporation sole'. The implication is that the minister took the decision that is complained of and that he is being asked, out of the goodness—or softness—of his heart to alter it. This bears all the mark of old-fashioned ideas of prerogative. It has the implication that a minister taking a decision either himself, or within his department, was so casual about taking the first decision that he can fairly readily reverse it when he has been approached, in the right spirit, to do so.

This is an undesirable situation for a number of reasons. First, as we have seen, an implication of prerogative is now totally out of date under our republican Constitution. Secondly, it is illogical to expect a minister, and the officers working on the case, to be effective in reviewing their own decisions. Thirdly, it gives the impression that appeals are decided on grounds of 'politics', or on the basis of some sort of personal influence. Finally, as a consequence of this, the impartiality of the minister and his department in trying to achieve a certain administrative end becomes highly suspect—especially to those who lose their appeals. The consequence of such suspicion, no matter how ill-founded, can be that resistance to such an administrative end becomes, over time, exacerbated, so undermining the *administrative* case for such an appellate system.

The second case is where a minister is appealed to to alter the decisions of another body. The most striking example here is the appellate functions of the Minister for Local Government, (now for the Environment), in relation to decisions of local authorities. There is more logic to this arrangement, but the arguments about 'politics', influence, etc. apply just as strongly. It was for reasons of this sort that the then Minister for Local Government decided to shed his powers in relation to planning appeals, and get established a statutory tribunal, An Bord Pleanála, under the Local Government (Planning and Development) Act, 1976.

Apart from these difficulties, there is a major complication in relation to the conflict of roles. A Minister for the Environment, for example, may be very concerned to get houses built. If somebody appeals against the proposal of a local authority to acquire his land compulsorily, he may have difficulty in accepting the impartiality of the minister in deciding on that appeal if the minister is already publicly on record urging the local authority to get more land! If the minister is scrupulous on this front, then he is less effective as a developmental minister. If he is not so scrupulous, he undermines his reputation for impartiality in considering appeals. Either way, there is less effective administration.

To get away from these difficulties, there has been an ad hoc growth of various kinds of tribunals for adjudicating on appeals. The first of these remedies has been, probably, that of setting up commissioners, outside the direct control of ministers, to look after certain services. Much the same arguments apply against commissioners being judges in their own causes as apply against ministers. There is the added argument that, while the commissioners may not be tarred with the 'political' brush, they may suffer from the bureaucratic tendency to maintain untenable positions, that ministers, with their greater political sensitivity, are free of. For example, one of the major recipients of appeals has been the Commissioner for Valuation. These appeals are against decisions taken by his own officers, so he seems to be deciding in his own cause. Moreover, we know that the whole modern basis for determining the valuation of domestic property, at least, is illegal and has been so for very many years (McElligott, 1955). However, the Commissioner's decisions are, of course, subject to further appeal to the circuit court.

A second expedient has been to define a group of deciding officers within a number of government offices – the Land Commission, the Taxes side of the Revenue Commissioners, and in the Department of Social Welfare. Appeals from the decisions of these deciding officers can be taken to an appellate body associated with the organisation, but independent of it – in the first case, to the special commissioners of income tax, in the second case to certain organs of the Land Commission, and in the third to specially designated appeals officers within the Department of Social Welfare.

Finally there have been set up in recent years special external tribunals, especially associated with the Department of Labour, which tend to be staffed from outside the public service and, indeed, to deal mainly with problems arising outside it, for example, the Employment Appeals Tribunal which deals with appeals under Redundancy Payments Act, 1967, and under the Unfair Dismissals Act, 1977. A number of organisational problems arise in relation to these various expedients.

The first is, of course, not only to ensure that the bodies are independent in deciding on their appeals, but are seen to be so. A number of them can be faulted on this ground. So far as the social welfare appeals officers are concerned, the Supreme Court spelled out for them the way they must maintain their independence, in the case of McLoughlin *v.* the Minister for Social Welfare.

Secondly, there is a fairly considerable problem about the staffing of these various bodies to ensure that those who decide the appeals have the knowledge, the skill and the training to deal with problems at a uniformly high level. Experience in Britain of the need to supervise the vast number of tribunals by the Council on Tribunals has shown this problem with some clarity (Street, 1968, p. 62; Herman, 1972).

Thirdly, there is the problem of the form that the tribunals should take – whether a single officer, as in Social Welfare, or an officer supported by those with specialised skills in more complex affairs, or a lawyer chairman supported by a number of persons with specialised skills, as in An Bord Pleanála; or otherwise. Some degree of flexibility and pragmatism – in adjusting the form of the appellate tribunal to the nature of the circumstances – seems to be well justified.

The big problem area, however, relates to those decisions taken in the public service from which there is no opportunity for a formal appeal. This is most notable in relation to the state-sponsored bodies as a class. This is all the more surprising in that, as we have seen, structures are now growing up, especially in relation to the Department of Labour, that provide appellate tribunals for persons in the private sector who have grievances against their employers and, in addition, there have been growing up under the Department of Industry, Commerce and Energy, various structures to assist consumers against suppliers mainly in the private sector. The ad hoc nature of Irish administrative appellate bodies is parallelled in other countries, notably the United Kingdom and to a greater or less extent in such countries as Finland, Sweden, the German Federal Republic and Portugal.

In other countries institutions and procedures are standardised under an Administrative Procedure Act. Examples are the United States (which has had one since 1946), Spain, Norway, Austria, and some east European countries.

The best developed system is where administrative legality is placed in the care of a judicial body, notably a *conseil d'état*, which, so far as is relevant to the present discussion, is a distinct system of administrative courts, independent of the ordinary courts. France and Belgium are notable examples (Brown and Garner, 1973).

Both the administrative procedure act arrangement and the *conseil d'état* represent very considerable degrees of sophistication, almost certainly too advanced for adoption in Ireland at the present stage of development. Given, however, the growth and the pervasiveness of government activity, the rising interest in human rights, the normal evolution of providing means for remedying grievances, it is likely that there will be fairly considerable development on this front in the coming years, especially to make more *comprehensive* the appellate system.

There are three principal forms of *review* of appellate tribunals.

The first form of review is that by the Courts. There has been a tendency in Irish legislation for some recent decades to try to keep the courts out of the business of reviewing decisions of administrative tribunals, whether these be ministers or otherwise. An early formula was that a decision of a tribunal was final. Later, the formula became that a decision of a tribunal on a point of fact was final, but an appeal to the courts on a point of law might be made. The courts, however, were in general, not prepared to accept the first formula, nor to an unlimited extent the distinction between fact and law, so far as that meant a limitation of their general right of review of the procedures by which the administration goes about its work (Beth, pp. 24–5). Nonetheless, the courts are equally reluctant to get involved in the large volume of detailed work discharged by these tribunals. Hence, the courts in their review tend to content themselves with scrutinising the procedures followed, to satisfy themselves that these are in accordance with the general principles of law and natural justice, and, of course, that the decisions have been given in accordance with the relevant statutory powers.

There has been some discussion in this country as to whether the High Court might not have an administrative division that would concern itself with these problems (Barrington, 1973); but the volume of work or the nature of the problems that have emerged so far has not called for such a development. On the whole the Ó Dálaigh committee concluded that the High Court ought to confine itself to a review of the law governing the decision given on appeal, and to a general overview aimed at the provision of remedies for the aggrieved citizen who sought a review of the way his grievance was dealt with. It proposed that there should be a means by which, at no cost to the citizen, an approach could be made to the High Court for clarification of the legal situation concerning the matter in dispute where this clarification seemed to be called for. It also proposed that there ought to be legislation to provide a simple and direct process of review by the court, to remove needless uncertainty about access in administrative cases, and about the variety of possible remedies (PSORG, pp. 452–3).

A second form of review is the general overview of the operations of the tribunals themselves, such as the Standing Committee on Tribunals in the United Kingdom. In that country, especially in relation to social benefits, there is a great number of such tribunals, usually consisting of three part-time members. There have been considerable problems in ensuring that these tribunals all operate at a uniformly high level (e.g. Street, 1968).

This problem was tackled, for this country, in the Ó Dálaigh report already referred to. The proposal there was that a Commissioner for Administrative Justice should be appointed whose task would be to look at the problems of administrative justice as a whole, where new tribunals were needed, what legislation was required, what sort of staffing they should have, and what kind of training would be necessary (PSORG, pp. 453–4). This was essentially an *administrative* solution to one of the major problems of modern government, indeed to the problems of a greatly underdeveloped part of the Irish administrative system.

Another method of review is parliamentary review. In the last analysis, of course, this is a sine qua non. But, generally speaking, parliament neither in this country nor in Britain is equipped for the general overview of the large volume of activity that requires, not only review, but action on the results of the review. A number of countries have now adopted the Scandinavian institution of a parliamentary officer who will review grievances that seem to have fallen through the net of the other remedies. In a number of countries, and this seems to be particularly true of Scandinavia, this net has a very small mesh so that not much falls through (Bexelius, 1961; Nielsen, 1973, p. 355). In other countries, where the mesh is very much wider, the volume of complaints dealt with by the Parliamentary Commissioner, or Ombudsman, is relatively minute (Mitchell, 1965). As events have worked out he now exists largely for cosmetic reasons.

The Oireachtas committee referred to above recommended an Ombudsman for Ireland. This would be useful, so far as it goes; but it goes a very short distance indeed. The committee do not even recommend a parliamentary committee to overview the whole question of administrative justice. They brush aside the question of *systems* for the remedying of grievances in the public service as a whole. They seem not to have grasped the significance of having an administrative focus of some sort, somewhere, concerned to bring practice and procedures in Ireland up to those of most other democracies, at least.

There seem to be few problems about remedy once the existence of a genuine grievance has been established.

Problems of compensation arise, for example, where land has been compulsorily acquired, or permission to develop land, in certain circumstances, refused. Old procedures for assessing compensation, that stretch back to the Railways Acts of the last century, seem to work with reasonable satisfaction.

These are all problems of what is now called 'access', the access of the citizen to rights, to justice, to benefits, to information in his relations with the administration. The trouble is that this problem of access—notwithstanding the objectives of many schemes—grows more acute the lower one is placed in the scale of affluence. Yet, it is precisely there that the need for access is often greatest.

This is a problem often obscured in the public mind because of the clamour—especially in times of depression—surrounding its opposite, the abuse by beneficiaries of, e.g. social welfare, benefits to which they may no longer be entitled. There is the problem, at the bottom of the wage scale, of social welfare benefits approximating to the wage on offer and so acting as a disincentive to work. Thirdly, there is the issue of 'Farmers' dole' which is a small farmers' income supplement system that, unfortunately, operates through a scheme for supporting those suffering from *unemployment*. Much of this indignation is, of course, highly selective—that the poor should benefit from ill-devised welfare schemes is regarded as much worse than that the well-off should evade ill-devised taxation schemes.

But behind the problem of abuse of welfare schemes is the problem of the large number of poor people who do not draw the benefits to which they are entitled. So far as Ireland is concerned the size of this problem has not been measured (NESC 38, Ch. 5): but in other countries where it has been studied the problem of 'take up', as it is called, has been found to be significant. More serious, perhaps, is the failure of policy makers to discern the emergence of major social problems and to devise effective policies for them (e.g. NESC 41, Ch. 2). These are parts of a much more extensive problem, that 'universal' benefits—e.g. free schooling—are availed of to the full by the relatively well-off but tend to be used—indeed may be relevant—to a decreasing extent as one moves down the scale of affluence. So, some members of the community are condemned to a self-perpetuating cycle of poverty and fail to gain access to many of the basic benefits of society.

When we think, therefore, of natural rights and natural justice we must also have in mind means by which the minimum rights of the most deprived can be identified and safeguarded.

Whether we consider disputes by individuals with the administration, or problems of the administration in relation to collective disputes within the society–and a lot of the worst of these disputes are, in fact, in the public sector–we are brought up once more against the problems of consensus within society and the means for the orderly resolution of such problems as seem to undermine that consensus. On the whole, given the special problems of the country, Irish public administration is not well developed in this area. If the consensus is to be maintained, and if possible widened–that is the mark of the development of the society–the importance of these issues needs wider recognition and the problems they pose need to be seriously and systematically tackled.

3. 'Open Government' and Representative Systems

The attitude of the people is a major dimension of government in a democratic society. If they are distrustful of government they can make the discharge of business extremely difficult by supporting dissidents, and by generally creating a climate of criticism that at best will upset smooth administration, and at worst will lead to a breakdown of order. In the last analysis, when election day comes around, they may sack the government. They do this, of course, by first sacking a crucial number of those politicians who support the government.

The state of public opinion is, therefore, a constant preoccupation of politicians. Less urgently, but in the long run just as significantly, the state of public opinion is an important feature of day-to-day administration. Both politicians and administrators may get rough treatment in the media, and both may see, through their correspondence, and from the activities of groups and meetings, that they have, at the least, a problem of public relations on their hands. The objective of government is the common good and it is a mark of failure in politicians and administrators if their well-meant efforts to contribute to this should lead them into avoidable controversy, much less suspicion and contempt.

It is a major interest, therefore, of politicians who wish to be re-elected to power, and of administrators who wish to achieve certain objectives in the public interest, that they have, at least, the tacit support of the public, and that there be a suspension of distrust and suspicion in relation to their motives and their actions.[1] The best way of allaying suspicion and of

[1] See Whitaker (1977), especially at p. 294. See also Raven, Whelan, Pfretzschner, Borack (1976). Some unpublished, and tentative, studies suggest that, in relation to administrators, this distrust runs very deep indeed. The extraordinary degree of recourse in this country to public representatives, and the extent of their 'clinics', suggests that, even in relation to statutory entitlements, people believe that they will not be treated fairly by public officials. There seems to be a widespread (but wholly unfounded) belief that most things can be 'fixed' if only one can get word in the right ear.

creating a suspension of distrust is to have a system for ensuring that the public are fully informed of the issues that are at stake and of the reasons for the proposed action.

Communication cannot, of course, be just a one-way exercise. There has to be a two-way communication before there can be a real meeting of minds. There can be failures on both fronts here. On the official front there may be failure to communicate clearly what is proposed and the issues that arise in relation to it. There may also be a failure to listen to the, perhaps uninstructed, reactions of the public. But the public itself may not make its reactions clear or give any real guidance as to what modifications it might be prepared to accept in a proposed operation. This makes the problem of communication from the official side all the more difficult, but it also impresses the need for the establishment of smoothly running channels of communication, and the building up of mutual confidence and tolerance. Because the initiative for most actions rests with the official side, and it is concerned to get things to happen, the primary obligation for establishing a good system of communications rests there.

One can put this in a more positive way. It was a notable feature of the last war that the degree of mobilisation of resources in the United Kingdom was greater than that in Hitler's Germany.[1] One could say that the populace were more wholeheartedly on the side of the war leaders in Britain than they were in Germany. One could also say that the system of war-making was more efficient there. A number of reasons were given for this paradoxical situation. One of them was the general democratic argument that in a democracy the people are prepared, once they have committed themselves, to defend themselves and their system à outrance. This is the famous spirit of Valmy. On the one hand, the German government, because it lacked an efficient and sensitive communications system—as one might expect in any dictatorship— never knew quite how far it could go in mobilising the resources of the society. A mistake made in this could do irreparable harm to their whole war effort. On the other hand, in a democracy, a government could rapidly learn when it overstepped the limits of public toleration—as the British war-time Government was to learn on the relatively minor matter of the rationing of electricity—and draw back in time. This meant that the democratic government could push issues further than the totalitarian one and, therefore, achieve a higher degree of mobilisation.

Something similar is true in the less dramatic circumstances of peace. Where there is general acceptance of the bona fides of the government and

[1]This is confirmed from the German side by Speer (1975) p. 300: '[It remains one of the oddities of this war that] Hitler demanded far less from his people than Churchill and Roosevelt did from their respective nations. The discrepancy between the total mobilisation of labor forces in democratic England and the casual treatment of this question in authoritarian Germany is proof of the régime's anxiety not to risk any shift in the popular mood'.

effective and sensitive communication when it goes too far, more progress can be made than can occur when these factors are missing. Hence, the crucial importance of communication and information in a modern democracy.

This is a subject that has not received adequate or comprehensive thought in this country. So far as the relationships of communication between government and public are concerned, we operate two entirely different traditions.

The first is a tradition of openness. The proceedings of the Houses of the Oireachtas are fully reported in the official reports and get extensive coverage in the newspapers. No doubt there will be a steady development towards the use of the other media when the legislators get over the fears that, in the eighteenth century, their predecessors had of newspaper reporting. Similarly, the courts, except in very exceptional circumstances, carry out their business in public, their proceedings are extensively reported, and it is normal for judges, in matters of some significance, to give their judgements, and the reasons for them, in writing, and these are subsequently published. We take it for granted that proceedings of local councils should be extensively reported, especially in the provincial papers. Where, occasionally, councils wish to carry on their discussions behind closed doors, they receive a lot of stick from the media. As a result of this openness in the Oireachtas, in the courts and in local councils those who care to read the newspapers with some attention cannot fail to have a reasonable grasp of a number of the issues of public affairs.

In a number of countries there has been established a legal right to know. Legal provision for ready access to documents of local authorities was made in Ireland in 1898, but has become a dead letter.

There is a long-standing right—since 1766—for members of the public or representatives of the media to scrutinise the correspondence of Swedish ministries. Other Scandinavian countries—Finland, Norway and Denmark—have recognised similar rights. Since 1966 there has been in the United States a Freedom of Information Act (Wennergren, 1971).

In a number of countries a lot of information gets out by means of deliberate or covert 'leaks'. For example, it seems to be almost impossible to keep anything secret within the administration of the U.S. Government. Hence the founding, under President Nixon, of the ill-fated 'White House plumbers' to prevent leaks. A former commissioner of the European Commission has said that the body works only because it 'leaks at every pore'! Apart from this, there is the occasional enterprise of newspapermen and other representatives of the media who uncover interesting, if embarrassing, pieces of information about the processes of government.

As has been indicated above, modern government can become impossible unless there is sufficient general information in the community to understand the necessity for various government initiatives. The problem is to know where to draw the line between 'the right to know' and the needs of day-to-day government. Lord Croham, who as Sir Douglas Allen, was, until 1977, head of the British civil service, has this to say: '. . . I do believe that, in present conditions, the degree of secrecy which was rigidly maintained until recently is damaging rather than helpful to good government' (*Listener*, 7 September 1978). Hence, a great deal of information is made available by public bodies by way of annual and occasional reports and briefings to the media. Very often, this is long-term information, where problems of public policy are beginning to be discerned, and possible options in relation to them to be clarified. A very striking example of this policy of public education in some major policy issues is given by the reports of the National and Economic Social Council which cover a remarkable range of problems, and, in consequence, have contributed to the general education of public opinion; but this falls very short of what the protagonists of 'open government' demand, and the practice of some countries.

On the other hand, there has been a great falling off, as compared with the practice of the last century, in the information conveyed in the annual reports of government departments, where they still continue to produce them at all. This shortfall means that essential information, figures, and continuity of information are no longer made available to students. Some of the state-sponsored bodies produce reports, but these are, occasionally, simply public relations exercises.

At the political level, ministers in replying to parliamentary questions, in making speeches on their estimates, and in moving the second reading of bills, as well as at various functions throughout the country, produce a great deal of information.

Nonetheless, there is a fairly widespread belief that, in this country, 'open government' is not practised. Some evidence for this belief comes from the fact that political parties, when they are in opposition or newly elected to office, often promise 'open government' but, when they take over, their practice does not seem to differ much from that of their predecessors.

It is no less the interest of administrators, in the partnership of government, that the public be well informed about problems, difficulties and policies, if the administration is to get the support of public opinion, the absence of distrust, and some form of active or passive assent to its activities. Administrators to not seem to realise the extent of this distrust. It is certain that much of it could be allayed if a great deal more were done in terms of communication of such matters. Government departments, local authorities and state-sponsored bodies could do more to inform the public about their activities, not only by means of annual reports, but also by means of occasional reports, the publication of reports of committees and research groups, talks to various specialist and community groups, and so on.

A delicate balance has to be struck between those things that politicians wish to communicate, and those where they are not so much concerned. In particular, they tend not to be concerned where officials set out to explain settled policy and its application to particular cases, provided this is done with reasonable discretion. In the same way, there has been a long standing tradition in this country that senior officials can, with discretion, discuss longer term problems of public policy, and the advantages and disadvantages of various alternative solutions, in the interests of informing responsible public opinion—a forum long provided by the Statistical and Social Inquiry Society of Ireland.

Bigger and richer countries can afford to support newspapers and periodicals of, perhaps, limited circulation, which will devote substantial space to the skilled and informed analysis of problems of government and of possible solutions, helped by usually responsible official background briefing. Unfortunately, Ireland has not, so far at least, been able to support publications of this kind, so that the opportunities for building up well informed public opinion are much reduced. For example, in recent years some major reports published by the National Economic and Social Council have received much less analysis and discussion than their importance to the future of the country certainly warrants. On the other hand, the smallness of the country means that it is relatively easy to communicate with those who, from time to time, play the role of leaders of public opinion in one area or another.

However, these are the problems of briefing an élite. In a modern mass democracy it is desirable, and often necessary, to reach out to the population as a whole and to explain to them the nature of the problems facing the country and why it may be necessary to have to adopt unpleasant policies. A striking example here has been the difficulties of successive governments in achieving what has been glorified under the name of an 'incomes policy', that is, sporadic attempts to persuade people as a whole that moderation in claims on the resources of the community is in the general interest. There are occasional successes on this front; but, overall, there have been significant failures to get this message effectively across, notwithstanding that, as in many countries, it has been a major objective of government. This illustrates the problem of public information seen as a means of achieving a general sense of public responsibility and a widespread acceptance of, and participation in, the policies that are held to be essential for the benefit of the community as a whole and of its individual members.

Notwithstanding this, other parts of public business are carried on in impenetrable obscurity. The operations within government departments and within state-sponsored bodies are almost entirely closed to public scrutiny. We know about what goes on within them only in so far as a conscious decision is taken to publish a decision or report, often presented as a remarkable act of magnanimity on the part of the body concerned.

There are, of course, certain areas where secrecy is essential. This is true over a significant area of national security. Delicate negotiations could be wrecked by premature disclosure. Much mumbo-jumbo has grown up about 'budget secrets'. In some countries, but less often in Ireland, there is acute debate about what 'official secrets' are essential to maintain in the national interest by some sort of official secrets act, and what pieces of information are kept secret simply because their disclosure would be embarrassing to certain persons. Then there are the various forms of overt and covert censorship. Examples are the prohibition on RTE against permitting programme time to representatives of certain subversive bodies, the British 'D notice' system, and so on. There is the extreme sensitivity of the Courts about what reporting is or is not 'in contempt of court'. The British House of Commons tends to show some sensitivity on so-called 'contempt of Parliament'.

Public servants, in the course of their work, often come to know much about the private affairs of certain citizens. It is, of course, a matter of professional honour to respect such confidential information. But there is another, controversial, side to such confidentiality.

One of the arguments that is used to support the exceptional degree of secrecy that applies particularly to the civil service is that senior civil servants are the confidential advisers of ministers and what they say or write within the confines of official buildings must be kept confidential. Otherwise, it is argued, ministers will not get the absolutely candid opinions of their advisers. The argument is that, if an official has to take into account that his advice may be published, he will, to a greater or lesser extent, play to the gallery. This is an argument that has received widespread acceptance, but needs more probing discussion than it has hitherto received.

It needs, especially, to be looked at in the light of the increasing tendency to make public records available to historians after a period that tends to shorten as the years go by. This period, in Britain (and now in Ireland), has become thirty years. In consequence, the British Foreign Office papers about the ghastly post World War II deportation to Russia of various kinds of Russian emigrés, under an agreement made because of Russian insistence, have now become available, and have been studied and analysed in a recent book (Tolstoy, 1977). Notwithstanding that the deportations were known to result in the slaughter of great numbers, it is apparent that certain senior Foreign Office officials – including some who still hold posts of considerable responsibility in Britain – stuck loyally to this policy, rejecting the protests of the soldiers who had to implement it, overcoming the disgust of American diplomats, and soothing the occasional scruples of their political masters. To these ends, it appears, they wrote minutes of advice that display a minimum of moral scruple and were factually wrong (Tolstoy, 1977, pp. 332–4, 345–51, 427, compare also pp. 359–60 with Chs. 8 and 9). Perhaps if the writers of these minutes had realised that they would come up for public scrutiny, they might have taken more care about the quality of the advice they gave.[1] Certainly, the argument for secrecy here cuts both ways.

This is an extreme example, but it is not wholly improbable that the tradition of secrecy does put ministers in the position of receiving advice that is, on occasion, based more on emotion and prejudice than on a detached analysis of the subject at stake. This is most likely to occur in conditions of conflict where ministers may find themselves subjected to the forces of 'dynamic conservatism' (Schon, 1973, Ch. 2), where the overriding consideration may be the preservation of the department's present position and past practices.

Apart from this, it says little for one's professional confidence if, being the holder of a secure job, one is afraid that one's honest advice should become public knowledge. This is a discipline that officers of local authorities have long had to live with.

Of course, it may be embarrassing for a minister if it becomes known that he has rejected well thought out advice for, perhaps, political reasons of his own. Part of the discipline of the civil service is to protect ministers from embarrassments of this kind. Such reasoning was behind the long struggle to prevent the publication of reports of inspectors who hold public enquiries about, say, the acquisition of land, or about planning appeals. The argument was that the minister must be left free (of embarrassment) if he decided to reject the recommendations of the inspector concerned. This issue was debated at length at the committee stage of the Local Government Bill, 1945 (Dáil Debates, Vol. 93, Cols 1814–26; 1840–66; 1966–2010). However, the courts are now requiring the publication of these reports and ministers seem to have survived this innovation (O'Sullivan, 1978, Ch. 2).

There is, behind all this, a major problem of the quality of the thinking and of the advice that is presented to ministers before major decisions are taken on policy. For that reason, a number of years ago, Professor Patrick Lynch suggested that senior officials should be encouraged to engage in publication so that outsiders might have an opportunity of assessing the quality of their thinking (Lynch, 1953). This proposal was attacked by a very distinguished official who, paradoxically, has given many public opportunities for assessing the very high quality of *his* thinking. He was

[1] Shortly after these events a senior Conservative spokesman said in the House of Commons, in 1947: 'If you are to make all confidential reports by civil servants disclosable, then the result will be that the State will not have the advantage of a clear, honest and forthright report from its civil servants as it would have if they were protected'. Quoted in Finer (1961) p. 921.

Dr T. K. Whitaker (1954, p. 43).

Let us be clear about this. The overwhelming volume of advice given to ministers is sensible, honest, and well thought out. Sometimes there are conflicts in the advice, and ministers have to make a choice. In fact, the existence of such conflict enhances the freedom of decision of ministers and only the most sensitive could consider that the existence of two or more points of view on an issue within a department would detract from its authority. It is inevitable, and right, that there should be differences of view. Certainly, the prestige of the courts does not suffer from the open disagreements of judges openly arrived at.

We can sum up this discussion by saying that generally the tradition of open government is well developed in some countries, grounded in what is believed to be a general democratic principle of the 'right to know'. In other less democratic countries, the information released tends only to be what, in the opinion of government, it is broadly good for people to know.

As we have seen, this is not in the long-term interest of effective government and administration and poses the need for an information policy to give effect to this 'right to know'.

The point about an information policy of this kind is that, except for clearly defined areas—such as national security—it cannot be selective. Outside those areas people have to be confident that they are being told the whole story. Responsibility in a modern mass democracy will prevail only if there is a conscious effort to create conditions of openness and trust. The ordinary man or woman cannot be expected to be a responsible citizen unless he is also an informed citizen.

This poses major responsibilities on modern government to have a comprehensive information system. In this respect, Ireland has significant failings.

Another method for having an informed and responsible citizenry is to have widespread opportunities for public participation and representation. As the business of government grows and becomes more comprehensive, and as the citizens become better educated, as they have a greater understanding of some at least of the issues confronting society, and as they have more leisure to take an interest in public affairs one might expect to see the principle of democratic public representation being extended throughout the society. On the contrary, as public business has grown, as the public franchise has been extended universally, the opportunities for standing for public office have in Ireland absolutely and relatively declined.

When the British in 1838 decided to lay, in Ireland, the foundations for what has become the main part of our social services, however limited their ideas may have been about the scope of these services, they took the extraordinary step of covering the country with a network of directly elected local bodies to administer these services. Our ideas of social services and of democratic election have moved on since those days; but who nowadays would think of evoking, from nothing as it were, such widespread opportunities for public service and public responsibility?

We have, as compared with other countries, relatively few opportunities for standing for public office. Notwithstanding this, there was what seemed to be a serious proposal by government to wipe out about half of the existing directly elected bodies in the country in the 1971 White Paper on local government reorganisation. The reason for this – and it was a valid reason – was that the smaller local authorities, so far as their traditional duties were concerned, had become largely irrelevant. In the choice as to whether they might be made more relevant to modern conditions, or be abolished, the decision went the latter way. This has been part of a long-standing tradition since the State was established. There is an alternative (IPA, 1971).

The continuance of this way of thinking about public elected office is all the more surprising in that there has been a growth throughout the country of various kinds of community and interest bodies who have been knocking on the door for opportunities for extending the range of public responsibility; but, notwithstanding that there has been some lip service to ideas of participation, the door has been kept firmly locked against them (e.g. Local Government Reorganisation, 1973). Of course, many self-appointed bodies make nuisances of themselves, behave irresponsibly, and may not represent, in effect, the people on whose behalf they claim to speak. Moreover, their lives are often short – they arise, make a lot of noise, run into intense frustration, and fade away. Deprived of the opportunities of responsible action on their own account, they tend to become pressure groups and, in the minds of existing public representatives and administrators, nuisances.

There are legitimate grievances on both sides of this tension and they are likely to continue, and to grow worse, until opportunities for further elected offices are made, opportunities for the discharge of appropriate degrees of local responsibility, and opportunities for determining, in a democratic way, who it is precisely speaks for what community or for what interest.

Part of national development is to ensure that there are opportunities for the citizen to exercise freely his democratic responsibilities as a citizen. This is an area of government that has been much neglected in Ireland. The basic problem is how to associate the democratic process, at each level, with an appropriate level of administration.

As the notion of the elective representative has declined, another form of representative has become very common, namely the appointive one. As a big part of the business of government is now being performed by state-sponsored bodies, the number of boards or councils of these bodies has also greatly increased. Almost invariably, the members of these bodies are appointed by the appropriate minister. This is, of course, a way of securing from the community as a whole various kinds of knowledge and skill that can be utilised for the better overall management of these bodies. This is necessary and desirable; but in the last analysis one can't help asking the question of what direction will our democracy take where the opportunities for our elected representatives to take part in the newer and more interesting tasks of government become less and less, while the opportunities for appointed representatives extend at a steady pace?

As the number of interest groups in the community grows, and as they become better organised and dispose of more resources, they necessarily play a larger part in the consultative processes of government. It has now become virtually unthinkable that government will take an initiative about, say, industry without consulting with the Confederation of Irish Industry, or about trade unions without consulting with the Irish Congress of Trade Unions, or about farming without consulting with the Irish Farmers Association and the Irish Creamery Milk Suppliers Association. To a greater or lesser extent this applies throughout the whole business of government. Consultation, discussion and, very often, negotiation with the appropriate interests are now almost essential preliminaries to political and administrative action.

On the whole, it is of advantage to public bodies to have responsible and representative interest groups with whom they can consult before they take action. In this way they can gain the benefit of detailed knowledge and attitudes that, otherwise, would be difficult for them to arrive at. Inevitably, of course, opportunities for conflict arise where interests diverge; but, over the long view, this tends to be a fruitful arrangement. But it is an arrangement not always easily arrived at. There is some evidence that considerable numbers of interest groups suffer from substantial frustration in their attempts to obtain openings to persuade public bodies of their points of view (Carty, 1970). (Needless to say, these points of view may conflict sharply with the public interest.) However, the stronger interest groups readily achieve a free and easy relationship with their appropriate official bodies.

Nearly every government department, for example, is flanked by advisory bodies of one kind or another (Leon, 1963). At the highest and most general level of policy a body such as the National Economic and Social Council, substantially representing the main economic and social interests in the country—the 'social partners' as they tend to be called in the EEC jargon—represents a very highly developed form of consultation and the role that the council has set itself in issuing a large number of reports advising about the major economic and social issues of the country, itself has the effect of involving a very much wider body of opinion in these problems.

The need to consult with various interests, or with public opinion generally, means that a lot of time must be spent on such processes. In a sense, every new project has its appropriate and minimum gestation period. Sometimes, this can be prolonged. Sometimes impatient politicians and administrators may wish to foreshorten this period by skipping some of the necessary steps. Occasionally this works, but often such impatience serves only to prolong the whole operation.

Consultation has two main purposes. The first is to pick brains, as it were, so as to get the best knowledge, experience and ideas available within the community for the best solution of the problem in hand. One of the time-honoured ways of doing this is by the commission of enquiry, supplemented, as it tends to be in modern times, by commissioned research projects. This, if the size of the commission and its period of operation, are kept reasonably restricted, can have a major informational effect in clarifying the problem, in setting out the options, and the arguments for and against each of these. (The setting up of an inquiry may also have the effect of damping the fuse of an explosive political issue.)

The informational inquiry leads on to the second aspect of consultation which is to inform public opinion, including the specialised opinion concerned with the problem in hand, of feasibilities, to evoke discussion and, eventually one might hope, a consensus. When this process has been completed, there remains the need for political and administrative decision and the preparation of the necessary legislation, etc.

This is, to repeat, essentially a twofold process—first, to assemble the available and relevant knowledge and experience within the community, and, secondly, to raise the general level of information and to achieve, hopefully, a consensus, before action is taken. This is, in all, necessarily a slow-moving process—the gestation period for a solution to any significant issue of this kind may take several years or more.

However, it is well to be realistic about this. The pace of administrative change in Ireland is not supersonic. For a variety of reasons, some of them purely technical, most new schemes of real significance take a long time from conception to birth. There are various desirable ways of speeding up many of these schemes, but one of them is *not* to cut short the time devoted to preliminary thought, and another *not* to do this in relation to the education of public opinion. There is a famous saying from the last century about 'educating our masters'. As our society becomes more democratic and more educated, the need and the benefits of at least informing our masters become greater and the penalties for not doing so more severe.

The complexities of this are neatly illustrated in a survey conducted for RTE about the proposal to build a nuclear power station in County Wexford (broadcast April 1978). Apparently, a majority of those in the sample considered that it was necessary to have this station. Nonetheless, an overwhelming majority of the whole sample thought that there should be a preliminary enquiry about it. Most people were prepared to accept responsible opinion about this matter, but were nonetheless anxious that the contrary view should be reasonably explored. This may involve delay, but it is, in the last analysis, what democracy is all about. The danger is that, otherwise, one can run into the kind of violent reactions that have been experienced in Germany, France and other countries in relation to projects of this kind.

The point of all this is that it is necessary for governmental systems to have a proper humility in relation to the people in the democratic society who are, when all is said, their masters. A major feature of modern government is discussion and persuasion. These face, in modern conditions, very severe obstacles unless they are supported by an honest and comprehensive information policy, by greater opportunities for local democracy, and for general consultation.

Chapter 8: Review

1. Consensus

The argument of this book is that there is a *system* of government, part of which is the *system* of public administration. The ramifications of the governmental system are very great, yet we can see all the threads gathered together by the fifteen men who sit around the cabinet table and constitute 'the Government'. All the immensely complicated actions of all the parts of the governmental system can be related back to the members of the Government. From their viewpoint one can most easily see, and speak of, a governmental system.

Can we speak of the administrative system in the same way? This is more difficult because the ministers are at the heart of the administrative system and they collectively are its essential link. But books on public administration normally assume – at least, this one does – that there is an administrative system within the governmental system, yet conceptually distinguishable from it. It is true that, in conception, the Minister and the Department of the Public Service were intended to be a focus for the Irish administrative system as a whole; but this has not, so far at least, occurred. Can we, therefore, discern any special forces that in fact bind together the administrative system in this smaller sense?

The most important of these forces, as I have been insisting, is the *consensus*. This exerts pressure, now vigorous, now deceptively restrained, on the parts of the system to operate in some sense systematically. It is the external sanction, if you will, on the system.

But inside the system itself there is an inherent drive for the systematic, difficult as it may often be to discern in practice. This is the urge of professionalism to review progress against objectives, to identify and remedy the causes of shortfalls. More generally, it seeks to take broader looks at the system as a whole, as well as significant parts of it, to assess internal coherence and overall direction or drift, and, from these to develop fresh insights. Finally, it seeks to look to the consensus, to its maintenance and to its development. It is through this internal, reflective urge that the sub-systems in their protean forms and the system as a whole can be seen as entities and that they and it are most effectively in communion with the various forms of consensus that surround them.

If we are to speak meaningfully of an administrative system, therefore, we have to recognise that the two main forces that link that system together – that of consensus and of professionalism – impose on public servants at least certain intellectual and moral obligations in relation to the general, as well as the special, conduct of public affairs. The root operation here is that of Review, and the demands it poses for reflection, knowledge and action.

The task is to get the system operating smoothly and effectively, not simply for its own sake but because it is a crucial element in, and force for, national development as a whole and because it cannot adequately fulfil its role unless it, too, develops as part of the total development process. The special internal dynamic making for the development of the administrative system, for administrative development, is what we have been calling *administrative professionalism*, and the special external dynamic derives from the implications of the notion of *consensus*. These are both linked into the process of development by means of the orderly practice of Review.

It is unlikely that there is some secret spring that, touched, will reveal the secrets of how the process of administrative development is to be kept sufficiently dynamic. If we are to discover how the system might achieve an adequate level of administrative development we must take a more laborious course. That is to review unsettled problems of the system, with particular reference to developing the two potential dynamics of consensus and professionalism.

Our task is, therefore, to review, in this section, issues that arise from the systemising forces of consensus, and, in the next section, from the forces of professionalism. First, consensus.

'Administration' is not an autonomous activity, notwithstanding that it plays a big part in the working of government and that, within its proper sphere, it exercises significant degrees of autonomy. To understand its role in that working we must – without getting bogged down in what seems to be an endless debate – consider more closely the issue we touched on in Chapter 1, namely the working relationships between politics and administration in the ongoing business of government.

It is the mark of a distinct political society that it is equipped with institutions – of a greater or less degree of formality – for taking decisions that are of concern to the society, and within its competence to take. These institutions are of two main kinds – political institutions and judicial/administrative institutions, the one concerned with unstructured issues, the other with mainly structured ones. A structured issue can be referred back to some major decision that will be accepted by those concerned as an authority for taking the new decision required. The most obvious institutions here are the courts which will adjudicate the issue on the basis of the interpretation and application of an existing body of law, constitutional or otherwise. An unstructured issue cannot be so referred, either because there is no such major decision or, if there seems to be, its application is not acceptable to the parties or to one of them. In one instance a formal procedure for dealing with the matter exists; in the other no such formal or agreed procedures exist.

If conflict of this kind is to be peacefully settled in the absence of a formal procedure, it will normally be resolved by the political system, which will attempt to conciliate the contestants, or, failing that, may arrive at some solution that, on the whole, public opinion will be prepared to accept.

In a functioning political society a vast amount of such conflicts are successfully dealt with by the political system. The unpatterned, unstructured problems of the community come crowding in upon the political system and, somehow, the necessary degree of conciliation is achieved, a structure is agreed for dealing with these and with comparable problems in the future, and the continual task of maintaining the structure is given to some institution (Miller, 1962, p. 288; Crick, 1964, pp. 141, 199). Thus the achieving of this consensus is, as we have seen, the foundation of public administration.

It is no part of the argument here that there is a single consensus in the society as a whole. There may, or may not, be; but that is for discussion somewhere else. So the grand notions that haunt the political philosphers of a 'universal consensus', a 'general will', various forms of social contract, universal ideology, and the rest, remain away above our heads.

On the practical level, some things agreed upon in the society may have a very high intensity of consensus as to their intrinsic importance – the rule of law, parliamentary democracy; others, like social justice, may evoke a high consensus in general, but much debate in detail; others, like heavy taxation, a bleak acceptance; others still, like the regulation of the greyhound industry, positive acceptance by most of those directly concerned, and passive acceptance, even indifference, by the rest of us. If we look at the vast jumble of things that the political system has processed to the stage of public administration, we can see that this degree of consensus varies with each.

These individual forms of consensus are not permanent – they can change quickly or slowly, often unpredictably. A small disturbance may precipitate drastic, sudden and perhaps irrational change in one, while stubborn adherence to another may continue long after the need for it may have disappeared.

It will be apparent from the examples that consensus is not the same as unanimity. The opposition of a minority may not disturb the consensus if that opposition does not gain sufficient or influential support, or if the minority are not prepared to carry their opposition to extreme lengths, or else do not deploy such tenacity and skill as to win the support of a significant number of the hitherto indifferent and the tolerance of a number of the remainder. Similarly, a consensus does not necessarily mean the support of a majority – it may exist where the majority are indifferent.

Again, the matters about which there is consensus vary widely in intrinsic importance. These range from major values that are largely immutable or that change very slowly over time – such as, in Ireland, national identity, Christianity, democracy – to important principles, like natural justice, or to mere matters of convention, such as driving on the left. A striking feature here is that the ease with which the consensus may be broken can often be in inverse proportion to the intrinsic importance of the issues. It may take time to mobilise dissent in relation to some major national event, but a minor matter may become speedily explosive.

The governmental system is, basically, a means of taking decisions on conflicts within the society and these decisions enhance the stock of consensus. When the society is poor its resources are limited, and so are the aspirations of its members. But when resources increase, when a broader range of human wants can be satisfied, when it is believed that the state should take a hand in providing these satisfactions, when the members of the society become more aware that the environment of their lives can be altered for good or bad by personal and social decisions, then the arguments about choice become more intense, and conflicts, and the opportunities for conflict, rapidly increase. There is a great deal more for the political system to do and the transfer from conflict to consensus, the adding to the stock of consensus, often becomes progressively more difficult.

We see, in short, a rising body of problems for resolution, and the committing of most of them to the administrative system to be dealt with in accordance with existing, or newly agreed, procedures. In the successful case, we see the following progression: increased resources – conflict as to their allocation – a clash, sometimes marked, even intense, of the interests that support different solutions – the intervention of political, placatory activity – the establishment of some kind of consensus – the agreement on a procedure for resolving conflict of this kind – the emergence of public administration. Wants lead to politics and politics lead to administration. That leads in turn to procedures. Does it stop there? The answer depends on how one approaches the problem of maintaining the procedures, for retaining the consensus.

The task of achieving a consensus in the first place is clearly a political one. The task of maintaining the consensus is, very largely, an administrative one: the way in which a service is provided may have a profound effect on the continuance or otherwise of the consensus. The conditions for the continuance of the consensus are seldom clear. Public opinion is like a sleeping giant, at one time sunk in imperturbable slumber, at another restless and stimulated to violent reaction by the slightest disturbance. But there seem to be three bench marks that it most frequently uses for determining whether to maintain the consensus or not.

The first of these is the responsiveness of the administrative system to changing needs, wants and demands of the public, or a significantly articulate section of it that can command at least passive support. Sometimes the system of government is so arthritic that it is unable to respond, with any real effect, to a demand of this kind. Sometimes it may be willing to respond but unable to resolve the clash of interest between that demand and some other.

The second condition for consensus seems to be, in varying measure, the quality of effectiveness of the operation of the system. For example, the public may, from time to time, be restless with the Electricity Supply Board; but, overall, will wash away its sins by reason of the normal accessibility of power at the pressing of the switch. No such source of absolution is, normally, available to the telephone service. The threshold of acceptable effectiveness may not be high in this country, but it exists and can be decisive so far as public opinion is concerned.

The third condition seems to be that of humaneness. Again, the threshold here may not be high. Certainly, a lot of absentminded indifference seems to be acceptable. But a positive disposition to what is felt to be heartlessness, or cruelty, or – as these failings often manifest themselves – arrogance, may have explosive effects.

One of the problems here is that of delayed reaction. Some happening may profoundly disturb the consensus, yet appear to be viewed by public opinion with passivity, only to lead to a decisive expression of dissatisfaction at a later time and, sometimes, on a separate issue.

The main argument about consensus is that the whole of the operations of public administration are encased in the notion. Breach the consensus, and politics and conflict come pouring in, unless the breach can be speedily healed. But if it cannot, then public administration becomes, in the extreme case, impossible or very difficult. The most notable feature of public administration, therefore, is that it is encased in the skin of political consensus and its actions are governed and modified by the conditions of this consensus. These conditions determine the whole flavour of public administration. When the conditions are widely drawn the public body has a wide degree of discretion and can carry on for a long time without jangling the nerve ends of the consensus. So it can be said, and seen, to be 'out of politics'. But should it press on those nerve ends, it will rapidly find itself in the political arena, in conflict.

These features are illustrated in chart 7 overleaf.

The point is that the maintenance of the consensus over a wide range of issues is an essential condition for the operation of public administration at all. For that reason, its whole mode of operation is governed by the need

CONSENSUS AND THE ADMINISTRATIVE SYSTEM

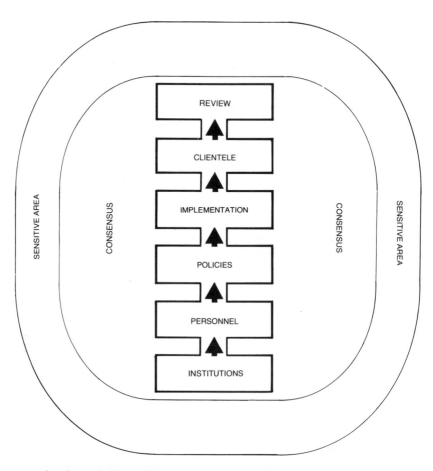

to maintain and, if possible, extend the area of consensus. This is a point the politicians as a whole are very well aware of; but the other partners in government, the officials, by the nature of their calling–with its thrust for order, regularity, and stability–are much less aware of it.

One comes back to the basic condition for all administrative behaviour, the consensus of the public. It may be that the conditions imposed for that consensus may seem, from time to time, to be unreasonable. Nonetheless the basic problem of public administration is to live with its consensus and, as in the parable of the talents, to use this consensus for the purpose of enlarging the original endowment.

Senator T. K. Whitaker, who has made the transition from the administrative system to the political one, has said: 'politics may be the art of the possible, but we should always try hard to extend the range of the possible, that is, the area of consensus for action' (Whitaker, 1977).

The problem of patrolling the consensus, as it were, is often put in terms of 'control'. This is an ambiguous term that could mean – and probably at the foundation of the state was intended to mean – that all actions of officials should receive specific political sanction; but in these times it is more generally taken to mean the existence of a system of review that will throw up for attention the unexpected and the undesired, leaving normal operations to be carried on within the bounds of general rules and a proper autonomy. The purpose of this kind of control is to provide a feedback, that is, to bring to notice those significant issues, those deviations from the expected, that call for attention. We speak of a 'negative' feedback when what is thrown up can be dealt with within the terms of the existing sub-system of consensus, as a thermostat, by discreet intervention, maintains temperature at about the required level, or as homeostasis operates within the human body. But where the necessary correction cannot be carried out within the existing conditions we must consider the possibility of 'positive' feedback – in our terms, steps to enlarge the consensus or establish a new one.

An effective system of review that allows these feedbacks to occur and to alert attention is an essential link between the political and administrative systems. It is also an essential link in those systems themselves. These feedbacks are also major dynamics of the two systems when they activate the policy process. Judicial controls have similar feedback effects but, for the sake of clarifying the argument, are not considered in what follows (Barrington, 1975, p. 38).

Briefly, as an issue moves from 'politics' to 'administration', or from 'conflict' to 'consensus', the administration works out policies to give* effect to that consensus. These are decided upon normally by the political head of the organisation, and, to that extent, implemented. So long as the policy as implemented gives satisfaction there is no further trouble; but, inevitably, snags appear that lead to a review of the original policies and their reformulation in whole or in part, the making of revised proposals, the gaining of approval, and the implementation of the revised policies as approved. And so the process goes on, the cycle repeating itself perhaps many times. This is roughly illustrated by chart 8 overleaf. One must see the figure on the top right as carrying a continual line of traffic, sometimes moving slowly, sometimes very fast indeed. It is from this traffic that most of the normal business of governmental administration – taking decisions on policy proposals – arises.

Eventually the traffic runs into trouble. Perhaps the conditions of the original consensus prove insufficient; perhaps the original problem has been solved, only to reveal a larger one; perhaps the basic issue remains unsolved, even though all that could be done within the existing consensus has been done; perhaps developments in another area require a major

THE GOVERNMENTAL PROCESS

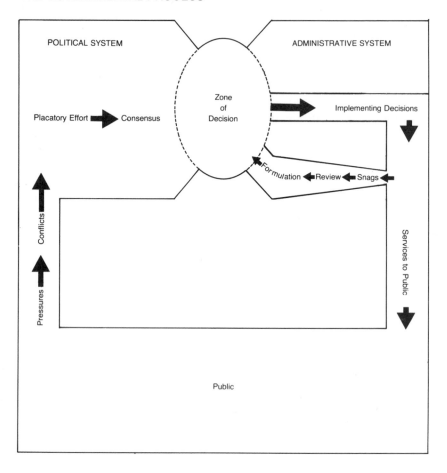

change in this one. In such events, the feedback mechanism is faced with the change from the negative to the positive. The task then becomes one, not of making changes needed to maintain an existing equilibrium, but of seeking out a new equilibrium. The task of administration becomes, not to do that which must be done to maintain the existing consensus, but to seek out ways to do what ought to be done to enhance it, or replace it with a new consensus at a higher level.

In all of this one can see the partnership of the political and administrative systems in the overall task of government. Significant policies that aim to maintain an equilibrium, or to replace an existing equilibrium by a new one, cannot be adopted without the decision and active intervention of the political system through a minister or the government as a whole; but the decision itself is often dependent on the proposals of the administrative system. If these are inadequate, or delayed, or simply not made, the political system may not be seized of the issues for decision until conflict breaks out outside the government system and the political system has to go back to its original placatory task of seeking a consensus on what is to be done. This situation may also arise where ministers fail to decide on a policy arising from proposals made to them from the administrative system.

The political system has its own ways of dealing with governments that do not exercise the responsibility of governing; but there is seldom such a direct system of accountability in the administrative system. Here we are in very large measure dependent on the professional promptings of the administrative profession itself. We are here in moral country, the territory of the 'oughts', not the 'musts'. But it is territory much given to mists and low-lying cloud, so that, often, clear perspectives cannot be gained. That is the case for more careful mapping of the ground, for a greater clarifying of the imperatives of the administrative profession. In this moral country, professional knowledge, if it is adequately developed, will reveal what needs to be done, the size and the significance of the gap before one. The other main constituent of professionalism – professional ethics – will lead one to do what can be done about closing, and crossing, this gap. Two basic professional imperatives are to know and to act, to know what has to be done and to act on that knowledge.

2. Professionalism

Let us now look more closely at the second of our systemising forces, the urge to professionalism. This urge can be stimulated by external pressure; but, at heart, it comes from internal promptings, from self-consciousness, from the concern for order, rationality, efficacy, and style. Within all the complexity of the system, through all this unruly matter, this is, in the Aristotelian sense, the 'form' that struggles to emerge. It is a form that has been only dimly discerned even by practitioners and described, when it has been described, in terms inadequate for conveying its significance and importance. The crucial factor, or link, in the administrative system, considered in itself, is this inadequately articulated concept of a professional public administration, of an administrative profession.

Here we should make a distinction between two ends of a continuum, between professional qualities and special qualities. For example, if we need medical or legal advice about a problem, we try to get it from a specialist in that problem, and we judge him according to the efficacy of that advice and the final outcome. But if we are considering the profession of medicine or law as a whole, we apply much less specific criteria. Nonetheless, there is fairly general agreement on what these criteria should be. In the same way, the administrator is primarily judged by his efficiency in special areas – perhaps agricultural administration, some part of social administration, financial administration, or whatever. But when we come to consider the profession of administration as a whole, we must stand back from these special areas and look to other, more general, criteria. What criteria?

But, perhaps first, we ought to ask the question, does it matter whether the professional side is underdeveloped if the special side is working well? When all is said, is not the important thing the delivery of services to the public, not the intellectual and ethical satisfactions of those who do the delivery? The answer surely lies in the claim that the quality of the services and of their delivery can be increased by greater concern for the tackling of general issues, partly because at some stage – sometimes sooner, sometimes later – the special always needs some sort of general support – financial, organisational, intellectual – and what is neglected in the general in one sector – say, in relation to the consensus – may prevent effective delivery of the special in another. One can be concerned, therefore, with the development of the general precisely because one is concerned for more effective delivery of the special. We have already considered numerous examples of less than effective special action because of less than sufficient concern for general issues.

Over fifty years ago Mary Follett, talking of the development of business management as a profession, began by saying: 'the word 'profession' connotes for most people a foundation of *science* and a motive of *service*. That is, a profession is said to rest on the basis of an approved body of knowledge, and such knowledge is supposed to be used in the service of others, rather than merely for one's own purposes' (Follett, 1940, p. 117).

These requirements are equally applicable to the administrative profession but here the concepts of science and service are of unequal strength. What is known is much less than what is done. That is to say that the moral imperative that comes from knowing what has to be done can operate only to a limited extent.

The doyen of American public administration studies, Dwight Waldo, has pointed out that these studies have constantly enlarged their range, but without any advance in insights into the heart of the study (Waldo, 1975, p. 185). The Open University in Britain has provided its students with a number of so called 'approaches' to the study of public administration, but not an indication of what it is one is approaching, or when one has reached it (Open University, 1974, Blocks II & IV). Waldo speaks of an 'identity crisis' and sees the solution to this in what he calls 'an overarching professional paradigm' (Waldo, 1975, p. 224). The analogy is with medicine which is practised as an art, based on the assimilation of the insights of many sciences, natural, human and social. We can see the great strides medicine has made since it allied itself with the sciences and since it gave those sciences a medical perspective. Can one say the same of public administration as a profession? Only to a very limited extent.

There is a long-standing subject known as 'administrative science', but it is woefully underdeveloped (Barrington, 1979). So far as 'service' is concerned the situation is much better, but the farther one moves from the direct provision of services to the more general and abstract issues that are inherent in effective provision, the more problems arise. If the two legs of a profession are 'science' and 'service' the latter is much the longer leg and the gait of the profession of public administration is handicapped indeed.

We see, therefore, something of a stalemate. Because the 'science' side of the profession is so underdeveloped the motivation and the capacity for 'service' are restricted and, because of this, the motivation for developing the 'science' is muffled, and so on. Yet it is not impossible to break this stalemate by a survey of the problems, by the development of systematic Review and, thus, by stimulating both 'service' and its handmaid 'science'.

Perhaps the first task of Review is to review itself, to see how far it is operating effectively, and then to carry the process down through each stage of the administrative system, to Clientele, Implementation, Policies, Personnel, and Institutions, to see how far each is contributing to the maintenance and the enhancement of the consensus and of professionalism, and is sensitive to developments that endanger them. In this exercise we are concerned only with the general, and not the special, areas of administration. Moreover, what follows does not purport to be a complete census of problems in even the general area – that would call for a book in itself.

From a review of Review itself it is clear that the Irish administrative system does not engage in any significant degree of review of its general effectiveness. Otherwise there would be lively professional discussion of general professional problems, there would be a substantial body of research into such problems, and there would be a long agenda for administrative change and development. The sort of external inquest by outsiders once a generation (Brennan, 1936; Devlin, 1969) is no substitute for this constant, internal process of review. The problem is, therefore, to find means by which the steady process of review and overhaul can be carried on at all levels of the system.

The Institute of Public Administration, founded in 1957, had as its primary aim to encourage this kind of informed and constructive discussion and a great deal has been done in periodicals, books, special reports, educational activities, extensive training courses, and, now, the building up of a research facility, to this end. Yet, somehow, no significant professional flame has been kindled. We know more now about the problems of our administrative system but it is hard to see any emerging determination that, in practice, they should be tackled. Similarly, the Devlin idea of a Public Service Advisory Council, commenting on the pace of administrative development, has likewise cast its seed on stony ground. The Council has published a number of important reports and one of these has been the subject of a Seanad debate. But the impassivity of the system remains. The most important instrument is, of course, the Department of the Public Service, but, here again, such influence as it exerts has not been decisive in stimulating a reflective, administrative self-consciousness. Outside the administrative system neither the Oireachtas (apart from the new committee on state-sponsored bodies as yet untried, the archaic system of the Public Accounts Committee, and the long moribund committee on delegated legislation), the media, nor any other instrument of public opinion, has put any pressure on the administrative system to engage in review of its general problems. It is clear, therefore, that we lack an adequate sub-system of Review as a crucial contribution to the whole administrative system. This, then, is a first main item on the agenda for a programme of administrative development.

A second main item emerges when we review the sub-system of Clientele. In a democratic society, at least, one comes back continually to the people for whose benefit all this administrative activity is engaged in. They have, through the law, through the political system, through their perception of correct administrative behaviour, laid down constraints within which all this activity must be carried on. It is likely that, at an increasing pace, these constraints will, notwithstanding (perhaps because of) the extension of administrative intervention in the community, be tightened. If unnecessary conflict is to be avoided significant improvements will be needed in at least three areas. The first of these is for more extended, and better, systems for the hearing and, where possible, the alleviating of grievances against the administration. The second is in relation to an active and comprehensive information policy, summed up in the phrase 'open government'. The third is in a more widespread and democratic system of public representation.

By these means some of the dangers and distrust facing the administration, as its duties extend through the community, may be reduced or obviated. There has been a comparative ignoring by the administration of indications of the deep distrust of the public of its motivation and actions (Chubb, 1970, pp. 312–3). The indications are that, if anything, this distrust is likely to be increased. There is a real need to quantify and assess this issue before it is too late. In addition to this problem one can see that, as countries grow more affluent and as middle-class values spread more widely amongst them, there has been a substantial rise in dissent in relation to the environment and cultural matters generally. So far as this country is concerned, this dissent may still be at an early stage. Should it extend, there could be a substantial further danger to the consensus on which, to repeat, effective administration must rest.

Action is called for in relation to two problems. The first relates to grievance procedures, information and representation where, already, Ireland lags behind. Action here would be in the hope of reducing the degree of distrust of the administration where, it would seem, Ireland ranks unenviably high. What needs to be done is relatively clear cut. The second relates to the need to be better informed on the emerging trends that seem to be imposing more stringent conditions for the consensus. Here the way ahead is not so clear. All one can say is that, if unnecessary conflict is to be avoided, new and basically democratic methods of coping with the anxieties of the public will almost certainly have to be devised. These may have significant institutional implications, especially in the areas of regional, local and community government.

Similar issues arise when we look at the Implementation of policies. Considerable conceptual problems emerge, and from time to time fall from view, in relation to the notion of 'development' and its implications for the role of the state and its responsibilities in national development. These in turn pose complex conceptual and practical problems in relation to the balance to be struck at any time between the various forms of development and the recognition to be given to the different facets – economic, social, cultural, etc. – of national development in the establishment of national objectives and their achievement.

At the practical level of 'administrative management' there are a number of issues. There are clearly severe problems of human and industrial relations, of productivity measurement on an objective basis, and of quantification generally; there is the survival of archaic practices in relation to 'common services'; there is the notable diffusion of responsibility and accountability – paradoxically, because of the efforts to concentrate them; there is the casual approach to management training generally; and there is the failure of analysis and synthesis in the approach to management problems in a public sector context. Generally, there seems to be insufficient professional concern to exert pressure to control costs and to achieve clear objectives over a defined period. There is a major problem of effective concertation where a large number of public bodies may be involved in a single project.

At the next level, the problems of Policy Formulation have received more attention than those of implementation, but they are so diverse that it is possible here to look only at two general areas – finance and planning – which pose this professional issue.

There has been, to repeat, a remorseless growth, notwithstanding occasional interruptions, in the proportion of the gross national product that passes through the hands of government each year. It is hard to see, if the present overall trends continue, just where this process will end, short of the 100 per cent proportion. As we have seen, this growth comes from three main sources.

The first is the increasing need, in every country, in order to have social equity, to reduce the gap between those in good employment and those who, for one reason or another, have small income or none. Even with full employment in Ireland two-thirds of those now receiving social welfare benefits would still require them.

The second reason is that most state services are highly labour intensive, so that, unless there is some at present unforeseen revolution in achieving dramatic rises in the productivity of labour in the service industries, the cost of state services will rise at a faster rate than the rise in the affluence of the community.

The third reason is that the state has found itself obliged to be responsible for great and increasing services, such as health, education, transport, housing, and communications. For some of these the price system, which, for most other services rationalises demand, is largely removed. These services, therefore, make dramatic increases in their demands on the resources of the community.

All this calls for an ever-increasing rise in what is called the 'burden of taxation'. A recent book points out that the growth in public expenditure in Britain, Sweden and Italy is now about to exceed the growth in GNP, so that, if it continues, there will be cuts in real take-home pay (Rose and Peters, 1979). There is also some evidence that people are, to an increasing extent, resisting having to pay increasing proportions of their income in general taxation, and pursue the self-defeating course of demanding compensating income increases. One can quantify the various social benefits into an average and call it a 'social income'; but few people are prepared to regard this as, in fact, part of their income.

This is a major problem of public finance that is likely to press with increasing intensity on all developed administrations in the coming years. So far as we are concerned in this country it is exacerbated by two factors. The first of these is what the 1976 Green Paper on social and economic development called 'circular transfers' (p. 38). By this is meant those so-called 'free' or subsidised services, the full costs of which in many cases are paid for by taxpayers, in advance of, and divorced from, the receipt of benefits. If this kind of circular transfer could be eliminated, the taxation bill could be reduced.

The second aggravating feature is the ad hoc way in which the various taxation systems have grown up. The most striking example of this is the increasing extent to which social welfare and health services are now being financed by direct contributions by employed people and their employers. So far as these were flat-rate contributions they constituted a regressive tax, which also had the effect of penalising labour intensive industries, in a country that has, normally, a chronic labour surplus. Where they impinge on the PAYE taxation system there are a number of striking anomalies (NESC 37). The proposals to integrate the two systems to obviate or limit the anomalies were firmly rejected by the government in 1978.

These problems illustrate in some degree two major issues in the Irish system of public administration. The first is the reluctance to adopt a professional stance and consider as a whole the effect of the various financial interventions and taxation systems so that they might be general- ised, simplified and made to achieve their objectives with economy. This is a matter of administrative style. The second is the failure to pay closer attention to the disturbing, and perhaps increasing, rumbles of discontent from the public – as in the case of rates on domestic dwellings. This is the problem of maintaining the consensus, or of altering systems in such a way that the consensus can be renewed.

The difficulties and failures that have been associated since 1958 with establishing a system that has been calling itself 'Economic and Social' planning illustrate some of the intractabilities of the Irish system of public administration, of its arrested administrative development. Let us name three examples. After twenty years we still lack, throughout the system, the specialised skills required for a reasonably comprehensive system of planning, notwithstanding repeated promises that this lack would be remedied. After more than a decade the conceptual difficulties inherent in the commitment to 'social' planning have hardly been identified, much less tackled (e.g. Programme 1978–81, paras 2.13–2.19). The institutional arrangements – or, more properly, lack of arrangements – for regional planning have barely begun to be touched upon even though this neglect undermines the credibility of our efforts to persuade the European Com- munity to play a larger part in the problems of regional imbalance.

The substantive problems before the new Department of Economic Planning and Development are truly formidable. Tough as they are, their difficulties are exacerbated by the long neglect of the administrative problems that have been thrown up by attempts to devise an effective planning system. Planning is, basically, an instrument of administration, calling for its own specialised skills. A former Taoiseach, Seán Lemass, in the early days of planning said that 'any plan of action is as good as and no better than the arrangements made to carry it into effect' (Lemass, 1961). A new, specialised department has now been established to deal with planning under a minister wholly committed to that task. It will be of interest to see how far there will be a planned approach to the administra- tive, as well as to the substantive, problems facing the task of national development in Ireland.

In the last analysis good policies and good policy-making systems are the products of good, lively people, of, in the jargon, Personnel. A major problem about people in institutions is that they tend to be 'cribbed, cabined and confined', and their native springs of originality and vigour tend to dry up. It is a major task of personnel management to counteract this phenomenon and to tackle those specific problems about which a good deal is known and that are amenable to good quality management. In the last analysis any system of administration comes back to the dynamism, the intelligence and the moral qualities of those who staff it. In this respect the Irish public service has a number of distinct advantages. The trouble is that Irish personnel management, on the whole, has not risen to the challenge either of this inherent quality or of the demands of the times on the Irish public service. There has been a preoccupation with order, with regularity, with controls. There are exceptions but, overall, what has *not* been encouraged and developed has been creativity, motivation, leadership, intellectual excitement, dynamism. One is reminded of the Roy Campbell quatrain on South African novelists:

> You praise the firm restraint with which they write,
> I'm with you there, of course:
> They use the snaffle and the curb all right,
> But where's the bloody horse?

For this lack of personnel development there is less excuse than in the other areas we have been reviewing. Personnel management may not be a very well developed activity anywhere, but a good deal is known, and elsewhere is done, about tackling the problems of human vigour in organisations.

There remains the level of Institutions and their interrelationships where the problems of neglect and failure of intellectual development are perhaps at their greatest. The work of public administration is carried on through institutions which deliver services to the public. These institutions use great quantities of national resources, human and financial. The techniques for measuring the return given by these institutions for the resources they use are still not well developed; but it is a matter of common observation, both by those who work within those institutions and those who have dealings with them from outside, that some improvements in their methods of working seem to be possible (Cogan, 1978; NESC 43). Most commissions of enquiry in many countries arrive at similar conclusions. Improvements are often suggested in the methods by which public institutions apprehend problems, by which they produce solutions for them, by which they implement these solutions, by which they relate to their clienteles, and by which they review the results of their operations for the purpose of learning from experience. In particular, because of the complexity of much public business and the number of bodies that may be concerned in any single operation, there are problems of the interrelationships of public organisations and of co-ordinating their operations. Overall, the problem of interrelationships calls for the tackling of two main issues — clarification and allocation of roles within the system as a whole, and the establishment, also within the system, of effective communications.

We have seen that there are over 400 public bodies directly involved in the business of public administration. Not all of these directly relate to one another, but all of them relate to the more important bodies and nearly all the important bodies relate to one another. There are, therefore, vast numbers of individual relationships. The situation is thus very complex. The complexities are made much greater by the fact that there has been nothing like enough definition of duties, responsibilities and relationships as between all these bodies.

A vast task of analysis and definition is required to achieve clarity and order. What sort of duties and responsibilities are appropriate to a central-ised government body? What sort of duties, responsibilities and degrees of autonomy are appropriate to a central functional body? What sort of duties, responsibilities and autonomy are appropriate to a local elected body? Where do regional bodies fit into this picture? Is it possible to rationalise the areas of operation of all sorts of bodies so that they will be built up from the same basic units and that orderly linkages can be established between them?

There is here a major task of devising a place for each body and, within that place, for using it to its full potentialities. The task is like that of moulding a large number of randomly selected recruits, some of them unruly, into a disciplined, expertly led frontline battalion, with a clearly defined mission and resources and back-up services sufficient to achieve that mission. But nowhere in our public administration is there an effective vision of using the institutions of government in this way so as to realise their full, inherent and co-operative effectiveness.

A second problem might, if tackled, mitigate the severity of the prob-lems we have been discussing. This is to establish effective systems of communication between the various bodies (O'Halpin, 1979, Ch. 8). One achieves high levels of co-ordination in extremely complex structures, for example in the human body, by, amongst other things, having effective systems of communication throughout the whole. In conditions of approp-riate autonomy good communications enable the various parts to react appropriately. But, in fact, the tendency is – where there is any tendency – to prevent this ready response by the maintenance of archaic, arthritic controls and the accumulation of new ones.

There has been a great growth in the number of administrative bodies, in the range of their duties, and in the sizes of their staffs. We see here not so much a system of planned growth as of proliferation. Far from having a programme of role definition and of fixing of focuses of responsibility and autonomy, we find, where we find any action at all, efforts towards a sort of creeping uniformity, as if the cure for proliferation were to drag the whole into a state of entropy.

It is no wonder that, both inside and outside the public service, one finds a sense of disappointment that performance so often lags behind both needs and potentialities, and that there is little evidence that things will get better.

The task of public administration in modern society is to adjust to change, to bring about an orderly response to it, and to stimulate ordered change, so that no matter where change comes from, it is transmuted by orderly means into overall development. It is clear that the public institutions, as they play a larger and larger part in the life of the community, cannot, whether they are responding to change or are stimulating it, themselves remain immune to such change and development. The problem is how to find what are the dynamics of institutional development.

The institutions are, of course, staffed by people, so part of the answer is clearly concerned with the dynamics and development of people. However, it is well known that organisational behaviour is different from the behaviour either of individuals or of unstructured groups. It looks as though the dynamics of groups of institutions are different from those of individual institutions. How, then, does one get this set of over 400 institutions working creatively and up to the potentialities of the individuals, the individual institutions, and the sub-systems of institutions that constitute the whole? The obvious solutions – the commission of enquiry, the setting up of a special government department, or whatever – seem not to work. Is there any device that will work in this context? Obviously, this is a major professional problem that requires urgent attention.

Even so summary an account as this of the general administrative problems that arise at each level of the administrative system shows the many failures to engage in, and to act on, systematic Review, both in relation to the consensus and to professionalism. The system operates under severe difficulties because of this neglect. The whole process of administrative development as an integral part of national development is correspondingly impeded. From the standpoint of Review the crucial weakness is in the professional area – the failure, both in relation to consensus and to professionalism itself, to identify certain problems, the failure to analyse those that have been identified, and the failure to act on those problems that have been analysed. These failures present a formidable barrier to effective administrative development.

3. Administrative Development
Is, therefore, administrative development an impracticable concept? This may be; its practicability or otherwise has yet to be demonstrated. For myself I believe that only as a last resort can we accept that all else in the society will and must develop but that the instrument on which so much of this development depends cannot itself develop. That is to see it as, strictly, a catalyst; it is to hold that the instrument that absorbs so large a part of the community in quantity and quality is not an organic part of that community. So let us, in a spirit of wary optimism, push this discussion further.

The purpose of our Review and the listing of problems and failures is not to criticise the system but to arrive at an outline of what might be on the agenda for a programme of administrative development. Even so rapid a survey shows two things. The first is how numerous and important are the problems – there is plenty for the agenda. The second is that these problems are not primary ones – how to get farmers to have more healthy animals; how to have better educational or health services, or whatever – that make up the day-to-day work of 'line' departments: they are second and third order problems that cut across, or transcend, the 'line' or, to repeat the term we have used in this chapter, the special.

It is well known that, in the business world, one of the most difficult transitions is from the small, one-man business into a corporate body. A further difficult transition is from that to the multi-national or conglomerate body. At each stage the growth in size solves some problems but presents new ones of a different order. This is what is happening to the Irish administrative system. It has changed from being the one-man, special type of business envisaged in the 1920s, to the substantial and complex operations of the post-war years, to the conglomerate, and incipiently multi-national, of the present time. The small business model, with its connotation of rugged individualism, may, or may not, have been appropriate for the twenties and thirties; it was, as so many vainly said, wildly inappropriate for the sixties and seventies; it will have no relevance to the eighties and nineties.

Just as complexity demanded new managerial frameworks and skills not needed in earlier times, so new skills are demanded at the conglomerate stage. The most significant of these is national planning. It is inherent in such planning that one attempts to take a comprehensive view of society as a whole and where it is going or might go. Once this insight has been grasped the perception of the role of government has been transformed. Both rugged individualism and managerial efficiency cease to be enough. An intellectual quantum leap has been taken revealing new imperatives for action. Amongst these is the necessity of administrative transformation and development.

It may be argued that Ireland is so small that the changes in administrative structures and systems required in other countries are not necessary here. We have to be concerned, however, not only with size but also, much more seriously, with complexity and comprehensiveness. The new perception of the role of government, even in a society in which the market and spontaneous action have a significant part to play, reveals the remarkable complexity and comprehensiveness of the duties of government. The significant factor here is not size but sovereignty. In a small society the bucks may be correspondingly small, but they are likely to be almost as numerous and equally diverse as in a large society and perhaps even more prone to stop on some governmental desk. In a small society the complexity and the comprehensiveness may be easier to grasp than in a large one. This, if seized, is a relative advantage to set against other relative disadvantages. The point is that planned administrative development is no less necessary for the small society and, if pressed ahead with, may yield some extra advantages.

To repeat, the accumulation of extra duties and responsibilities in itself calls for administrative change where the special must be supplemented by the general. When, arising out of this accumulation, new insights are achieved on national objectives – such as national development – and on new techniques – such as national planning or monetary policy – with their domestic implications for the role of government, the general itself is transformed into the comprehensive. Government has grown not only big but *different*. Instruments devised for when government was relatively simple become inadequate when it becomes complex; those that were appropriate when it was complex are insufficient now that it has grown comprehensive. Government has evolved onto a different plane. Because of this evolution issues that were implicit in the situation have now become explicit and this explicitness brings further issues onto the agenda.

One of the issues that grows in importance with this development is that of co-ordination. At the operational level horizontal co-ordination is relatively simple, yet in practice it poses the administrative system with significant problems of the integration of the activities of numbers of public bodies, as we have seen in the Rossaveal example (p. 77), and the problems of vertical co-ordination are more difficult still. At the policy level there are problems of communication and integration between e.g. 'parent' departments and state-sponsored bodies. Other problems cut right across the administrative system. For example, in modern conditions defence, certainly in a small, neutral country, is only partly a matter of soldiers and their equipment. To a large extent it is also a question of transport, communications systems, civilian safety and morale, hospital services, and so on; their effectiveness in time of war depends on how well they have been prepared in time of peace. These services are not the direct responsibility of the Department of Defence and that department in time of peace is dependent on the willing co-operation of those to whom the problems of defence do not bulk large. This is no inconsiderable problem, especially at times when its urgency does not match its importance. At the highest level, the existence of *four* central co-ordinating departments presents, at least, opportunities for conflict and cross-purposes between the co-ordinators and the operators, and also between the co-ordinators themselves.

At these levels machinery for co-ordination exists or can be identified, and there is usually a department that can take a 'lead' role in co-ordination. There are other levels where such machinery has barely been assembled, or does not exist. We have seen (Chapter 5) the difficulties there have been in working out even the rudiments of coherent social policy. What department can take a lead role in relation to social policy or even significant interdepartmental elements of it? Here and there an ad hoc solution has been adopted, as when the Department of Health in 1974 was given a lead role in relation to children; but five years later something decisive has still to happen.

Given the present system by which ministerial responsibility – and hence the administrative system – is divided according to broad functions it is extremely difficult to devise ways of tackling problems of this kind. Solutions tried in the United Kingdom of 'overlord' ministers – those without direct departmental responsibility but with some sort of supervisory and co-ordinating roles in relation to departmental ministers – did not work: political power flows out of the departmental file. The experience with 'giant' ministries has been mixed. In any event neither solution has been tried in this country. In the United Kingdom, also, cabinet committees are much relied upon. Some use has been made of these in this country, but they have not emerged as a significant feature of the Irish system.

At the administrative level the methods for bringing to light problems for attention that cut across departmental functions are mostly haphazard. A fully operating planning system would be an important instrument here, but we have seen (Chapter 5) the difficulties that lie in the way of achieving any such thing. When such problems have been brought to light, whether because of interdepartmental conflict, or financial issues, or external pressures, the task of producing interdepartmental policy is usually committed to an interdepartmental committee. Sometimes this has the help of non-departmental experts; but usually these committees are closed corporations. Where a serious problem of co-ordination exists the interdepartmental committee is the principal instrument that is relied upon. (There is also the special case where embarrassing questions are referred to a committee in the hope that they will cool off).

This is not the place to engage in a study of the roles, strengths and limitations of the interdepartmental committee. We have already touched on this in Chapter 5. The immediate point is that we have had in Ireland no studies whatever about the efficacy of this most important administrative tool. There are, clearly, circumstances in which it is a useful tool, but others where it, equally clearly, either does not work at all or does so with inordinate delay or with minimal creativity.

An interesting example is that of the interdepartmental committee to study sub-national systems. We have seen (Chapter 2) that there is great confusion about the roles and potentialities of various bodies at the sub-national level – regional bodies, local authorities, community groups, field services of a large number of government departments, state-sponsored and other public bodies. This confusion impedes the government commitment to regional planning and development. It is posing big issues for the future shape and flavour of Irish democracy. The Devlin group (13.4.8) recommended in 1969 that an enquiry into these issues be pressed ahead with. Eventually, in 1975 a cabinet committee and a parallel inter-departmental committee were set up. The cabinet committee was abandoned on the change of government in 1977 but the interdepartmental committee continued. Up to June 1979 it had not produced a report. In 1976 NESC (22, p. 32) pointed out that a previously existing interdepartmental committee for co-ordinating regional policy had not met since early 1972. It is clear that there will be no hasty or impetuous decision-making about sub-national systems.

The point here is not to criticise but to review. How far is the interdepartmental committee an effective instrument for administrative co-ordination? We do not know; but there is some reason to believe, as was indicated in page 112 note 1, that it cannot operate effectively where what is at stake is the repartition of departmental functions. This, in part, may be because of the basic ambiguity in the role of the departmental representative. Whatever about this, the fact remains that in very many instances the main instrument of administrative co-ordination is unable to perform that task with speed or creativity. What is to be complained of here, in the context of administrative development, is not that a major but unsuitable instrument gives poor results. The cause of complaint is that no research is being engaged in to find out why, or in what circumstances the instrument can be effectively used, in what circumstances it becomes ineffective, and, where it is ineffective, what better instrument might be put in its place. This is all the more deplorable in that co-ordination has become an increasing problem of the Irish administrative system.

Often business cannot wait until knowledge can be fully accumulated. Power and impatience can be effective for action. But in these interdepartmental problems exactly whose power and whose impatience and what systems exist for giving effect to them? The problem of sub-national systems is only one of those relating to regional policy as a whole to which there has been repeated and explicit government commitment in 1965, 1969, 1972 and 1979 (NESC 4, App. IV; Programme, 1979, p. 66). We have effective policies for industrial location in regional areas that date back to the thirties at least, and for specific regional areas (Shannon and the Gaeltacht) that date back to the fifties; but to implement the newer and more comprehensive concept of regional development there are no corresponding policies, institutions or effective courses of action.

There are many other areas where as a consequence of the comprehensiveness of government responsibilities similar problems, and similar lack of knowledge of how to tackle them, exist. To repeat, there is a significant agenda for administrative development. The problem is how to get this development underway and to give it a sophistication to match the nature of its agenda. One thinks of consciously evoked development in the economic and cultural areas as in good measure the task of devising policies that will release in the private sector native sources of enterprise, creativity and dynamism. In the infrastructural and social areas development is more difficult, in one sense, because action for the most part lies in the public sector itself: but, once plans have been evoked, usually in response to public demand, action is likely to follow the release of resources. In the administrative area neither private creativity nor public demand normally exists to provide a dynamic for administrative development. If, therefore, we consider that administrative development is a crucial part of the whole developmental process, what do we do to get it moving? As we have seen from Chapter 3 the exogenous approach through 'administrative reform' has not given heartening results. Neither has the hope that, somehow, the political system would make a sustained effort in that direction. The reality is that the public are not much concerned about, or even aware of, the need for administrative development but they are very much concerned about many other things at the level of the special and the concrete and the political system responds accordingly. There is no corresponding pressure on politicians at the abstract levels we have been considering. It is unrealistic to expect of them, at this stage at least, more than to create the conditions in which administrative development can take place.[1] That leaves us with the task of somehow discovering and releasing the endogenous dynamics of administrative development.

That these dynamics have not hitherto operated consistently cannot be put down to a conflict between the value systems of the bureaucrats and those of the public as a whole; in this the bureaucracy can be taken to reflect closely the values of Irish society. Perhaps a more telling explanation is that the bureaucracy is too well adapted to the prevailing climate of wary anti-intellectualism and of general scepticism about the efficacy of administrative self-consciousness.

It seems that only by evoking a concern for the intellectual standards of the administrative profession within the profession itself would it be possible to work a way out of this impasse. It is reasonable to expect the political system to create the conditions in which professional dynamics can grow, and to give resulting projects an adequate degree of backing,

[1]'We can almost speak of an implicit and unwritten non-aggression pact between politicians and officials in Britain. The former generally have little direct experience of administration and few definite opinions about problems of structure, methods of operation and personnel management. They are content to express preferences and requirements on very broad issues, usually where a clearly defined political interest is at stake . . . Thus we can fairly speak of a certain indifference on the part of politicians to the substance of administrative reform and development: provided some of their broadly defined political requirements are met they are ready to leave the handling of administrative change to the professionals' (Johnson, 1976, pp. 290–1). For a different approach see Whelan, 1979.

but if the profession itself does not exercise developmental initiative it is hard to see who or what else can do so.

To get these dynamics to operate there are, I think, two main forces — knowledge and responsibility. What exactly needs to be done, at the various levels, in the interests of administrative development? How to express these needs so that the administrative system will be constrained to act on them?

A big breakthrough in the efficacy of modern government was the grasping of the concept and the means of economic development. Something similar is happening in the social area. Would these developments have occurred if there had not been, first, a science of economics and then other social sciences with appropriate resources and departments in the universities oriented to problems of public policy? Notwithstanding the importance of public administration in this country no similar intellectual infrastructure exists in the area of administrative studies. A good deal is done about public service training and some beginning has been made on education for public service; but, otherwise, there has been little development. There is virtually no research — apart from the work of the new research unit in the Institute of Public Administration — into administrative problems, especially into the sorts of problems we have been identifying. Indeed, the most important problems calling for research have barely been identified.

At the level of knowledge of, and thought concerning, its own problems, therefore, the Irish administrative system is at a grievous disadvantage. For this the blame must lie, fairly and squarely, on the administrative profession itself. It has not concerned itself to any sufficient degree with its intellectual base. The first step in the programme of administrative development, therefore, is to tackle this problem on a scale commensurate with its size. Even so far as we have been able to uncover it the detailed agenda is long and onerous. It contains a big backlog of neglected items; new items continually emerge; and there are certainly many more beneath the surface.

The mere existence of an explicit agenda for administrative development would be a stimulus to action. To this could be added an appeal to the positive in the pride of the profession itself. That pride usually reveals itself in the negative, the defensive response to what is conceived of as attack. But it should be possible to evoke it in a creative form, to harness it to the basic thrust of the profession itself. We have said (p. 206) that this thrust is towards order, rationality, efficacy and style. These qualities, to the degree to which they can be achieved, are legitimate sources of pride and, within reason, given their heads, a major dynamic for our programme were it to be realised. The existence of an agenda for administrative development that shows the system to be afflicted by such a degree of disorder, irrationality, ineffectiveness and absence of style would pose a fundamental challenge to the profession to put its house in order, to establish at least outposts of rationality, to use more efficaciously the great resources at its disposal, and by such means to achieve a level of professional style of which it could be legitimately proud. This last is the synergy that emerges when the other three qualities are practised to the full. The philosopher Whitehead said that 'style . . . is the contribution of specialism to culture'. The national culture is enriched and developed when the specialism of administration submits to its own inherent drives so as to develop itself to such a degree of sophistication that what it does is consistently done with style. The first stage in this internal liberation is, I believe, the drawing up of a First Programme of Administrative Development. The second stage is, of course, to harness professional pride to inflexible determination to carry through the programme decided upon.

The task of public administration, therefore, is to achieve creative responses to the problems of the community, including the problems of public administration itself. The public servant cannot serve the community at all until consensus is achieved and maintained. He has a significant part to play in the maintenance of the consensus, by the quality of his service to the community, by his adherence to its values, by his concern for human rights and dissent. He has a heavy load of responsibility to discharge in developing the professionalism of his work, and by adopting and applying new skills and methodologies that will make it more effective. Within his own sphere he has considerable responsibilities of leadership, and of using and inspiring great human resources to the best effect. In the last analysis, people, whether as the persons to be served by public administration or the persons who are staffing the public bodies, are the beginning and end of the story. They are both the motivation and the ultimate control – the engine and the brakes – of the instruments of government.

There is another sense in which the profession of public administration has to be concerned with its limitations. Over the centuries, as we have seen, an objective of government has been the transition from personal rule, dynastic rule, class rule to, one may hope, rule in the general interest. This has been accompanied by a vast expansion in the role of government, from limited intervention at the early stages to extraordinarily comprehensive intervention now. If inherent in this is the evolution of a responsible society, how does one square the inescapable responsibilities of the state with the dissemination of a sense of responsibility amongst the population at large? One of the objectives of a Christian, democratic society, is a wide sense of personal and group responsibility. On the other hand, the drift of our society is towards a concentration of responsibility in public offices. Is it possible to devise means by which, as new duties and responsibilities come in at one end of the governmental machine, at least a corresponding number are discharged to individuals, groupings and localities at the other? Is the professional task of public administration, in this sense, to accept readily new responsibilities, to intervene effectively, and to move on leaving orderly, healthy and autonomous activities behind, just as a doctor intervenes temporarily to get his patient back on his feet, or to deliver a new child into the world? In this sense, the task of public administration may not be so much to do things, as to discover and release dynamics within the society that will lead to spontaneous creativity.

Two extremes of development are conceivable. The first is the steady growth of the activities of government so that virtually everything within the society becomes a matter for public administration. The other extreme is a reversion from this where well-educated affluent people will conduct most of their own affairs for themselves (Myrdal, 1960, pp. 67–70). So far as Ireland is concerned, and for some period ahead, some middle position will be struck. If so, vast responsibilities will have to be discharged by public administration and a great burden of responsibility will lie on those who practise that profession to raise its performance to a level commensurate both with the levels of the national value system and of the quality of the people that it has been so fortunate as to recruit.

References

Note: Unless otherwise indicated, titles were published either in Dublin or London.

Administration Yearbook and Diary 1979
Administrative Justice: Report of All Party Informal Committee May, 1977
Adult Education in Ireland: Report of (Murphy) Committee 1973, Prl 3465
Albrow, M. *Bureaucracy* 1970
Andersen, R.B. 'A Danish study of the functioning of the system of social security' *Jnl Soc Pol* I, 4
Andren, N. 'Programme budgeting: the Swedish experiment' in Leemans, 1976
Argyris, C. *Personality and Organisation* New York, 1957

Baker, R.J.S. *Administrative Theory and Public Administration* 1972
Baker T.J. & O'Brien, L.M. *The Irish Housing System: A Critical Overview* 1979
Banking Commission Report, 1938 (Report of Commission on Banking, Currency & Credit)
Barnard, C.I. *The Functions of the Executive* Cambridge, Mass, 1938
Barrington, D. 'Private property under the Irish Constitution' *Irish Jurist* 8 (1973) 1
Barrington, T.J. *Notes for Interview Boards* 2nd edn, 1964
  From Big Government to Local Government 1975
  'Can there be regional development in Ireland?' *Administration* 24 (1976) 2
  'Can administrative science aid the administrative profession?' *Administration* 27 (1979) 4
Beth, L. *The Development of Judicial Review in Ireland, 1937-66* 1967
Bexelius, A. 'The Swedish institution of the justitieombudsman' *Administration* 9 (1961) 4
Biendenkopf Report 'Co-determination in the company' trs D. O'Neill, Belfast, 1976
Brennan Report, 1936 – see *Commission of Inquiry into the Civil Service*
Bristow, J. 'State enterprise and economic planning in the Irish Republic'

Jnl Statistical & Social Soc 1964-5
Brown, W. *Organisation* 1971
Brown, L.N. & Garner, J.F. *French Administrative Law* 2nd edn, 1973
Browne, R.G.S. *The Administrative Process in Britain* 1971
Bunreacht na hÉireann 1937
Byrne v. *Ireland* [1972] IR 24

Carty, F.X. *Government and People – Creative Dialogue* (Report of 1969-70
    Communications Conference) 1970
Caiden, G.E. *Administrative Reform* Chicago, 1969
Capital Investment Advisory Committee *1st Report* 1957; *2nd Report* 1957;
    3rd Report 1958
Central Policy Review Staff (CPRS) *Review of Overseas Representation*
    HMSO, August 1977
Chapman, B. *The Profession of Government* 1959
Chapman, R.A. 'Merger of ministries in Britain' *Administration* 25 (1977)
    1
Chapman, R.J.K. 'The Irish public service: change or reform?'
    Administration 23 (1975) 2
Chubb, B. *A Source-book of Irish Government* 1964
    The Government and Politics of Ireland 1970
    Cabinet Government in Ireland 1974
    The Constitution and Constitutional Change in Ireland 1978
Chubb, B. & Lynch, P. (eds) *Economic Development and Planning* 1969
Civil Service Report of (Fulton) Committee, 1966-68 Vols I-V, HMSO,
    Cmnd 3638, 1968
Clark, C. *Taxmanship* 1964
Clarke, R. *New Trends in Government* 1971
Cogan, D.J. 'The Irish services sector: a new challenge' *Administration* 25
    (1977) 4
    The Irish Services Sector 1978
Colley, G. 'State-sponsored bodies – roles and issues' with comments by
    T.J. Barrington and N. Whelan *Management* Jan-Feb 1973
Collins, J. 'The bond and the free' *Administration* I (1953) 1
    Local Government 2nd edn by D. Roche, 1963
*Commission of Inquiry into the Civil Services 1932-35, (Brennan) Report,
    1936,* P. 1844
    Coombs Report see *Royal Commission*
Council for Social Welfare *Planning for Social Development – What Needs to
    be Done* 1976
Coyle, P. 'Public enterprises in Ireland' in *The Evolution of Public
    Enterprises in the Community of the Nine* Brussels, 1973
Crick, B. *In Defence of Politics* Penguin, 1964
Crozier, M. *The Bureaucratic Phenomenon* 1964

de Buitleir, D. *Problems of Irish Local Finance* 1974
de Jouvenel, B. *Sovereignty* 1957
Development for Full Employment 1978, Prl 7193

Devlin Report – see *Public Services Organisation Review Group*
Dicey, A.V. *Law of the Constitution* 10th edn, 1961
Dogan, M. (ed) *The Mandarins of Western Europe* New York, 1975
Dooney, S. *The Irish Civil Service* 1976
Drucker, P. *The Practice of Management* 1955

École Nationale d'Administration (ÉNA) Paris, 1975
Economic Development 1958, Pr 4803
Economic and Social Development, 1976-80 1976, Prl 5758
Engelbert, E.A. 'Guidelines and standards for education and training
     programs in public administration' National Association of Public
     Affairs and Administration, USA, 1975
European Development Fund *1st Report* Brussels, 1975
Expenditure Committee *Eleventh Report* HMSO, 1977

Fanning, R. *The Irish Department of Finance, 1922-58* 1978
Fayol, H. *General and Industrial Management* 1949
Finance, Dept of, *Outline of Irish Financial Procedures* 1976
Finer, H. *The Theory and Practice of Modern Government* 4th edn, 1961
Fitzgerald, G. *State-Sponsored Bodies* 2nd edn, 1963
     'Seeking a national purpose' *Studies* Winter, 1964
     Planning in Ireland 1968
FitzGerald Report – see *Outline of the Future Hospital System*
Follett, Mary P. in Metcalf & Urwick (eds) *Dynamic Administration* 1940
     in Urwick (ed) *Freedom and Co-ordination* 1949
Fougère, L. *Civil Service Systems* Brussels, 1967
Frankfurter, F. *The Public and its Government* New Haven, 1930
Franks, Oliver (Lord) *Central Planning in Peace and War* 1947
Fulton Report, 1968 – see *Civil Service Report of (Fulton) Committee*

Galbraith, J.K. *The Affluent Society* 2nd edn, 1969
Garret, J. *The Management of Government* 1972
Geraghty v. Minister for Local Government [1976] IR 153
Goodnow, Frank J. *Politics and Administration* New York, 1914
Grogan, V. *Administrative Tribunals in the Public Service* 1961

Haldane Report – see *Machinery of Government Committee*
Health, *Restructuring Report* 1973, Prl 3445
Henderson, D. *Listener* 24 November 1977
Herman, M. *Administrative Justice and Supplementary Benefits* 1972
Herzberg, F. *Work and the Nature of Man* 1966
Hill, M.J. *The Sociology of Public Administration* 1972
Hughes, O. 'Rates equalisation' *Administration* 9 (1961) 2

Industrial Development Authority (IDA) *Industrial Plan, 1977-80*
Institute of Public Administration (IPA) *Mobility in the Public Service* 1960
     More Local Government (Chubb Report) 1971
     Administrative Justice: Report of Working Party

Local Authority Finance 1977

Johnson, N. *The Government of Western Germany* Oxford, 1973
  'Recent administrative reform in Britain' in Leemans, 1976
Katsiouni, O. 'Planning in a small economy: the Republic of Ireland' *Jnl
  Statistical & Social Soc* 1977-8
Keatinge, P. *A Place among the Nations* 1978
Keeling, D. *Management and Government* 1972
Kelly, J.M. *Fundamental Rights in Irish Law and Constitution* 2nd edn,
  1967
Kennedy, F. *Public Social Expenditure in Ireland* 1975
Kennedy, K.A. & Dowling, B. *Economic Growth in Ireland* 1975
Keynes, J.M. (Lord) *The End of Laissez Faire* 1926
  The General Theory of Employment, Interest and Money 1936
Kiezun, W. *Autonomization of Organisational Units* Warsaw, 1977
Kotarbinski, T. *Praxiology* 1965

Lawrence, P.R. & Lorsch, J.W. *Developing Organisations* Reading, Mass,
  1969
Leemans, A.F. *The Management of Change in Government* The Hague,
  1976
Lemass, S.F. 'The role of the state-sponsored bodies in the economy' with
  comments by C.S. Andrews & J.P. Beddy, *Administration* 6 (1958) 4
  'The organisation behind the Economic Programme' *Administration* 9
  (1961) 1; reprinted in Chubb & Lynch, 1969
Leon, D.E. *Advisory Bodies in Irish Government* 1963
Local Government Reorganisation, White Paper 1971, Prl 1572; *Discussion
  Paper* 1973
Lynch, P. 'The economist and public policy' *Studies* Autumn, 1953;
  reprinted in Chubb & Lynch, 1969

Machinery of Government Committee (Haldane) Report 1918 reprinted
  Administration 20 (1972) 2
*Manpower Policy—Administrative Arrangements for Implementing Report of
  Interdepartmental Committee* 1965, Pr 8260
McCarthy, C. *The Decade of Upheaval* 1973
McElligott, C.C. 'The problem of revaluation' *Administration* 3 (1955) 1
McGinley, M. 'Pay negotiations in the public service' *Administration* 24
  (1976) 1
McLoughlin v. *Minister for Social Welfare* [1954] IR 1-28
Massé, P. 'French planning' *Administration* 10 (1962) 3
Miller, J.D.B. *The Nature of Politics* 1962
Minister for Local Government v. *Ennis Mental Hospital Committee* [1939]
  IR 258
Mitchell, J.D.B. 'The irrelevance of the ombudsman proposals' in
  Rowatt, D.C. *The Ombudsman* 1965
Molitor, André *L'Administration de la Belgique* Brussels, 1974
Monnet, Jean *Memoirs* trs R. Mayne, 1978

Moulin, L. 'The politicization of the administration in Belgium' in Dogan, 1975

Mundow, H.J. 'Organisation and methods in the civil service' *Administration* 1 (1953) 1

'Management in the civil service' *Administration* 3 (1955) 2-3

'Organisation and methods at work' *Administration* 4 (1956) 2

Murphy v. *Dublin Corporation* (No 1) [1972] IR 215

Murray, D.P. 'An ombudsman for Ireland' paper submitted for Diploma in Administrative Science, IPA, 1976

Myrdal, G. *Beyond the Welfare State* 1960

National Development, 1977-80 1978, Prl 6836

National Economic and Social Council (NESC) Reports:
  4. *Regional Policy in Ireland: A Review* 1975, Prl 4147
  8. *An Approach to Social Policy* 1975, 4438
  12. *Educational Expenditure in Ireland* 1976, Prl 4730
  16. *Some Aspects of Finance for Owner-occupied Housing* 1976, Prl 5273
  20. *The Future of Public Expenditure* 1976, Prl 5337
  21. *Public Expenditure* 1976, Prl 5479
  22. *Institutional Arrangements for Regional Economic Development* 1976, Prl 5407
  25. *Towards a Social Report* 1977, Prl 5706
  28. *Service Type Employment and Regional Development* 1976, Prl 5841
  30. *Personal Incomes by County in 1973* 1977, Prl 5933
  31. *The Potential for Growth in Irish Tax Revenues* 1977, Prl 5840
  37. *Integrated Approaches to Personal Income Taxes and Transfers* 1978, Prl 6684
  38. *Universality and Selectivity: Social Services in Ireland* 1978, Prl 6802
  40. *Policies to Accelerate Rural Development* 1978, Prl 7127
  41. *Rural Areas: Change and Development* 1978, Prl 7159
  42. *Policies for Agricultural and Rural Development* 1978, Prl 7201
  43. *Productivity and Management* 1979, Prl 7252

National Industrial and Economic Council (NIEC) Reports:
  3. *Manpower Policy* 1964
  9. *Comments on Report of Interdepartmental Committee for Implementing Manpower Policy* 1965, Pr 8475
  24. *Comments on Second Programme Review of Progress, 1964-67* 1968, Prl 311

Nationalised Industries White Paper, HMSO, 1978, Cmnd 7131

National Prices Commission *Report No 71* March 1978

Nielsen, N. 'The Danish ombudsman' *Administration* 21 (1973) 3

Northcote-Trevelyan Report: The Organisation of the Permanent Civil Service reprinted *Administration* 2 (1954) 2

Northcott, C.M. *Personnel Management* 1960

O'Doherty, E.F. 'Responsibility of the public servant' *Administration* 6 (1958) 2

O'Donnell, J. *How Ireland is Governed* 6th edn, 1979

OECD *Investment in Education* 2 vols, 1965 & 1966
OECD *Observer* Paris, May, 1977 and May, 1978
O'Halpin, P. *The Chief Executive in State Enterprise* 1979
Oliver, J.A. *Working at Stormont* 1978
O'Mahony, S. 'Programme budgeting in the Department of Education'
   Administration 19 (1971) 3
   'The working of the first programme budget in Education'
   Administration 20 (1972) 3
Ó Nualláin, C. *Personnel Assessment and Selection* 1971
   'Public service reform' *Administration* 26 (1978) 3
Open University *The Study of Public Administration* Blocks I-IV, Milton
   Keynes, 1974
O'Sullivan, P. *Irish Planning and Acquisition Law* 1978
Outline of the Future Hospital System (FitzGerald Report) 1969

Papal Encyclicals *Rerum Novarum* 1891; *Quadragesimo Anno* 1931; *Mater
   et Magistra* 1961; *Pacem in Terris* 1963; *Populorum Progressio* 1967
Plantey, A. *La Fonction Publique* 3rd edn, Paris, 1971
Posts and Telegraphs Review Group, 1978-9 (Dargan) Report 1979, Prl 7883
President's Committee on Administrative Management (Brownlow) Report
   Washington, 1937
Programme for Economic Expansion—First, 1959-62 1958; *Second, 1963-70*
   Part I, 1963, Pr 7239; Part II 1964, Pr 7670
Programme for Economic and Social Development—Third, 1969-72 1969, Prl
   431
Programme for National Development, 1978-81 1979, Prl 7618
Public Expenditure, Control of, (Plowden) Report HMSO, 1961, Cmnd
   1432
Public Service Advisory Council (PSAC) *1st Report* 1974, Prl 4509; *2nd
   Report* 1975, Prl 5453; *3rd Report* 1976, Prl 6274; *4th Report* 1977, Prl
   7138
*Public Services Organisation Review Group, 1966-69, (PSORG), (Devlin)
   Report* 1969, Prl 792

Raven, J., Whelan, C.T., Pfretzschner, P.A. & Borock, D.M. *Political
   Culture in Ireland* 1976
Review Body on Higher Remuneration in the Public Sector, Reports,
   1972 Prl 2674; 1978, Prl 7259
Revue Française d'Administration Publique (RFAP), 5 (1978) Paris
Roche, D. 'Outline of the regional situation in Ireland, Britain, France,
   Italy' *Administration* 21 (1973) 1
Roche, J.D. *Planning in the ESB* 1978
Roes, Th.H. 'Establishment of the social and cultural planning office (in
   the Netherlands)' paper presented at conference of European Group of
   Public Administration at Tampere, Finland, 1976

Roethlisberger, F.J. & Dickson, W.J. *Management and the Worker* Cambridge, Mass, 1939

Rose, R. & Peters, G. *Can Government go Bankrupt?* 1979

Royal Commission on (Australian) Government Administration (Coombs Report) Canberra, 1976

Ryan, R. 'The role of the state-sponsored body in the new public service' *Administration* 21 (1973) 4

Schon, D. *Beyond the Stable State* Penguin edn 1973

Self, Peter *Administrative Theories and Politics* 2nd edn, 1977

Simon, H.A. *Administrative Behavior* 3rd edn, 1976

Speer, A. *Inside the Third Reich* Sphere Books, 1975

Steering Committee on Regional Technical Colleges, (Mulcahy) Report 1969, Prl 371

Street, H. *Justice in the Welfare State* 1968

Sutton, M. *Irish Government Aid to the Third World* 1977

Taylor, F.W. *Principles and Methods of Scientific Management* New York, 1911

Tolstoy, N. *Victims of Yalta* 1977

Transport and Power, *Restructuring Report* 1974

Tussing, A. Dale *Irish Educational Expenditures – Past, Present and Future* 1978

Urwick, L. & Brech, E.F. *The Making of Scientific Management* 3 vols, 1945, 1946, 1948

Vinde, P. 'An introduction to the Swedish civil service' *Administration* 16 (1968) 2

Waldo, D. 'Education for public administration in the seventies' in F.C. Mosher (ed) *American Public Administration: Past, Present, Future* Alabama, 1975

Walker, D. *Local Government Finance and County Incomes* 1964

Walsh, B.M. *The Employment Problem in Ireland: Background Analysis and Policy Options* 1978a

'National and regional demographic trends' *Administration* 26 (1978b) 2

Walsh, B.M. & Copeland, J. *Economic Aspects of Local Authority Expenditure & Finance* 1975

Wennergren, B. 'Civic information – administrative publicity' *Administration* 19 (1971) 1

Whelan, N. 'Reform (or change) in the Irish public service 1969-75', *Administration* 23 (1975) 2

'Public service adaptation – its nature and requirements' *Administration* 27 (1979) 1

Whitaker, T.K. 'The finance attitude' *Administration* 2 (1954) 3; reprinted

in Chubb & Lynch, 1969
'The civil service and development' *Administration* 9 (1961) 2
'Planning Irish development' *Administration* 25 (1977) 3
Seanad Debates, 23 November 1977. 87.456
Wilson, Woodrow 'The study of administration' *Political Science Quarterly* 2, June 1887
Wraith, R.E. *Guggisberg* 1967
Wright, M. 'Public expenditure in Britain: the crisis of control' *Public Administration* 55 (1977) 143

Index

Brown, L.N. & Garner, J.F., 184
Brown, W., 168
Browne, R.G.S., 163
Brownlow committee 164
Bula Mines Ltd 57
Bunreacht na hÉireann 19, 171-6
bureaucracy 81-2
business as model 8-9, 32-3, 43-4, 58-9,
    65-6, 157, 217
Byrne v. Ireland 174

Caiden, G.E., 80
cameralism 14
Canada 67
capital expenditure 117, 132
Capital Investment Advisory
    Committee 117
Carnsore nuclear project 148-9, 197-8
Carty, F.X., 196
Central Bank 122, 130
centralisation
    democratic 39
    efficiency of 40-42
    and Ministers & Secretaries Acts 31-2
    of policy-making 28, 145
Central Policy Review Staff 74
Chapman, B., 14, 74, 92, 173
Chapman, R.A., 83
Chapman, R.J.K., 87
Chubb, B., 20, 210
civil service
    British 31
    classes
        administrative 30, 36
        executive 30, 36
        professional 30, 101, 108
        others 30-31
    depoliticisation 32, 37
    executive agencies 25, 33, 61
    management in 36, 156-163, 163-70
    numbers in 19, 30-31
    of government 30
    of State 30
    profession 36
    professional constraints 36-7
    professional secrecy 37, 191-4
    role of 16-17, 33, 34-5, 37, 38-9,
        60-61
    staff units 33-4
Civil Service Commission 34, 36, 43,
    92, 93
Civil Service Commission Act, 1883, 14

Clark, C., 118
Clarke, Sir R., 25, 83, 101, 116
clientele
    controls 171-2
    redress 172-187, 210
        Administrative Procedure Act 184
        administrative tribunals 172,
            177-8, 182
        alienation 15, 81, 82
        appeal 179, 181-4
        conseil d'état 13, 172, 184
        courts 174, 175-7
        decision 179-8, 183
        ombudsman 15, 172, 185-6
        'representations' 34, 175
        review 177, 184-6
        see also Administrative Justice,
            Commissioner for,
Cogan, D.J., 82, 111, 162, 214
Colley, G., 61
Collins, J., 44, 60
Comhlucht Siúicre Éireann 58
communication systems 22, 187-9, 215
community bodies 39, 195
Comptroller and Auditor General 116
Confederation of Irish Industry 196
consensus 6, 7-8, 29, 81, 89, 139-40,
    176, 199-207, 223
Constitution(al)
    balance 177
    constraints 20, 172, 175
    executive and courts 175-6
    executive and legislature 174-5
    sovereignty 173-4
consultation 133-4, 196-8
Coombs report (Australia) 112n, 113
coordination 23-5, 27, 37-8, 131, 142-3,
    215, 218-9
    interdepartmental committees 112-3,
        219-20
Córas Iompair Éireann (CIE) 19, 25,
    39, 49, 57, 58, 65, 77
Córas Tráchtála (CTT) 25, 65
Council for Social Welfare 138n
Council of Europe 68-9, 70
Council on Tribunals (UK) 183, 185
county councils 25, 42-3
county development teams 44, 144
courts 20, 30, 174
    and executive 175-7, 183
    and legality 175
    and legislature 174